"Ross Ellenhorn has given us an elegant, ([...] ch to understanding our resistance to change— [...] ne it. Engagingly written and scientifically rigo [...] ion to the literature of mental wellness."

—David A. Kessler, MD, bestselling author of *The End of Overeating, Capture,* and *Fast Carbs, Slow Carbs*

"Finally. Someone who understands that change—changing anything about ourselves—isn't a mechanical process, and takes more than a YouTube video and willpower (whatever that is). Ross Ellenhorn explains why making even a simple personal change is so damn hard: it stirs a deep existential crisis and takes great courage—we have to take responsibility and face the terrible prospect of disappointing ourselves. The great big secret in this book is that the capacity to change grows not out of staring down our shortcomings but in showing kindness and compassion to our imperfect selves."

—Hara Estroff Marano, editor at large, *Psychology Today,* author of *Nation of Wimps*

"This groundbreaking book invites you to consider the existential issues that affect all human beings, which cause us to resist change when we know it is good for us. Ross helps you to let go of the shame involved in not reaching your goals despite your best intentions, and leads you on an insightful journey to find how to create lasting, positive change from within rather than follow a mechanical prescription. . . . Reading this book will supply you with the courage and wisdom you need to bravely confront your limitations and turn them into strengths for the journey ahead."

—Judy Ho, PhD, author of *Stop Self-Sabotage,* clinical and neuropsychologist, and cohost of *The Doctors*

"Countless self help books claim to help people change. But Ross *Ellenhorn's How We Change* actually does it, not through pithy slogans and relentless bullet points, but by encouraging readers to confront their own behaviors, patterns, setbacks, and fears. Erudite, funny, and highly accessible, *How We Change* is one of those books that stays with you for a long time. By the end of it, it's safe to say you'll be a different person."

—Abby Ellin, author of *Duped: Double Lives, False Identities, and the Con Man I Almost Married*

"*How We Change* provides a sound framework for examining our longings to become better people while contending with the barriers that prevent it from happening. With wisdom, compassion, humility, and humor, Ross Ellenhorn takes us inside the mind for a closeup view of this tug-of-war and the strategies for winning it."

New York Review of Books

ALSO BY ROSS ELLENHORN

Parasuicidality and Paradox:
Breaking Through the Medical Model

ROSS ELLENHORN

HOW WE CHANGE

(And Ten Reasons Why We Don't)

HARPER WAVE

An Imprint of HarperCollins*Publishers*

Twelve images from *Harold and the Purple Crayon* by Crockett Johnson, illustrated by: Crockett Johnson. Text copyright © 1955 by Crockett Johnson, copyright © renewed 1983 by Ruth Krauss. Text copyright © 1955 by Crockett Johnson, copyright © renewed 1983 By Ruth Krauss. Used by permission of HarperCollins Publishers.

A hardcover edition of this book was published in 2020 by Harper Wave, an imprint of HarperCollins Publishers.

HarperCollins books may be purchased for educational, business, or sales promotional use. For information, please email the Special Markets Department at SPsales@harpercollins.com.

FIRST HARPER WAVE PAPERBACK PUBLISHED 2023.

Library of Congress Cataloging-in-Publication Data has been applied for.

ISBN 978-0-06-296110-5 (pbk.)

23 24 25 26 27 LBC 5 4 3 2 1

TO MAX AND REBECCA

Suppose, for example, that I am climbing in the Alps, and have had the ill-luck to work myself into a position from which the only escape is by a terrible leap. Being without similar experience, I have no evidence of my ability to perform it successfully; but hope and confidence in myself make me sure I shall not miss my aim, and nerve my feet to execute what without those subjective emotions would perhaps have been impossible. But suppose that, on the contrary, the emotions of fear and mistrust preponderate; or suppose that . . . I feel it would be sinful to act upon an assumption unverified by previous experience, why—then I shall hesitate so long that at last, exhausted and trembling, and launching myself in a moment of despair, I miss my foothold and roll into the abyss. . . . *There are then cases where faith creates its own verification.* Believe, and you shall be right, for you shall save yourself; doubt, and you shall again be right, for you shall perish.

WILLIAM JAMES

No hope without fear, nor fear without hope.

BARUCH SPINOZA

CONTENTS

THE INFINITE POWER OF SAMENESS

I went to a bookstore and asked the saleswoman, "Where's the self-help section?" She said if she told me, it would defeat the purpose.

—George Carlin

You're eager to make the change. You know all the ways it will benefit you. Your life will be smoother, happier, more successful; you'll finally reach that perfect crow pose, lose that beer belly, schedule your time better, finally get out of the house and meet your perfect match, take that long-awaited step into a new career. The change will make you proud, raise your self-esteem, align your life with your values, bring you fulfillment and a sense of accomplishment. So you plan. You set up a daily schedule, enlist the help of a trusted ally, set reminders on your cell phone, buy a journal so you can record your successes. *This* time, you're going to do it.

And then . . . nothing. No follow-through, no breakthrough. As much as you wish to change, you just don't do it.

If this sounds familiar, then you probably also know the feeling that comes when a well-intentioned friend or relative suggests a few "easy" things you can do to make that change: "Why don't you just (drink less, eat less, work out more, go on Match.com?)," which always sounds suspiciously close to "What's wrong with you? Why *can't* you?"

When someone suggests that personal change is easy, only requiring a bit of knowledge or skill, they usually mean well. But they're also usually missing a very important point. Sadly, a lot of experts miss this point too.

We're often presented with well-intentioned self-help programs, as if a set of prescribed tactics works for all. For most of us, however, change isn't a follow-the-instructions sort of thing. That's because there are no simple answers to personal change. As we've learned from over a century of psychotherapeutic thought, change isn't as superficial as doing what an expert tells you to do, or learning new skills.

True self-help is just that: helping yourself. It's an act of personal leadership and direction. It certainly requires that you consider advice and contemplate the ideas of others. But being a sheep—following the newest advice as if it will magically spur your change—is not engaging in self-help. Instead, truly helping yourself requires that you courageously grasp the shepherd's crook in your own fist on your own journey. In fact, of all the behaviors you engage in life, changing is the one that most brings you face-to-face with your sole responsibility to make your life work.

That's why change isn't easy or simple. As you forge your own path, changing is often strenuous and can leave you vulnerable: The act of even attempting change makes you repeatedly—and uncomfortably—aware that the success and failure of your actions belongs to no one but yourself.

There's wisdom in that old joke: *How many therapists does it take to change a lightbulb? One, but the lightbulb has to want to change.* No matter how many experts you follow, how many therapists and counselors you see, or how many friends and relatives support you, you are alone and responsible for the change you make.

Aloneness. Responsibility. These aren't words we necessarily embrace with gusto, and they are hardly a match for books and talk-show interviews guaranteeing that success is a matter of easy steps toward "a thinner," "more blissful," "more powerful," you—even if, deep down, you know those guarantees are empty promises. Instead, our responsibility to, and for, ourselves is at the very core of all personal change. That makes change difficult; never *easy.* As you walk toward change, you also walk toward feelings and experiences most of us try to avoid—profound adult things like the anxiety stirred by realizing you are the master of your own fate—and away from feelings and experiences that we typically find attractive, like comfort, a sense of certainty, the shirking of responsibility, the blaming of others, and the painlessness of a numbing routine.

The kind but misguided suggestions of your friends and relatives and the "easy, step-by-step" how-to instructions of experts typically ignore the fact that there are very real, very powerful forces holding you back from changing. These forces don't represent some weakness or laziness in you, but are central struggles we all deal with all the time.

And here's the clincher: That force within us that's happy to maintain the status quo usually wins the battle more often than does change. That's why we often don't change, despite our longings to do so and all the evidence that we should.

Consider drug and alcohol abuse. Today, addiction treatment in the United States is a $35-billion industry,[1] with over a million active members of Alcoholics Anonymous.[2] Yet only a third of people with an addictive habit kick it successfully.[3]

Let's look at exercise. We spend more than $30 billion annually on whipping ourselves into shape,[4] but 73 percent of us do not reach our fitness goals.[5] The weight-loss industry rakes in $66 billion a year,[6] while 69 percent of us quit our diets.[7] And those brave souls who stay loyal to kale and quinoa? Eight out of ten of them end up regaining whatever weight they lost.[8]

New Year's resolutions? Ninety-three percent of people who make them, break them.[9]

The pull to stay the same doesn't just keep you from achieving those big wellness and behavioral goals, like more exercise, dieting, or breaking a dangerous habit; or deeper personal goals involving your growth as a human being, such as greater fulfillment in your work and love life, or even your pursuit of greater meaning and purpose. That pull is also present in the very minutiae of your life. How many times have you told yourself you need to turn off Hulu and read more, pay more attention to your kids, order less takeout, or put the dishes in the dishwasher and not the sink? And how many times have you stuck to these new changes for a week or two, only to find yourself back to square one? I place my money on more often than not. Staying the same is the norm, not the exception, no matter the size or gravitas of the goal.

Now consider this: Even though sameness is the winner in most of your battles to change, the actual consequences of staying the same are typically riskier than the outcomes of changing. People die of heart attacks for all kinds of reasons, but nobody has ever keeled over because they *stopped* eating cronuts.

The negative results of sameness aren't just personal; they're global, witnessed most clearly in every inch of rising sea levels. We've received the definitive diagnosis regarding climate change, and the experts offer realistic strategies to fight it,[10] yet we keep collectively engaging in old and destructive habits.

Despite all the potential risks of staying the same, and regardless of innumerable rewards we can attain by changing, we typically don't alter our behaviors. And Lord knows, it's not from lack of trying. In fact, trying to change, feeling guilty that we aren't trying hard enough, or feverishly planning the next strategy to try again often consumes us. So why does all our effort seem to end up in failure more than success?

The answer is that sameness has its own logic. While there are often very good reasons to change, there are often equally if not more attractive and even sensible reasons to stay the same: wanting to feel secure and stable in the predictability of old patterns, avoiding seeing yourself as a failure, or avoiding the pain of disappointing your friends and family if you don't change. There are other even more powerful reasons to stay the same as well—deeper reasons that mostly lie below the threshold of your awareness.

Advice and instruction speak to none of that. In fact, when you follow advice without fully and dispassionately considering whether you really want to change, you treat the choice to change as the *only* reasonable one to make, and sameness as an unreasonable option.

That view of change as a foregone conclusion—as the sole definition of success—typically doesn't work.

Research shows us that deep and lasting change is typically the result of contemplation,[11,12,13] the dispassionate weighing of the pros and cons of a situation. That doesn't mean advice is totally useless. It's just that you're not going to take and use it in a way that actually helps until you've contemplated both sides of an argument in which sameness has been winning so far.

Pick a diet, any diet. Follow it and you'll lose weight. Choose a gym routine. You'll get more fit if you follow it. Follow advice on quitting a habit. Habit gone. How-to instructions are as easy as one, two, three. But *following* them isn't. That's because personal *change only happens from within.* To make a personal change in your life is to make a decision and to commit to that decision. The only way to make a committed decision that can lead to change is to do the hard, very human work of contemplating the pros and cons of your situation *before* you act. There's no chicken-and-egg riddle between contemplation and advice. Contemplation always comes first when you succeed in making the change you want to make.

The Strengths of Contemplation, the Weakness of Advice

Here's a statistic that might startle you.[14] It's about a behavior we commonly see as the most difficult one to change: addiction. It turns out that most people in the United States who quit habitual drinking do so *without* treatment. That's right: Most people quit this highly addictive habit on their own. What's more, people who quit drinking on their own stay sober longer than those who enter treatment. They take a serious, hard look at themselves and decide that not drinking is better for them than drinking. Their sobriety likely lasts longer than that of people who achieve sobriety in treatment because the self-propelled sober person holds firmly to their own internal compass throughout their recovery, instead of following someone else's advice. In other words—it's an inside job.

You're that lightbulb in the therapist's office: To change, you have to want to change, and *you can only get to wanting change by considering the reasons you're resisting it.*

This book helps you do just that.

I offer you Ten Reasons Not to Change, which will help you to contemplate your situation no matter the change you want to make. By getting up close and specific about why we resist change, the Ten Reasons give you the ability to locate why you may be choosing to stay the same in a particular situation. No longer does your resistance to change feel like some giant mysterious force you can't control. Instead, it is framed in ten portraits—a gallery you peruse while contemplating which portrait might match your experience. If you can match the portrait with the reason (or reasons) for not changing that you're struggling with, your path to change will be much more effective.

HOW THE TEN REASONS NOT TO CHANGE HELP YOU CHANGE

"If you know yourself but not the enemy, for every victory gained you will also suffer a defeat," Sun Tzu famously wrote in *The Art of War.*[15] Sun Tzu's adage applies to the struggle for change. Knowing what you want—healthier lifestyle, happier relationships, more engaging work—is only half the battle. Knowing what roadblocks you erect (the enemy) that thwart these changes and keep you stuck is the crucial complement. We tell ourselves we oppose sameness—same sedentary lifestyle, same unfulfilling social connections, or same unsatisfying work. But in reality, there are some not-so-obvious reasons for our stuckness. Exploring these reasons and letting yourself identify, understand, and even embrace the seductions of sameness is tremendously helpful if you want to change.

Here are four ways this exploration of the intricacies of sameness will get you closer to making the change you want to make:

1. *Killing shame with open air.* When one or more of my ten portraits matches your experience, that means there is, at the very least, a community of you and me. If we are in this together, then I can help you feel less shameful about failing to change.

Unlike guilt—a bad feeling you have when you've done something wrong or immoral—shame is the feeling that there's something broken or soiled about you as a person. Ridding yourself of shame about the things you want to change is important, since shame is a sneaky, dangerous feeling. A wolf in another wolf's clothing, shame is often regarded as a scary motivator—a kind of psychic threat that compels you to move forward. But it's actually a motivation killer. "You're broken," it tells you, *"so give up."*

As a self-kept secret about a feeling of singular taintedness, shame is harbored and cultivated in the dank gloom of isolation. In the darkness, undisturbed by reality and a sense of commonality, it grows bigger. Thus, the more you can view seemingly shameful behaviors in the open air of others, the less power shame has over your life.

Imagine that you're in a support group for people who want to quit smoking. The counselor instructs you and the other participants to engage in a process of guided imagery. Eyes closed, you envision the success of quitting smoking, and how you would feel, both psychologically and physically, on that successful day. Eyes open, you look around at your fellow support group members. Do you now feel any closer to them, any sense that you and they are on a similar journey? Perhaps a bit. Do you gain any motivation to quit smoking during this exercise? Maybe a little. But what if the instructor asked the group to list the reasons they don't quit, putting these on the board and finding their similarities? Someone says the delicious first drag; someone else, the way it calms them down. Another talks about the ritual of pulling a cigarette out of the pack and lighting it. You mention how it helps you focus while working. Heads are nodding in recognition; there are some smiles of agreement. How would you feel then? Probably connected and, as a result, less ashamed. Your shameful act, in other words, is brought into the light and shared, and that sharing lessens the shame. Even though you would be talking about something you might believe is a mark of your bad character, you might feel a lift in your morale as the burden of shame lifts.

By decreasing shame, feelings of connectedness are fuel for motivation—the feeling that "I can do this"—and they are stoked when we find that otherwise personal issues are actually things others experience too. There's a reason people introduce themselves at AA meetings with "I am an alcoholic." Admitting to something that causes them shame in a group of others with the same problem bonds them in a fellowship of mutual support toward change.

By showing you ten ways in which others wrestle with change versus sameness, I offer you ways to feed motivation by lifting the smothering effects of shame with the recognition that you are not alone.

---

2. *Taking a both-and position toward change.* When you attempt to alter your behavior, the resistance to change always makes itself felt. Always. You can't escape it. This leads to an important insight: If change inevitably involves resistance to change, we can see the orientation toward sameness as part of changing. Thus, change and sameness are not in an either-or relationship, but a both-and one. They are equal parts of a whole.

That concept of two opposing forces that are segments of one thing is a difficult concept for us in the modern Western world to swallow. We have a tendency to think in dichotomies: clean-dirty, success-failure, beautiful-ugly. That tendency is only exacerbated by the omnipresence of advertising, much of which projects a fictionalized reality of unambiguously clean, healthy, successful people in order to sell goods (with much of self-help literature suspiciously fitting this mold). While I don't want to dwell too much on the dichotomy between Western and Eastern thought, it's worthwhile to consider that there are parts of Chinese philosophy, in particular, that counter black-and-white thinking and offer us a different window on change. The yin and yang symbol is the most famous embodiment of this approach.

In yin-yang, dark is found in light, and light is found in dark, and together they form a whole. Two seemingly opposite things are in dialogue with each other and are impossible to fully comprehend without being seen as connected.

Let's take this notion down to earth: Think of an artist. She can't express light without painting shadow; and she can't portray shadow without capturing light. It's called *chiaroscuro* in Italian, the word's literal meaning embodying this duality: *bright-dark*. Art is always a both-and process.

The art of change is no different. You can't understand change without understanding sameness; you can't really grasp what it means to stay the same without getting to know change; and you can't deeply comprehend change or sameness without seeing them as parts of a whole.

Change comes more easily, and the change you enact becomes more sustainable, if you do the hard work of understanding this marriage between change and staying the same. In the following chapters, you'll see how recognizing this duality helps you move forward in your life.

---

3. *Seeing the universal in the personal.* There's an important message about our humanity in the bottle of sameness. In

full yin-yang mode, grasping that message will help you deal with the most minute behaviors you want to change.

"The more specific you are, the more universal you are," says novelist Nancy Hale.[16] That idea is certainly true for all art. But it's also true for the therapeutic professions ("What is most personal is most universal," writes the great humanist psychologist Carl Rogers[17]). As this book guides you to get extremely specific about why you resist change, you'll discover the universal reasons for sameness.

Each of the Ten Reasons explored in the next chapters originates in the same philosophical basin. Each carries something about what it means to be human. Taken as a whole, they honor what all of us struggle with as conscious human beings: our accountability for our lives, the pain of our aloneness, our tendency toward shame, the call to be courageous in the face of vulnerability, and our struggle over hope and faith. Understanding the Ten Reasons as a whole offers you a portal into these very human, profoundly existential issues and how they play out in your life. I hope that by understanding these issues, you'll gain new clarity about why you resist the currents of change, whether it's your repeatedly failed attempts to organize your closet or your unmet vow to volunteer on a political campaign and help change the world for the better.

I like to think of the Ten Reasons Not to Change as similar to those paintings by the master artist Chuck Close. Each of his late portraits is actually made up of smaller works of art. When you stand close to Close's paintings (yes, a pun-like surname), these smaller works can be appreciated as precious individual works of art. As you back up a bit and look at the small pieces next to one another, each actually makes more sense and gains more value—like beads in a bazaar, an abundance of tiny things to compare and contrast. Then, as you back up even farther, they become part of a lovely portrait, at once a little abstract but also uncanny in its accuracy. Step back farther, viewing the piece on the wall of the museum, and it's almost indistinguishable from a photograph. Change is like that. It's serious business, because even the smallest attempt at behavioral change is intimately connected to larger, deeper issues.

This concept of smaller pieces contributing to a comprehensive whole reminds me of something written by the sixteenth-century rabbi Simcha Bunim Bonhart.[18] He wrote that people should carry in each of their pockets a slip of paper. On one piece, they should write, "I am but dust and ashes." On the other piece they should write, "The world was created for me." The secret to life is knowing that both are true, knowing that they are only true when held at the same time (in each pocket), and knowing when to read which piece of paper.

We are made of stardust. Each of us contains the universe, while each of us is also powder. Our special circumstances are a yin to the yang of cosmic issues. In regard to personal change, sometimes it's fine to try to make it happen by looking only at the dust of isolated behavior, but often it's better to see your behavior as connected to and responding to a world created for you.

Associating smartphone addiction, getting organized, or losing weight with the deepest issues of our humanity might seem like an awfully serious take on change. But life is serious, and the fact is, we all do approach often seemingly minute issues about change rather seriously: They are in the background and forefront of our minds all the time. Let's honor the minutiae as a way to enhance, rather than diminish, the beautifully complex world we call the human experience.

You might feel I'm asking you to take your eyes off the target when I suggest you place the specific content of the change you want within the realm of universal concerns. I know that feels risky. I know this because I see it in myself all the time. The minute I want to change something, it's like I'm playing darts: I tend to squint my perspective, focus myself on the target, and cut out any possible distraction as I aim for the bull's-eye. And you know what? That approach is great on a Friday night at an Irish bar. It never works with personal change.

Let me give you a guarantee: I promise you will not get fatter, uglier, more lonely, or less fulfilled if you consider universal issues while you attempt to make personal change. In fact, I promise you that understanding a bit of what it means to be human, and connecting your humanity to the reasons you resist change, will help you move forward. Who knows: It may even help you change some of your ideas on what needs changing. Once you have a picture of larger human concerns and how these concerns connect to your own ability to change, you might discover that the issue isn't your weight, but whether you can find better ways to love your body; isn't your looks, but worrying less about your image; isn't loneliness, but your inability to rest in solitude; isn't a lack of fulfillment, but the need for you to love the sameness-loving part of you. Then again, maybe you do want to lose a few pounds. Either way, you're more free to move forward toward the change you want when you see it as part of larger issues.

A famous TV personality and self-help guru clearly had "work" done recently—some sort of plastic surgery to bring back his youth. He does look a bit younger, but his face now appears almost inhuman—a permanent, distorted mask, a cartoon version of his previous self. To me, it's the image of change without depth: an alteration that's askew, unconnected to bigger issues of his humanity, a mutilation. The result of age removed with a scalpel, it's a warning about the lure of silver bullets and magic pills. Neither is offered in this book. Instead, I'm looking to help you achieve a different kind of change, one that is more gentle, more nurturing, less violent or forceful, but likely more profound and more satisfying. That kind of change happens in the context of other human experiences, including the experience of staying the same even though every bone in your body aches to change.

---

4. *Untying the sameness knot.* When you see that sameness is part of being human, you're also *not* doing something else: seeing your resistance to change as an abnormality. If you want to enter the change-generating space of contemplation, you need to release the knee-jerk belief that change has to happen and has to happen now. It's important for you to get rid of the idea that there is something wrong with you if you don't change. Contemplating change means contemplating all the options, including sameness.

You're not going to do the important work of contemplating change if you tip the scale toward change, seeing it as the only correct conclusion, and sameness as only a dead end. To abide by the contemplative's motto "On the one hand; on the other," you have to give sameness the weight and seriousness it deserves. There's nothing to contemplate if you don't.

That means that sameness—the force that frustratingly halts that seemingly positive change you're attempting to make—isn't really an enemy. Truly knowing yourself means knowing the part of you that will always find reasons to stay the same. The more you know this part, the less likely you are to "suffer defeat," to paraphrase Sun Tzu.[19]

Of all the ways the Ten Reasons Not to Change can help you, this idea is the most important: *Sameness is something to consider as reasonable, and by considering it so, you have a better chance of changing.*

Understanding ten reasonable reasons to stay the same gets you out of the self-fulfilling knot tying you to change as the only legitimate option. Sameness is in your life for good, and it's in your life for good reasons. As you'll read, it comes from your self-love, and from that, your wish to protect yourself from some really awful feelings.

As an expression of your self-love, sameness often does a lousy job of showing it—halting important changes, getting in the way of your unalienable right to grow. Nonetheless, it's part of you, not apart from you. And it's definitely not out to hurt you, even though it often does end up hurting in some serious ways. I want you to avoid placing sameness in a box of defective things. That's the wrong place for it to be. Sameness deserves your affection, since it comes from an affectionate part of you. If you reject its caring, broken reach and exile it from your consciousness, you won't be able to contemplate changing.

Which, as I've already mentioned, means you won't be able *to* change.

Here's some breaking news: Humans aren't machines (at least yet!). If you treat them as machines, each one the same and so simple that one instruction manual works for all their broken parts, not only are you acting in an inhumane way regarding their needs, but the interventions you use won't work.

They won't work because the source of change resides in the human *being part of you*—right at the center of how you experience and interpret the world around you—not in *a doing part*, the mechanics of thoughtless, robotic action.

How We Change calls out for you to do the complex and often painful work of making changes in an actual, thinking, feeling, and autonomous human *being*. That's not easy, not by a long shot. And it's made more difficult by a world in which people are increasingly treated as things.

From Persons to Machine: The Loss of Contemplation

Over forty years ago, the great psychoanalyst and social critic Erich Fromm wrote about the growing threat of a society that preferred "having" to "being."[20] In the world of "having," not only are you oriented toward getting more things, but the *doing* part of you—how you behave, look, reason—is a sign of your usefulness *as a thing*, as a device through which you and others can achieve goals. In fact, Fromm, along with many public thinkers in the 1950s, '60s, and '70s, was worried about a threat that today might seem all but quaint: "conformity." These thinkers were scared about a coming world in which everyone would try to act and look like one another. What worried them about conformity also worried them about many other things they saw emerging in the twentieth century: a vast trend in which efforts to fit in or fit an ideal caused people to neglect their own unique humanity and made them increasingly blind or disdainful of the unique humanity in others. The term for that phenomenon, when people become disconnected from themselves and from others, is alienation, which Fromm defined as "a mode of experience in which the person experiences himself as an alien."[21]

Concerns about conformity and alienation enjoyed a good thirty-year run as part of the zeitgeist, easily deciphered in the Beat generation, the women's movement, the antiwar and civil rights movements, even *Mister Rogers' Neighborhood* and the central philosophical groundwork for Martin Luther King. It was expressed in movies about loners and rebels, from *Twelve Angry Men* and *The Graduate* to *One Flew Over the Cuckoo's Nest*.

But the times they are a-changin'. A Banana Republic on every corner, the Kardashians on every screen, *Say Yes to the Dress*, liposuction, CoolSculpting, Botox—all now as accessible as shampoo; the push to brand yourself as a product not only accepted, but celebrated; all the books, videos, and YouTube channels giving instruction on how to mold yourself into some ideal; and, most glaring, a triumphant presidential campaign largely based on shamelessly dehumanizing others. Can you agree with me that the warnings of our humanist forebears about people becoming things were on the mark?

The world of "having" seems to have won the culture battle over the world of "being," so much so that we now live in a kind of collective amnesia, in which we no longer recognize that there is a more humane, more connected option than buying and selling things, and buying and selling ourselves *as things*. In this climate, we become obsessed with our packaging and neglect the contents of our being.

So what does this have to do with personal change? In the world of having, we tend to approach personal change as if it were an item on a shelf at Home Depot, judging ourselves for our uniformity and usefulness. Are you a beautiful, well-oiled riding mower? Or are you rusted and corroded inside and out? In this consumerist world, personal change means you fix what you then *own and trade*: A new body! A new skill! A new attitude! A NEW YOU!

How We Change hearkens back to a bygone era when books like Fromm's were read by a wide and general audience. This was an era in which deep thinkers like Rollo May,[22] Martin Buber,[23] Paul Tillich,[24] and Ivan Illich[25] joined Fromm in writing books for the general public about reaching their potential through acts of courage, not by following step-by-step instructions. It was a time when May's book *The Meaning of Anxiety*,[26] which described anxiety as an important part of human experience (and not—as we do today—a disease to cure with the quick fix of a pill), was read around the world.

These authors celebrated the *being* part of what it means to be human. They resisted approaches that saw humans as merely things to fix. Addressing the humanity in their readers, their goal was to help them contemplate their situation, in the hope that they might make decisions that would bring their lives more depth and meaning. That's a far cry from telling them the steps they need to take in order to function better so they can fit in.

Now I'm going to take an educated guess: I place good odds on the fact that you're reading this book because you want to make some sort of change in your life. That change may be about habits—like eating healthier, or sticking with a meditation practice. It might be about getting better at something or learning something new—like improving a skill or learning a craft. It could be about reaching deeper goals having to do with growth—like finding a romantic partner or taking a different career course. Or the change you seek might be about even deeper stuff—like your struggle over building a meaningful, purposeful life.

In any of these cases, you're likely not interested in the philosophies of the postwar public intellectuals. That's more than fine. I promise you that you're in the right place: I wrote this book to help you make such changes. But the fact remains that change doesn't happen if you're treating the thing you want to change as if it's, well, *a thing*, alien from you, separate from your humanity.

This book would have been so much easier to write if I didn't have to dive into the trench of our humanity. It would have ended up being such a nice, concise tome of advice if I wasn't so focused on you as a human being, and on helping you do the very human act of contemplating. I have to admit, I was tempted at times to stay on the surface and just tell you "how to." Wouldn't that be paradise? A world in which change is a grape I can peel for you. But life isn't paradise. Life is beautiful, awe-inspiring, and deep, and it's also a struggle with ugliness, emptiness, and superficiality. Life is a both-and proposition. So is change.

The Road Ahead

How We Change is divided into two sections. Section I gives you a bird's-eye view of change: what gets in the way of change, and what pushes you toward it. You'll learn about important existential concepts regarding experiences of aloneness and accountability and their influence on anxiety, and you'll read about "fear of hope," a concept I've developed and researched with a team at Rutgers University that I believe is central to change. In Section II, I zoom in on the Ten Reasons Not to Change, a gallery of distinct portraits of why we sometimes stay the same that will help you contemplate your particular situation in regard to change. The final chapter presents an eleventh portrait that depicts the importance of the social resources one typically needs to change.

THE INEVITABLE TENSION OF CHANGE AND THE FEAR OF HOPE

CHAPTER 1

HOW I GOT HERE

To him who feels himself preordained to contemplation and not to
belief, all believers are too noisy and obtrusive; he guards against them.

—Friedrich Nietzsche

My appreciation for the awesome power of sameness comes from
over thirty years of clinical experience, first as a social worker
helping people who had been treated for extensive periods of
time, then as the founder and CEO of a program that works with
such individuals. While I've always had a small, private psychotherapy practice in which I work with self-sufficient people who
need nothing more than a weekly visit, it's the former group,
those dealing with severe psychological conditions, who truly
taught me about the hidden appeal, the seductive reasonableness,
of staying the same.

It is not easy being a psychiatric patient. Our society tends
to stigmatize mental illness; neglects to accommodate people
experiencing difficult psychiatric symptoms in schools, work-
places, and neighborhoods; and adopts an overly medicalized
approach to behaviors and feelings that don't fit some idealized

norm. Shunned by the world, limited in their opportunities, and receiving the unspoken message from so-called mental health experts that they're hopelessly "broken," my clients are at the very limits of what we humans can withstand in regard to experiences of personal disappointment and social exclusion. Pushed to these limits, they have important lessons to teach us. While most of us have been lucky enough never to need to learn these lessons so acutely, they are nonetheless filled with universal wisdom.

Many of the people I work with find miraculous ways to make changes that enable them to move forward in life despite crushingly demoralizing personal experiences. They get back to school, work, and careers; start exercising again; make friends; enter romantic relationships. Many others, however, turn away from change, seeing *sameness* as their most trusted sanctuary or ally. Whether propelled to change or to remain the same, all of them have something to teach us about the complex, often paradoxical dynamics of personal change.

I started formulating ideas about the dynamics of change as a young social worker in Waltham, Massachusetts, facilitating a therapy group in a day treatment program for people with extensive histories in the mental health system. This was an open group, so new participants were always arriving and old ones leaving. Over time, I began to wonder about a specific issue: *Why did participants in the group consistently resist changes in their lives that seemed so obviously positive?*

I asked the participants this question repeatedly over the years. No matter who was attending my group, their responses were remarkably similar.

One night, I sat down and categorized these responses. As I looked at the list, I came to see that each reason a person resisted change had its own internal logic, its own *reasonableness*. Staying

1. Staying the same protects you from awareness of your aloneness and sole accountability for your own life.

2. Staying the same protects you from the accountability for "what's next."

3. Staying the same protects you from the unknown.

4. Staying the same protects you from your own expectations.

5. Staying the same protects you from the expectations of others.

6. Staying the same protects you from seeing where you are.

7. Staying the same protects you from the insult of small steps.

8. Staying the same protects a monument to your pain.

9. Staying the same protects you from changing your relationship with others.

10. Staying the same protects you from changing your relationship with yourself.

the same began to make sense to me as a course of action, a solution for certain experiences that, in fact, could *not* be attained by changing. This was true even in situations in which changing seemed like such an obvious choice. I called the resulting document "The Ten Reasons Not to Change" and shared it with the group.

The Ten Reasons operated as a powerful tool as we contemplated the places where they felt stuck. Freed from the Tarzan dichotomy of "change good/same bad," we were able to place sameness on the table, think about it, approach it with curiosity, and let it play in our minds. Once we could do that, something remarkable occurred: *By imagining sameness as a potentially sensible course of action, my clients often found it easier to make changes in their lives.* Thinking about not changing and why they may have wanted to stay the same seemed to loosen the restraints to motivation, and to do so in a more effective manner than all the advice or instruction *to* change. Like Houdini in a straitjacket, relaxing in order to escape, his body compressed in alliance with the pressure of belts, chains, and canvas, moving in the opposite direction from where you want to go often frees you to get there.

I began to see the key to change waiting for us within this paradox.

Later, I brought the Ten Reasons into my private psychotherapy practice, with those folks who see me once a week. The Ten Reasons had similar results, freeing people up to see their resistance to change as tied to the attractive reasonableness of sameness. I also welcomed the Ten Reasons into my own life, finding them to be instrumental in making changes I'd long wanted to make but never could.

My realization about the paradox of change is not new. In fact, it's a reflection of a central value in social work. The adage to "Start where the client is" is a root concept in my field, and suggests that professionals understand and sit with a person's experience in a nonjudgmental manner rather than push them toward change. The Ten Reasons also reflect values in other therapeutic fields, from paradoxical interventions[1] (a fancy term for reverse psychology) in family therapy, where clinicians tell their clients to continue behaviors the clients say they wish to resolve, in order to help these individuals see their often destructive behavior as having its own logic; the tenet in humanistic psychology of "unconditional positive regard"[2]; the notion in psychotherapy, mirrored in Buddhist-oriented approaches, of "going with the resistance"[3]; to an approach used in the addiction field called "motivational interviewing,"[4] in which the pros and cons of substance use are weighed in nonjudgmental conversation with a clinician, as opposed to using a strong confrontational approach for a supposedly hijacked, and thus unreasoning, brain.

The idea of approaching a person "where they are," being inquisitive about why they may want to stay the same, and even thinking about sameness as a reasonable course of action, is not my invention. But I do see the Ten Reasons giving form to these larger traditions by breaking resistance to change into ten smaller units. By doing so, change and sameness become objects you can mentally hold, manage, and shape.

Why the Ten Reasons Are Reasonable

For over two decades, I kept the Ten Reasons in my front pocket, an effective tool I would pull out time and time again that gave me and my clients an understandable frame around experiences of stuckness. There was something reassuring and comprehensible about this tool: the Dewey-like tidiness of a decimal. But over time, I grew to feel the Reasons were also a little too pat to capture the very deep and often dark processes undergirding change. What began as an attempt to give form to the behavioral results of the formless anguish of massive disappointment was now something you could count on two hands.

It's not that the Ten Reasons ever existed in a theoretical vacuum: I always knew they were linked to certain important experiences related to our capacity to hope, and to the power of disappointment to injure us in a way that makes us actually fear hoping. In fact, the idea that we could fear hope, and that this fear makes us want to stay the same, was something I would talk about freely with people when I discussed the Ten Reasons. But it remained theoretical, an interesting idea.

That all changed recently.

FEAR OF HOPE RESEARCH

In the fall of 2018 I gave a guest lecture on the Ten Reasons at a course at Rutgers University at Newark called the Psychology of Emotions, taught by Professor Kent Harber, a social psychologist who studies psychological resources. Kent lit up when I mentioned my ideas about fearing hope, and suggested my otherwise theoretical concept could be scientifically measured and studied. And so began a research collaboration that is confirming lessons I learned from clients regarding their troubled relation to hope.[5] Our research group has been able to show that fear of hope can be reliably measured using a unique scale that lets us determine whether and to what degree people fear hope, knowledge that is giving us new insight into the relationship between fear of hope and an array of other emotions and ways of thinking.[6] *Everything we've discovered provides a very strong explanation for why sameness can appear—and can even be—a reasonable choice.*

Our research began to color in the spaces outlined by the Ten Reasons Not to Change for me, illuminating the reasons behind *the Reasons.* Why would we actually resist changes that will so obviously enhance our existences? Because something in our lives has made us fear hoping. That "something" doesn't have to be some giant disappointment—in fact it might be something we can't even identify—but it is an experience that whispers to us that it's dangerous to follow hope into action.

I'll discuss this in much more detail later, but when you hope, you *hope for* something that you feel is missing in your life. Hope is thus always wrapped up in a kind of tension. The mother of yearning and longing, hope is about wanting something you lack.

That makes hope risky, since acting on your hope and "going for it" raises the real possibility that you won't succeed at attaining something you feel is missing in your life. And nowhere is the hope-generating tension between where you are right now—not having something you feel is lacking in your life—and where you want to be—having it in your life—more perilous than when you hope for personal change.

So that's the brief story of how the Ten Reason Not to Change formed in my mind, and then became a tool to help people contemplate the changes they want to make. There are, of course, lots of missing elements to this story, ones you don't know about now; many you will learn about later. For now, let's just say it's a very typical story of how one mind noticed something unexplained in its environment, took what it noticed and tried to explain it, forming an idea about it, then playing with that idea, sculpting it into something meaningful and comprehensible. We all do that all the time when novel information appears to us in worlds that seem well-worn and settled: We make this information fit, our minds often obsessively seeking to contain it within an understandable whole.

As you'll read in the next chapter, our minds are built with a drive toward wholeness at their core. Understanding that drive is central to understanding personal change.

CHAPTER 2

THE WHERE YOU ARE/ WHERE YOU WANT TO BE TENSION

We need the sweet pain of anticipation to tell us we are really alive.

—Albert Camus

It's the early 1930s and Kurt Lewin, a psychology professor at the University of Berlin, is sitting in a café with a large group of his students.[1] They give their orders to the waiter, who listens carefully but writes nothing down, then goes off to fetch their separate selections. He returns fifteen minutes later, tray in hand, and places each plate in front of the person who ordered it. Later, after their table has been cleared but before the check has been paid, Lewin asks the waiter what each of their party ordered— and the waiter provides a perfect recounting. Then Lewin asks the waiter what a large party at a nearby table ordered. "Why sir, I have no idea," replied the waiter, astounded at the question. "Those people already paid!" For Lewin, who had a genius for seeing the profound in the mundane, this was a major aha moment. *How is it,* Lewin wonders, *that the waiter remembers everything in such detail, but only before the bill is paid?* Lewin postulates that between taking the orders and settling the bill, a tension is created in the waiter that promotes recall. But when the task is finished (i.e., the bill is paid) the tension is gone, and the memory immediately disappears.

Lewin's musings about the mundane task of remembering orders at a café led him and others to theories about how people pursue goals in general. Lewin is the father of modern social psychology and a pivotal figure in organizational psychology. Much of his most influential work focuses on the tension between where we are in relationship to a particular goal, and how the strength or weakness of this tension influences our motivation to reach that goal.[2]

Lewin was influenced by what is called gestalt psychology,[3] which was a radical approach to understanding human vision, learning, and problem solving. Understanding the concept of a gestalt is important in grasping Lewin's ideas about motivation. And understanding his ideas about how tension, goals, and motivation work will help you understand my insights on personal change.

"Gestalt" means "shape" in German, indicating something complete, identifiable, and comprehensible. Gestalt theorists see our minds as designed to look at groups of separate things and construct wholes out of them. You enter a room and see four cylindrical pieces of wood standing upright, on top of which is a horizontal wooden slab, with more but smaller wooden cylinders projecting from one side joined at the top by a flat wooden piece. Your mind does not say, "bunch of connected wooden pieces." It says "chair," and you also see a chair; that's a gestalt—a whole made up of individual parts. When you entered the room, your mind took in the walls, the ceiling, and the floor, and you knew you were in "a room," rather than "drywall, sockets, sashes, hinges." That, too, was a gestalt. And the experience of the "you" that entered the room? A gestalt.

Since the mind is always looking to form this kind of whole, it doesn't like discrepancies in our lives—some disparity between two or more things that we feel should fit together. Indeed, some psychologists believe that all emotions arise when we encounter a discrepancy between what we expect and what we encounter, and that those emotions stay active until the discrepancy has been resolved.[4] When the psyche encounters these discrepancies, it wants to fix them, to integrate them into something complete, to reduce the tension that they create. To make discrepant things *meaningful*. We need that. Without it, the world would look completely dispersed and undifferentiated, the chaos and formlessness of dust in the light: no chair, no room, no you.

And here lies a delightful paradox of humanity. Our psyche abhors discrepancies and compels us to remedy them. Yet rather than living in quiet complacency, what do we do? We set goals. We aspire to change. Setting a goal inherently involves a discrepancy—between where you are now and where you want to be. The tension caused by this particular discrepancy, and your drive to rid yourself of this tension, often leads to a good thing: the motivation to reach the goal. If you can get to the goal, the tension is resolved. That's why the waiter is able to keep the memory going during his task—he's motivated to end the discrepancy between taking the order and announcing the bill, and his memory is the means to get there. That's also why the waiter forgets the orders once the bill is announced. There is no longer a discrepancy—and therefore no tension—once he's completed his task.

So, successfully reaching a goal is one very important way a person can relieve the tension between where they are in relationship to that goal and the goal itself. Of course, there is another, less effortful way to rid this tension: by giving up. No goal means no discrepancy, which, in turn, results in no tension. Giving up and surrendering are important elements of this book, and I'll return to them. But for now let's stick with the motivating fuel of the tension between your current state and where you want to be.

The idea that your motivation depends on the tension between where you are now and your goal, and the fact that your motivation ends once you reach your goal, may seem obvious. You crave your favorite bacon burger. You're motivated to cook it because you want it for dinner, and there thus exists a discrepancy between your present hunger and your final, satisfied swallow. Once you finish the burger, however, you are no longer motivated to cook it, because there is no longer a discrepancy between your metabolic need and the satisfaction of that need. You were hungry, you ate, and the burger is no longer on your mind. That's the theory: You want something, the tension between wanting it and getting it motivates you to action, and you no longer feel motivated to achieve the goal once you've attained it.

It's that simple.

Well, actually, it's not. The transition from doing nothing to doing something, or from doing something negative to doing something positive, involves a complex array of forces and counterforces. Lewin referred to these pushes and pulls as vectors,[5] a term he adopted from math and physics and applied to human action.

A vector is something that has both a level of force (called *magnitude*) and a direction.[6] The classic SAT math problem about when two trains will pass each other, one leaving Cleveland at 45 miles per hour and the other leaving from Wichita Falls at 60 miles per hour, is a story of vectors. Let's say you're coming to visit me in your car, and I ask when you think you'll get here. If you answer, "I'm taking the Ventura Freeway south," you're only giving me a partial answer, since you haven't told me how fast you'll be going. The same is true if you say "I'll be going sixty-five miles an hour," but neglect to tell me your present location. But if you say, "I'm taking the Ventura Freeway south from my house, and I'm going sixty-five," you will have described a vector, and I'll know when to start shaking the martinis.

When it comes to thinking about personal goals, vectors are quite handy, allowing us to look at both where a person wants to go and the level of energy or strength they have to get there. Yet human endeavors cannot easily be reduced into neat little math problems. Both the strength of our motivation and the direction in which we are going are too complex to fully map or measure. A car going 65 miles an hour on the Ventura Freeway exists in an easily rendered vector. But the complex, meaning-making person driving the car has all kinds of things affecting the course she takes, such as the magnitude of the force pushing her forward on this course, and even changes in the magnitude of that force. Why is one driver racing to meet a client, and why is another racing to escape an unhappy marriage? Both motivations are vectors, yet neither is easily translated into the algebra of velocity and direction. Fiction writers, such as Marcel Proust, William Faulkner, and Philip Roth, have dedicated pages upon pages to all the multiple forces that push someone toward or away from some particular action. For us humans, goal attainment is, therefore, rarely as simple as a line between Cleveland and Wichita Falls. That is why Siri can tell us how to drive across country, but not why to get out of bed. For those of us seeking to make changes, the vectors of our inner drives and often vague directions are far more complicated than instructions to "walk 10,000 steps" or "weigh out 10 ounces of ground beef" would suggest.

Fields and Force Fields

Let's return to that 1930s Berlin café. Lewin's aha moment comes when he perceives a sort of invisible bubble around the waiter, a "life space," or "field," as he later calls it.[7] This field consists of the waiter's own psychological strengths and weaknesses, what's happening around him in his environment, and the ways he responds to the environment and the environment responds to him. Lewin even came up with a formula for these fields: $B=f(P, E)$, meaning behavior (B) is a function (f) of a person (P) and his or her environment (E). This was a radical formula for the time that defied the stimulus-response model popular then. Humans, for Lewin, were not simply organisms zapped into action only by external rewards and punishments. They were "persons" with inner lives, inner thoughts, hopes, and fears that could act on their environments, and not just be acted upon by their environments. Thus, Lewin saw our movement toward goals as directed by dynamic thoughts, forces, and emotions that shifted depending on our own interaction with the environment around us.

This was also a radical departure from psychoanalysis,[8] the other major approach to human psychology, which regarded behavior as reflecting personalities formed by neurotic worries and repressed impulses, and focused less on how people negotiate the very real challenges of day-to-day living. Lewin was arguing that our movement toward goals is partly a reflection of our current state, rather than strictly based on psychological traits. The present situation matters, said Lewin, a dictum that shaped modern social psychology. *How many social psychologists does it take to change a lightbulb?* The answer: *Depends on the situation.*

Sitting at the café, Lewin postulated that the waiter's memory of the ordered items was dependent on a psychological field. This field was made up of the waiter's desire to do a good job, the general demands of his job, and the specific task before him (i.e., getting schnitzel, sauerbraten, and Pilsner to that raucous table of psychologists). The waiter's behavior, his remarkable memory, and his equally remarkable forgetting after payment all make sense when regarded in terms of the field he inhabits: the person he is (a waiter) and the situation he is negotiating (waiting tables). This is the gestalt of "waiter," and it creates the memory-enhancing tension of the discrepancy between the order for food and drink and the delivery of the bill. To put it another way, there's no tension between taking the order and remembering it without the waiter also carrying out the responsibilities of his job.

But what happens when the field changes? What happens when the waiter, let's call him Fritz, shifts from being a waiter to some other role, and when the goals of that other role become salient. Suppose that Fritz the waiter is also one of Lewin's students, and seeing his professor and classmates entering the café, he transitions from busy waiter to excited student. As Fritz plunks himself down with his schoolmates, their food orders—given to another waiter—do not register with Fritz at all. His mind is on the theory of vectors and psychological fields, not on skeins of ale. He might not even recall what anyone ordered, because he is, quite literally, "not in that space." Fritz's mental state changes by simply taking off his apron and sitting with his classmates, and now he is engaged in different goals.

Once Fritz puts his apron back on, however, he's actually still not guaranteed that he'll remember all orders. In his field there are not only forces pushing him toward his goals, but ones resisting him getting there too.

For Fritz, the forward vectors helping him to remember are his need for gainful employment, his intrinsic desire to please his customers, his pride in his ability to mentally remember diverse and even complicated things, the strong cup of coffee that focuses his attention, and his desire for a big tip. Together, these forward vectors engage the tension between recalling customers' orders and collecting their payments. Lewin called the sum of these positive vectors that keep Fritz focused on his goal driving forces.

Coexisting with these driving forces are other things that impede Fritz, many of which would also restrain him in the task of being a good student: He just received horrible news from home, was hit on the head the previous night, recently received a poor review by his superior, is preoccupied with news of an alarming political development, or just has a naturally poor memory. Lewin called these liabilities and negative influences restraining forces. When you measure the magnitude of things preventing a person from reaching their goal, you're looking at these forces. Restraining forces are the reason why we can't reach our goals with the snap of a finger. If there weren't things restraining us, there wouldn't be any tension, and we'd just get what we want without any effort.

To understand how we reach goals, Lewin developed the force field analysis (fig. 1). For him, a person's behavior exists in a dynamic (changeable state) between the driving forces toward a goal and the restraining forces that obstruct a person's path to the goal.

The picture Lewin painted is like those party gifts with the pipe and ball. You blow in the pipe, and the ball rises. As long as you keep your breath even, the ball stays in one place, floating above the pipe, between the driving strength of your breath and the restraining power of gravity. For Lewin, humans can only reach their goals when either the restraining force is weakened or the driving force is strengthened.

This idea of a force field is not really Lewin's invention. It was Sir Isaac Newton[9] who posited that "a body at rest will remain at rest, and a body in motion will remain in motion unless it is acted upon by an external force." Lewin recognized that these fundamental laws affect not only falling apples but also striving humans.

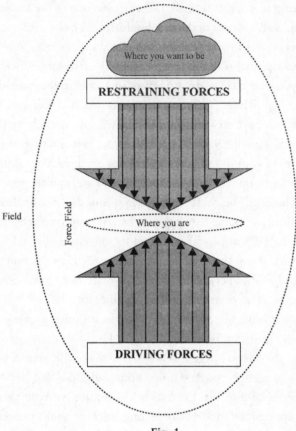

Fig. 1

Right now I'm sitting in a chair typing away. The reason I neither sink into the ground nor float off into space is the tension between mass and gravity. I'm that ball above the pipe. Whether in nature, or in the complex space we call the human psyche, inertia is dynamic. We don't stop being bodies at rest until the relative strength of the countervailing forces of drive and restraint changes.

Sometimes your driving forces are so strong that you get to your goal quickly, but sometimes your restraining forces keep you from getting to your goal at all. Other times, one of the forces is very weak, and it doesn't take much effort from the countervailing one to push it in a new direction. Always, your state in relationship to the goal is the very spot where the two forces meet.

Have you ever driven on a freeway in L.A.? Traffic jams day and night. So while you're plenty motivated to meet me for drinks, that doesn't mean you'll get to my house as easily as you might think. Luckily, you have strong forces contributing to the momentum of your movement forward, for example, your skill at driving, your sunny attitude, Waze. But there are, as well, powerful things holding you back, their force pushing against the direction you want to go: the slowpoke in the fast lane, your tendency to ignore the GPS until you've missed the off-ramp, the fact that rush hour has slowed driving from a flowing 65 miles per hour to a creeping 10 miles per hour. That's your state right now, determined by the clash of driving and restraining forces.

But it's not quite *that* simple. You see, the meaning of the goal for you has significant influence on the field.

Back to the bacon burger. You want to make the perfect one to impress someone you're dating. You really like this person, and you're looking to seal the deal of a commitment with them. Yet they are hesitant, and you're feeling insecure about the relationship. So much so, in fact, that you're beginning to feel like everything you do is an audition for their approval. That includes making your favorite bacon burger. You bring the meal to the table and you both bite in. Your potential mate does not seem impressed with the burger. In fact, they're growing a little tired of these insecure displays, your constant seeking of approval beginning to turn them off. So your goal to prove that you're a good catch clearly isn't being achieved.

In fact, your misguided strategy to reach it has even moved you a little further away from it. You're physically full, and the burger tastes the same as always, but you're even hungrier to make this relationship work. Thus, the motivating tension between the starting point and goal doesn't end with the consumption of a bacon burger, and it likely continues, since your burger-based strategy for ending the discrepancy between wanting a commitment and having one was pretty cockamamie to begin with. Your insecurity and the responses to this insecurity from your potential mate are restraining forces that undermine you.

If someone were watching this bacon burger scenario play out without knowledge about your insecurity, your concerns about commitment, or your counterproductive approach to securing the relationship, they would see a simple event of one person making dinner for another: Goal achieved. But your actual goal is different from how it appears. In fact, it's based on some rather neurotic needs, known only to you and invisible to others.

The fact that the meanings of our goals are often hidden, and that our own psychological state matters in regard to the tension between starting point and goal, means that we can't really understand a person's motivation without understanding *why* they want what they want. Every field—that space, in Lewin's terms, comprised of driving and restraining forces—is therefore as idiosyncratic as a snowflake, formed by the interaction between a unique personality with unique motivations, and a distinct social situation.

By seeing all motivation as existing in a field of influences and recognizing that the meaning of a goal is different for each person, Lewin takes a Thor-size hammer to most self-help advice regarding making personal change.

How-to advice typically ignores the complex workings of motivation, acting as if a specific goal has only one meaning for everyone, and assumes that every person lives in the same field. It's thus intended for a person who is psychologically consistent, whose actions completely speak for themselves with no deeper meaning than what they observably aim to achieve. A make-believe person, in other words.

Imagine Jim, Carla, and Lee seek the same weight-loss goal, but for very different reasons; Jim is lonely and wants to improve his social desirability, Carla is a tennis player and seeks to improve her athletic prowess, Lee has high cholesterol and seeks to improve his cardiovascular health. Sure, banning unhealthy foods from the kitchen will help all three. But addressing underlying goals—a richer social life, a quicker approach to the net, less fear about cardiac illness—are particular to each of them. And the motivating tension between where each of these individuals is and where they want to be is largely designed by the meaning of their particular goals. Jim might end up finding a mate who loves a man with "a little extra heft" and no longer feel the need to diet, Carla may move up the competitive ladder at her tennis club and experience an extra push to lose those pounds, and Lee could end up getting news from his doctor that his statin drugs are working and feel like he can ease up a little on his diet. All three set out to lose weight, but the meaning of their goals controls the level of tension between each of them and their goal, and thus the power of the motivation to get there.

As I'll argue throughout this book, the strongest enabling factors and the strongest restraining factors often reside in these sort of underlying, very unique, very personal goals. How-to instructions don't get at these meanings-based goals, and don't tell you how to negotiate them, because they aren't informed by you and why you want to achieve what you want to achieve.

Not to say that popular advice is totally useless in the real world of complex, unique individuals. Combined with a good dose of contemplation, it can help you make a desired change by providing a road map built on collective wisdom, and thus giving a little extra push to your driving forces. (It can also hurt when you follow the map, nothing changes, and you become discouraged.) But popular self-help advice is far from enough to get you from where you are to where you want to be.

And, hate to say it, but Lewin's force field alone can't get you there either.

The force field provides an aerial view of all fields and how they influence the motivating tension between where a person is and where they want to be in regard to an infinite amount of goals—from waiting tables to grander ventures like fighting wars, making peace, or surviving political oppression. Personal change sits squarely in this landscape. But it also has its own unique kind of strain, with its own specific forces that are always part of this strain whenever you set out to change. When you aim to quit a habit, improve your health, learn something new, seek deeper spiritual or psychological goals, or step out of your comfort zone in order to help change the world, particular restraining and driving forces enter the scene, forces that aren't always present when you strive to complete many of the other goals in your life, like remembering orders at a café or making your favorite bacon burger.

Between Hope and Death:
The Uniquely Tense Force Field of Personal Change

Remember when you were a kid and someone asked you what you wanted for your birthday present? Maybe you thought about it for a while before coming up with an answer. Let's say you wanted a new bike. After you made your request, did you all of a sudden feel like you just had to have a bike, that having ex-pressed this desire suddenly made it more urgent, that your life was incomplete without the bike and that the bike was essential to your happiness? As you waited for the gift, did both these feelings about having a bike grow: the pain of its absence, its promise of fulfillment? If so, that's a kind of tension that occurs when you hope for something. *When you hope, you assign a positive value on satisfying the hope and a negative value on not realizing the hope.*

Like birthday presents, there are all kinds of goals in life that include the tension of hoping and that don't involve the act of working toward personal change. Hoping that you'll win at the blackjack table tonight or that your neighbor will stop blasting Metallica at 1:00 a.m. are aspirations that don't necessarily involve change on your part. But personal change is definitely a process of goal attainment that triggers the hope-generating experience of wanting and needing something you feel is important to have and the pain of knowing you don't have it. The thing that makes the inherent tension of personal change different from, and often more intense than, other goals you hope to reach is the nature of the goal itself.

APPOINTING WHAT'S IMPORTANT, POINTING TO WHAT'S LACKING

When you hope for personal change, you hope for a change *in* you, not for a particular item, like a bike. And that means that the thing you now feel is important to attain, which is also lacking, is something *about you*—something you may have minimized as unimportant or ignored before you decided to make the change. That creates a difficult, complicated kind of tension, requiring that you both notice something you find dissatisfying about yourself that you've now made important, and risk the disappointment of failing to change an aspect of yourself that you identified as valuable the day you set course to change it.

Take dieting, for example: When you diet, you think as much about getting thin as you do about how heavy you are right now.

And if you fail at the diet, you'll likely become more aware of your weight than if you never dieted.

You can't hope for change without noticing that you are incomplete in some area in your life. Let's say you want to learn how to draw, so you take a drawing class. By taking the class, you're giving value to becoming good at drawing. By bestowing value on this goal, you are also clarifying that you're currently lacking something on your own palette of skills that you value. If you fail at this class, you will be right where you were before you enrolled, as far as your skills are concerned. But you will notice your lack of these skills more than when you began, because you gave them worth by pursuing them.

So how do we humans—programmed to completing anything that feels unfinished—satisfy the tension of hoping for personal change? How, in other words, do we deal with the push-pull of the unpleasant feeling that we're deficient in some way and thus need to change, while coping with the possible disappointment of not changing, which leaves us facing our self-designated deficiency head-on? There are two distinct ways to do so.

The more difficult way to relieve this tension is to try your hardest to reach the goal. You stick with the drawing class, finish all the assignments, and keep working at it in your spare time. That means a long haul of practice without a lot of immediate satisfaction until you finally reach your destination of being better at drawing (and even then, a tension will likely remain, since you'll know there is more improvement to be made ahead).

The second, easier way to end the tension is to give up on your plan and stay the same. Sure, you'll feel lousy about it for a couple of days. But in the end, by not aiming at becoming good at drawing, you don't place a high value on this attribute, thereby reducing your sense of lacking something. This is one reason why most of us choose to stay the same over change. Whenever you move toward something you want and need, the stakes become much higher than if you are complacent.

This is why personal change is such serious business. No matter how small or frivolous the change ahead of you might seem, it's always tangled up in the experience of seeing something you've appointed as missing in yourself, while knowing that getting it is not a foregone conclusion. That's a profound discrepancy. And it threatens to raise the veil on an even more profound one: a discrepancy so powerfully irreconcilable that our brains—made to complete all circles—heat up and go haywire when they face it.

I've been waiting to tell you about this discrepancy. It's a tough one. Take a breath, because here it comes:

You are alive right now, one day you won't be, and that day could be today.

This discrepancy can't be bridged. It's a tension you have to live with (well, until you don't—live, that is).

Now that I've given you this lousy news, what do you want to do with it? "Take that cooking class I always wanted to take!" "Finally lose those ten pounds!" "Follow the advice of country songs like 'Live Like You Were Dying.'" Good for you! But I also have to warn you about something: When you make such changes, that grand kahuna/great reaper of all discrepancies is going to nag at you much more than if you stay the same.

Personal change is always about how we exist within the shadow of the giant, completely unpredictable hourglass of our mortality. It's never *not* about this.

Heading toward a change, you probably don't say to yourself, "I'm learning how to knit because someday I'll be six feet under." But you *will* feel a kind of pressure that you don't feel when you stay the same. You'll feel that you *need*, not just want, to learn to knit. With this hoping will come a sense of responsibility to yourself, and a concern that you'll fail in getting what you lack in your life, and in yourself, before it's too late. Behind this experience of responsibility will be a quiet acknowledgment that you don't have all the time in the world.

Your mind will go into overdrive to try to smother this ac-knowledgment, in order to protect itself from going mad over a puzzle it can't solve. While it's really good at sweeping ashes to ashes and dust to dust under the carpet of denial—often making your greatest terror, and the one irrefutable fact in your life (other than taxes), feel like something sort of abstract, obscure, and theoretical—your mind can find the ever-present threat of death if it knows where to look. The undeniable pressure to make things happen now; the urgent but unseen force that focuses your mind; your impatience with delay; the guilt of all those "should haves" and "what could have beens"; the constant drone of potentials unmet; the dread of boredom and emptiness—these are concerns only for the species of mortals that knows they are mortal.[10,11,12,13]

And while you feel them profoundly, and experience them daily, your mind does a very good job disconnecting them from their root: your impending death. "Oh, there's remorse again. There's impatience, regret, and boredom entering my experi-ence," as if they have no shared source. But they do. These emo-tions have to do not only with the fact of your death, but also with how this fact highlights your *existence*, and what you want to do with it before it's over. *Existential* concerns, in other words: ones about your aloneness as your face your singular accountabil-ity for making something of your precious life.

The combination of the fact that when you hope for personal change you designate as important the target of this change (e.g., a new skill, a better relationship with family, an important work goal, a deeper existence), and thus also notice that this character-istic is lacking in you right now, combined with the ticking clock of your existence and the fact that its alarm could go off at any time, are what make the goals of personal change different from other things you hope to attain in life. You might notice that you lack a bike when you hope for one, but you don't feel that something about *you* will be missing if you don't get it. Likewise, you might have a hankering for a bacon burger, but you won't feel that you missed an important opportunity to improve your finite life if you burn it on the stove (unless the purpose of that burger was to somehow change your life).

This difference causes your process toward goals to abide by three laws specific to personal change, but still contained within Lewin's force field. You must proceed within the rules of these laws in order to propel yourself forward and make truly long-lasting change.

These three laws, one about your anxiety about your accountability and aloneness, the other two about your capacity for hope and faith, are foundational. They are completely baked into the driving and restraining forces that arise whenever you want to change. They influence what drives you and restrains you, and they often lead you to stay the same.

CHAPTER 3

ANXIETY, HOPE, AND FAITH

The Three Laws of Personal Change

We are our choices.

—Jean-Paul Sartre

- LAW ONE: The "Dizziness of Freedom" and Its Restraint
- LAW TWO: The Driving Force of Hope
- LAW THREE: The Driving Force of Faith and the Restraining Power of Helplessness

Change is about tension—between where you are now and where you want to be. Let's say the change was trivial: You decide to put your house keys in the same place every day before you go to bed. Tension like this is easy to manage. It's like holding a rubber band between the index fingers of your two hands, with just a slight pull between them (fig. 2). But if you are attempting a more substantial change that has to do with changing something about who you are—a new diet or different way of dealing with coworkers—the tension will be greater and harder to sustain (fig. 3). It's not just that the goal is larger and therefore more demanding; it's not a simple linear increase, like going from a 10-pound weight to a 40-pound weight. Rather, when you pursue a truly life-altering goal, much more is added. First, you ascribe more importance to this goal than before you decided to reach it, and you also recognize that this goal—newly minted as important—is lacking in your life. In other words, the goal gains importance and becomes a challenge simply because you have made it a goal and hoped for it.

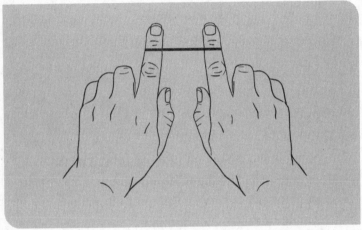

Fig. 2

The stakes in reaching the goal thus go up once you target it. You have this feeling of yearning, as if you can't live without achieving the goal, and a simultaneous worry about what it will mean about you if don't achieve the change in your life. So the tension of making personal change is greater than the mild strain you feel when you set out to reach for other goals that aren't life altering—like the new habit of keeping your keys in a findable spot (fig. 3). You can't hold this tension constantly, all day—but you can handle it for a while.

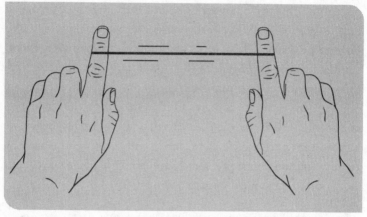

Fig. 3

When you head toward a major personal goal, you are always also sensing the pressure to make your finite life as meaningful, healthy, and deep as possible. What I mean by that is, you are no longer on autopilot; you are now flying the plane and that means that selecting a course, charting it, and reaching it require decisions big and small. That means the band strains even further (fig. 4). As much as you try to hold your shaking fingers upright, they precariously tip toward one another. You can't wait long before a *snap!*

The hardest, most painful way to end this tension is to ploddingly keep working toward your goal. There is a painless and easy way to reduce the tension, and this is to stay the same.

Considering the attractive simplicity of sameness, and comparing it to the disorienting complexity of change, it's no wonder we tend to choose the former more often than the latter. Sameness is our go-to place. In Lewin's force field,[1] there are all kind of things pushing us upward toward our goal, such as our talents and competencies, the support we get from others, our exalted place in society, and our material resources. And there are all kinds of forces restraining this drive upward, like our ineptitude at a particular task, a lack of social support, oppressive political forces, and a poverty of material resources. Those upward-downward arrows shift and change in regard to their importance—some often absent as driving or restraining energy in our field—depending on what we are trying to achieve. Our anxiety about our aloneness and accountability, on the other hand, is always present when we head toward personal change. They are the central influences on our driving and restraining forces, differentiating personal change from other acts requiring motivation.

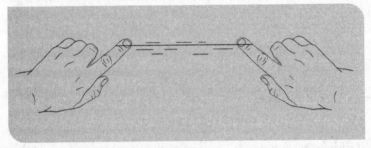

Fig. 4

Harold et le Crayon Violet

Years ago, as I was putting my young son, Max, to bed, I picked up the children's book *Harold and the Purple Crayon*[2] to read to him. I was also working at that time on the development of Ten Reasons Not to Change, and dusting off my graduate-school books on existentialism to help me put the Reasons in a philosophical context. As I read along, I was amazed by how efficiently this little book captured what drives us toward our goals, what restrains us from reaching them, and how these drives and restraints operate in a particularly existential kind of way. When I think

about existentialism today, I think less about Camus and Sartre, and more about Harold. Harold is my existential hero.

In the book, Harold is always alone with his giant purple crayon. When he doesn't use his crayon to draw, the pages are blank. When he does deploy his crayon, he draws the world around him.

Some drawings help Harold along his course (for example, a policeman pointing the way); many more are frightening and restrain him from moving forward (such as a monster, a stormy ocean, or a cliff). Faced with the most dangerous of these forces, Harold is always able to draw a way to push forward despite them. Sometimes he just keeps going in the same direction, head down, facing the challenge in front of him. But most often he draws new and inventive ways to work around the obstacles in his path.

Harold and the Purple Crayon is about both the awe and the angst of authoring a life, the wondrous human blessing of decision, the weighty responsibility to decide on lives that are meaningful and fulfilling, the ways in which that weight can hold us in place, what we need to do in order to keep going despite it, and how we can pick ourselves up when we feel the crush of our self-responsibility at moments of disappointment and failure.

There's a sequence in the book that depicts remarkably well the kind of fortitude we need in order to grow, despite the restraint of our concerns about being in charge of our lives. Harold first draws a tree. It's beautiful, full of fruit: open, exposed, and real. Harold wants to protect the tree. So he draws a monster as a guard. But then Harold forgets that he drew the monster.

He becomes anxious and begins to tremble. His hand shakes so much that he involuntarily draws wavelike marks. The waves become an ocean.

He falls into this literal sea of anxiety. Soon he is drowning in it.

But then Harold reaches out of the water, draws a boat for himself, and gets on it. He sets sail. All is well . . . but only for a while. There are other challenges ahead that he will have to meet, and all he has is his purple crayon to meet them.

That's one of the most important lessons you need to know about change: When you change, it's you drawing your life, and you are accountable for making the change happen. That means you take a big risk every time you change, since failing to make that change means that you don't get what you feel you need— because of you. And you now see this thing as lacking in your life and lacking in you. Attempting change is also risky because you're never sure you will be able to handle this feeling of anxiety and accountability: Can you build the boat you need to keep you afloat as you deal with setbacks and failures, and can you steer toward your self-selected destination? Like Harold, your ability to keep going—both to believe in yourself enough to set the next course, and to keep navigating around obstacles in your path—depends on your ability to keep hoping.

All of us are Harold, and we experience the anxiety over our own accountability for our lives all the time; we do so when we awake bleary eyed at 3:00 a.m., wondering what's happened to our lives; when we feel lost at work or adrift in our relationships; or when we just want to change some simple thing and feel something pushing back on our success. At those moments we are confronted with our own blank pages—and it's up to us to draw a meaningful path. We all also find innovative ways to keep going, and despite the weight of responsibility, our "purple crayons" of change sustain us, keep our heads above water, and help us build the kinds of crafts that will get us to where we want to be. For all of us, our purple crayon—our freedom to choose and decide—is the source of both terrible anxiety (it creates the waves of uncertainty and doubt about goals and our ability to reach them) and significant hope (it provides us the means by which goals are reached).

How do you feel knowing you have all kinds of choices to make, and that the consequences of deciding on only one of them led you here, to reading this book? Maybe a little uneasy and restless? Maybe a little agitated? That's anxiety tap-tap-tapping on your psyche. It's the "dizziness of freedom," as the Christian existentialist Søren Kierkegaard[3] called it: the anxious feeling you experience when you awaken to the fact that you have choice and that you're in charge of your time—and your life.

The dizzying anxiety of freedom can sink you, overwhelming you in a sea of worry. But this very same dizziness is also present at the starting line of change: the "go" in "ready, set, go." The anxious sense that you are a decider in your fate both restrains you and drives you forward.

Law One of Personal Change is about the restraint part of this equation—the anxiety of freedom to change.

Law One of Personal Change: The "Dizziness of Freedom" and Its Restraint

When you head toward personal change, you are following the call to take hold of your existence and make it better. That means that pursuing personal change confronts you with your existential accountability and your aloneness, and it does so more than staying the same does. These realizations typically produce existential anxiety. Thus every movement forward toward personal change often carries with it the counterforce of existential anxiety pushing against it (fig. 5).

As I wrote, when you move toward a change you want, all kinds of things will get in your way. But one restraining force will always be present, no matter who you are, and no matter what's happening to you at that particular time or what goal you want to achieve. This restraining force comes from your awareness of your existential *accountability and aloneness*; the confrontation with the fact that you hold that purple crayon, and you're in charge of what happens next.

When you become aware of your accountability and aloneness—these two facts that your death-fearing brain tries to smother—you get anxious, and sometimes overwhelmingly so.

Although way too complex and varied to address here, an existential approach[4] to our psychology offers us a few important

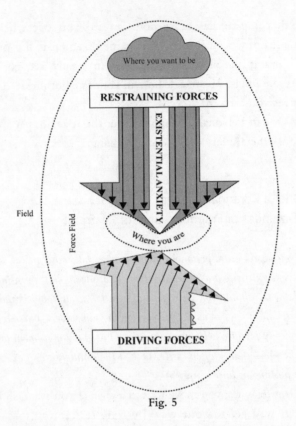

Fig. 5

and somewhat tidy ideas in regard to the fundamental restraint of our existential anxiety. Existentialism asserts that we all live for a certain amount of time and then we don't. To this fact, we can add the assumption that, on our route between birth and death, we're basically on our own. Even when we are deeply connected and have great moments of love, community involvement, and spiritual merging, what we gain from these events depends on *us, our individual selves*. And even when we face significant moments of oppression and trauma, we are ultimately alone in how we choose to deal with these challenges, and with the injuries we might sustain. Our choices in such situations are limited, and the results of these limited choices may move us toward goals that are very limited in regard to satisfaction, but we still have choices to make.

The word "existential" likely evokes an image of a French philosopher gloomily smoking a Gauloise at a Paris café. He's feeling what the existentialists call *angst*: the anxiety you experience when you recognize your own accountability to act and your own aloneness in doing so. It's a scary thing to think that your outcomes ultimately depend on yourself, that you are the final author of your life. That's why accountability is such a frightening awareness. "What if I blunder in shaping my life?" "What if the path I take leads to meaninglessness?" "What if I die empty and alone?" "How do I deal with myself, if all I have is myself?" "How do I handle stark experiences of loneliness and isolation?" "What do I do to get comfort for myself when it's up to me to get that comfort and feel that comfort?" These sorts of questions are at the root of existential anxiety.

Whether you choose to notice them or not (and for most of us it's "not"), these kinds of questions tend to emerge when you head toward personal change. In fact, personal change is an ultimate existential moment: It's the point when you independently help yourself, the site where you take responsibility for your life by placing a value on something and making a decision to act on its behalf. It requires that you look at yourself in the mirror and stare into the reflection of yourself standing there alone—often unbearably so.

Think of a time when you pursued an important personal goal. The moment you decided on that target, even if you made this decision in conversation with someone else, did you not make a mental handshake with yourself? Then, as you engaged in this change, did you not feel a growing sense of aloneness, a sense that you were by yourself? Even if you were surrounded by a marathon of others as you pushed toward the finish line, were you not also aware of a sense of profound solitude?

Now think about a goal you failed to reach. You probably felt a sense of despair (maybe slight, maybe intense) about yourself, heard the echoing clatter of your own incompetence. Now think about a time you reached your goal. "*I did it!*" You felt a reverberating pride in your own powers—perhaps tinged with a little anxiety about keeping it up. In either case, and no matter how minute your goal, the process gave you a stronger awareness of your singular responsibility to master your life.

When you make changes in your life, no one else is making those changes. It's you out there, alone and accountable. If you fail at making the change, you face your accountability for that failure—and, by extension, are reminded that you are solely accountable for your entire life. If you succeed at making the change, you must acknowledge your accountability if you are to continue on the new course. Either way, once you put your toe in the waters of personal change, you are deeper in the tides of eternal aloneness. That's why we stay on the dry land of sameness more often than not.

Sameness is our sanctuary from the overwhelming experience that we are in charge. In other words, it's a hidden choice we make to feel like we're not in charge. And that tendency to avoid our accountability is a central element in our lives, even when the challenges to our accountability are much less powerful than the powerful act of changing yourself.

GOOD AND BAD FAITH

My friend's birthday is coming up, and I *have to* buy her a present. Driving to the store, I *have to* stop at a couple of stop signs. At the store, I pick out just the right thing. I now *have to* get a nice gift bag and some pretty tissue, and I then *have to* get in line. Once at the register I *have to* pay. All of these moments when I feel compelled to do things are actually choices: *I don't want to disappoint my friend. I'd rather not get a ticket. I want my friend to like what I get her, and I want her to appreciate that it's wrapped nicely. Cutting in line is not worth all the problems I'll create. If I steal the item I may go to jail.* As it turns out, I didn't *have to* do anything. Behind the scenes of my play, there's a stage manager weighing the pros and cons of my decisions.

Jean-Paul Sartre, the famous French existentialist, called this form of self-deception, in which you conceal your agency from yourself and from others, "bad faith."[5] Bad faith comes in packages both small and large, from something as mundane as buying that present to the very big lies people tell themselves, the most ominous one being: "I was only following orders."

Sartre called the alternative to concealing your agency "good faith." It is the posture in which you consciously face life as a series of choices you alone make as a responsible actor. Good faith is about authorship; you're writing the play, not simply acting in it, when you behave in good faith. Most of us choose the route of good faith more rarely than we do bad faith, preferring to read lines rather than write them, and to protect ourselves from the anxiety that inevitably springs from an authentic approach to our authorship and aloneness.

Personal change raises the blinds on the harsh daylight of your accountability and aloneness. So you're acting in more of a good-faith mode than a bad-faith one when you attempt it. That means that trying to make this kind of change always comes with its own restraining force baked in. When you engage in personal change you are automatically facing big dilemmas about your existence—the very ones you're often trying to avoid. And so a bad-faith stance, one in which you stay the same, disempowered, supposedly unable to take charge and move forward, appears as a reasonable alternative.

Luckily, there are driving forces baked into your field too. These are your capacity to hope and to have faith.

Law Two of Personal Change: The Driving Force of Hope

Hope is the counterforce to existential anxiety. It keeps you going despite your awareness of your lone accountability for your life (fig. 6). Part of hope is faith, and without faith, hope's sustaining power can collapse, increasing your anxiety regarding your accountability and aloneness, and causing you to see the energies that typically drive you forward as dangerous.

Sure, freedom comes with the burden of responsibility and the threat of anxiety. But only fascists and fundamentalists see freedom as a dirty word. Freedom is the root of democratic aspirations, and the very thing many of us will fight and die for. It's something we enshrine and protect as sacred in the American Declaration of Independence and in the U.S. Constitution, especially in the Bill of Rights. Freedom, like flight, might frighten us, but it also dizzyingly exhilarates us. It may confront us with our aloneness, but through freedom we can encounter and realize our deeper selves.

I subscribe to the Jeffersonian belief that we are all born with the inalienable right of human agency: the ability to make decisions that can have major consequences for the quality of our lives, for the experiences and quality of the lives of others, and for our environment, both natural and human. While this fact can pose an anxiety-provoking threat, it can also offer an exciting prospect, since it proffers the chance for self-invention and the ability to make our lives deep and rich. When you face your accountability and aloneness, there is a real chance for you to develop your own self more fully, and realize potential strengths and gifts which you may only have suspected you possessed. But

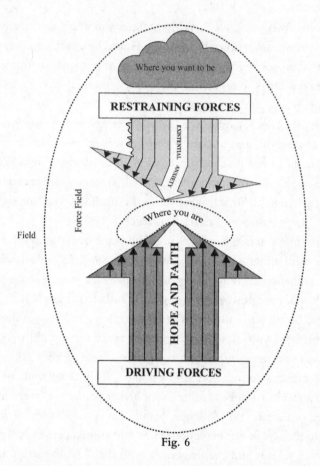

Fig. 6

to take flight on freedom, rather than take a nosedive into over-whelming anxiety, requires the propulsive emotion of hope.

The Second Law of Personal Change says that every movement forward is propelled by this powerful yet delicate emotion. When you set off to change something about yourself, there are all kinds of things driving you forward—friends who encourage you, your own self-confidence, material resources like money and a stable job, your innate talents, your position in society. And these driving forces are as idiosyncratic as your particular Lewinian field: sometimes you have them, sometimes you don't, sometimes they're strong, sometimes they aren't. Hope, however, is always present when you are trying to move forward toward something. It's as baked into the process of change as existential anxiety and pushing up against that restraining force.

Hope is a concept often used in the spiritual realm, the language of religion, and poetry. I see it, however, also as an integral element in our psychological and physical survival. In fact, I believe hope informs that most secular of concepts: evolution. It is what prompts us to act, what sustains our efforts to adapt and change, despite powerful restraining forces.

Every time you target some change and you move toward it you grapple with either a threat (*If I don't quit smoking, I'll probably die young*), a challenge (*Withdrawing from nicotine isn't going to be easy*), or both. It's your posture toward threats and challenges that determines both your willingness to try to change and your ability to persist once you start changing. Hope is the force within you that gives you the gumption to try, the fortitude to keep going, and the capacity to pick yourself up and try again when you fail.

The notion that hope is central to whether you act or freeze in the face of threats and challenges brings this often ethereal term down to the soil of our evolution. How any animal perceives and deals with threats and challenges is a central and basic part of its own survival and the evolutionary progress of its species.

A deer that thoughtfully weighs the pros and cons of fleeing whenever it hears the snap of a twig will likely grace a mantelpiece someday, and an ant that kvetches about the slope of every hill will create significant chaos in the very ordered world of ants. We humans, on the other hand, have more than a factory setting for survival. We often contemplate and decide what to do when we see threats and challenges. Our options exceeding the binary of fight or flight mean our decisions are guided by personal preferences, cultural norms, and our collaboration with others. Programmed for uncertainty—including the profound uncertainty caused by our unique ability to know we die, but not when or how—our filter for threats and challenges is dependent on our choices. That means we must deal constantly with the potential danger of failure. Hope enables us to muster the energy to hurtle ahead despite our uncertain future. What's more, it gives us the power to engage in the most human behaviors: to relate freely with others, explore, be curious, imagine, innovate, and discover. Hope is as much a means of survival in an uncertain world as it is the attitude that makes withstanding uncertainty a particularly human gift—our ability to handle the unknown, to even turn it to good and often beautiful use, without becoming immobilized by fear.

So what is this attitude that is so relevant to whether you succeed in making changes in your life?

Hope, Alternative Pathways, and Agency Thinking

In *Harold and the Purple Crayon*, Harold is not on an open-ended wanderlust of an adventure: he's searching for his way back home. He thus has a very clear destination in mind, and he's trying all kinds of ways to get there. So, for Harold, there is definitely that Lewinian tension between where he is and where he wants to be. His hope to reach his home creates that tension, but continuing

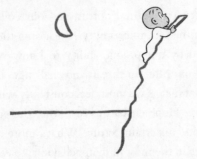

to hope—finding different ways to get there when he hits roadblocks—is also his means to withstand this tension and keep
going.

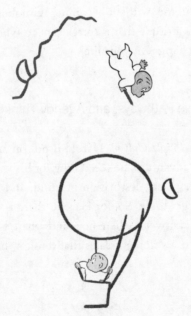

Like my earlier example of the hoped-for bike, the inevitable
result of hoping is that it appoints something as important and
makes you notice that you lack that thing. But the purpose of

hope—it's raison d'être—is to deliver you from the here of wanting, and the targeted *someday* of *getting*. Hope, in other words, exists within an anticipatory sense of time. A "time perspective," as (you guessed it!) Lewin[6] would put it.

A time perspective, according to Lewin, is "the totality of the individual's views of his psychological future and psychological past existing at a given time." Hope, in this light, is a little like the waiter's memory. It's generated by the tension of betweenness: *I'm further along than I was yesterday, I'm taking a step toward something right now, and I know what goal I want to reach.* It's about the past, the present, and the future.

Hope holds you together while you struggle with feeling that you lack something important—something you *need*. And it keeps you going, even when you don't get this need met immediately.

Winston Churchill[7] captures this understanding of hope in his most famous speech, given at Britain's darkest hour when it stood alone against the seeming unstoppable Nazi onslaught. "We shall go on to the end," he proclaimed,

> *we shall fight in France, we shall fight on the seas and oceans, we shall fight with growing confidence and growing strength in the air, we shall defend our Island, whatever the cost may be, we shall fight on the beaches, we shall fight on the landing grounds, we shall fight in the fields and in the streets, we shall fight in the hills; we shall never surrender.*

Churchill is speaking more about fighting than winning, not giving up or giving in. His speech combines a longing for something better with a call for moving forward in the present toward a goal whether things get better or not. That's hope.

Churchill's speech is also basically a list of alternative ways to fight. Thus, like Harold and all the different ways he draws a means back home, Churchill ties hope to "never surrendering" and inventing and locating innovative new routes to reach your home. That's a central element of hope: finding ways around, below, above, and through obstacles.

ALTERNATIVE PATHWAYS

According to Charles Snyder,[8] a leading social-psychological theorist on hope, this capacity to find all kinds of pathways to desired goals is the gift hope gives us. When your hope is high and you see a barrier in front of you, you figure out a different way around it. When you lack hope, you give up quickly if the path you're on is blocked, since you only believe the one route you're on can get you where you're going. In my mind, that means that hope is connected to contemplation—that ability at the very center of personal change to stand back and, with as much dispassion as you can muster, study all the alternatives in front of you.

Hope keeps you going, and keeps you going in as creative a way as possible, despite setbacks. Hope, in this light, is the antidote to despair. You *never surrender* to despair when you hope, because there is always the possibility of an alternative when you face a barrier. You've just got to know how to use your crayon to figure it out.

And yet, in another difficult paradox, hope comes with a warning label: Hope is the leading cause of despair. Hope and despair are in a both-and relationship. You would have no need for hope if not for the hot breath of despair always at your back, *and* you would never fall into despair if you never risked the aspirational heights of hope.

Hope doesn't negate or erase or dispel despair. Hope keeps you moving despite it, driving you forward even if you despair that you can acquire the thing you want right now. That push forward can be profound, giving you the strength to keep going, and keep contemplating how to go, in tunnels of darkness without any perceivable light at the end. However, by pinpointing important, valuable things, and showing you that you're lacking these things, hope also sets you up to feel like you're missing something life-giving if you don't attain your goal. Thus hope is not only the thing that pushes you ahead in moments of despair: it's the main route *to* despair.

If, as I believe, despair is the desperate, utterly helpless experience of not getting something you see as lacking in your life, and feel you deeply need, then you don't reach despair without first traveling toward hope—the attitude that ascribes importance to goals, and clarifies that you're lacking them.

The both-and relationship between hoping and risking despair is a lot like scaling a cliff. The more you hope, the more you feel you need the thing you hope for. That means the injury from the fall from hope—that experience of unmet life-sustaining needs—is greater the higher you've climbed up that cliff.

My client Mark[9] provides a dramatic example of what happens when you hope for something and are stymied in reaching it.

MARK AND THE RECORD PLAYER

Mark was in his late forties when he came to me for help following a difficult breakup with his girlfriend. His main complaint was about an experience of being fractured—"not knowing what I want, or even what I like: I can't make up my mind about anything: I often can't move because I can't figure out what to do. I only move when I have to, when there's some sort of crisis."

Mark experienced significant emotional abuse by his parents when he was young. Both insulted him, belittled his efforts, and treated him as unwanted. Mark's adult life was marked by this sense of being fractured, that is, unconnected to his inner core and unable to meet even the smallest goals he set for himself. During one session, Mark related a story from his youth:

"I was in my room, by myself, and someone put on the record player in the den," he said. "I loved the song it was playing, and went to the den to listen. I began to dance to the music. At first I barely moved, since I didn't want to get anyone upset. But then I let myself go, and I just danced, playing air guitar, that sort of thing. I felt so happy and joyful, totally myself. It was so rare for me to feel this kind of freedom. Usually, I stuck to myself, since it just felt way too risky to do anything fun, but that day, I went just a little wild. While I was dancing, I bumped into the record player, and the record began to skip. My father came running into the room, screaming at me."

Considering all the horrific abuse Mark endured as a child, this incident seemed minor. Yet it expressed a central motif in our therapeutic work, becoming something we returned to over and over, as a metaphor for experiences Mark still had as an adult. When Mark danced to that music, he was reaching for feelings he rarely tried to attain, but that are actually essential to childhood: play, wildness, joy, spontaneity, make-believe. Mark had taken flight, for a joyous moment, and the fall made such flight perilous. Suddenly his gift for joy and freedom became, for him, a liability. His story was about the deep pain we suffer when hope opens us to life unshielded, having abandoned our defenses as we try to attain what we need. And then we get hurt in this most vulnerable of states. It was a story about desperation and despair. It became a motif in our therapy because it captured how these feelings blocked his ability to hope.

It also caused Mark constantly to doubt himself and others.

I believe that at the center of hope is an attitude of confidence without certainty, something Mark lacked in his adulthood, a lack that splintered his experiences. This is a belief in oneself, in others, and in the cosmos, with no proof or certainty in the reliability of this belief. That's how hope pulls you through despair and uncertainty, and why you're willing to risk failure when you hope: you have a sense of confidence that getting through to the other side of despair is worth it, that you can handle uncertainty, and that if you fall, you'll still be intact and be able to recover. There's a second half to Snyder's concept of hope that points in the direction of this kind of confidence. He calls this "agency thinking."

AGENCY THINKING AND SELF-EFFICACY

For Snyder, hope is not only comprised of finding pathways. It's also the ability to "motivate oneself via agency thinking to use those paths." Agency thinking, according to Snyder, is a kind of confidence in one's own mastery: "High-hope people," he writes, "embrace such self-talk agency phrases as, 'I can do this,' and 'I am not going to be stopped.'"[10] Hopeful people, in other words, not only know where they want to go and how to get there—and innovatively work around obstacles along the way—they believe they have the wherewithal to make the journey. It's precisely the lack of this agency thinking that Mark found wanting in his adult life, caused by all the points when hope failed him when he was a child.

The social psychologist Albert Bandura's work goes directly to this kind of unprovable confidence in one's own mastery. He calls this "perceived self-efficacy." As Bandura puts it, self-efficacy is "people's beliefs about their capabilities to produce designated levels of performance that exercise influence over events that affect their lives." "A strong sense of efficacy," writes Bandura,[11] "enhances human accomplishment and personal well-being in many ways.

> *People with high assurance in their capabilities approach difficult tasks as challenges to be mastered rather than as threats to be avoided. . . . They set themselves challenging goals and maintain strong commitment to them. They heighten and sustain their efforts in the face*

of failure. They quickly recover their sense of efficacy after failures or setbacks. They attribute failure to insufficient effort or deficient knowledge and skills which are acquirable. They approach threatening situations with assurance that they can exercise control over them.

It is difficult to imagine actually acting on your hope without also having perceived self-efficacy. You must believe in yourself, and believe the world is shapable by you, to move forward.

The concepts of agency thinking and self-efficacy bring me to another term, which—like hope—is more often associated with sermons than social science lectures: *faith.* Faith is a kind of confidence that may rely on facts, but in the end is based on belief. You can't really act on hope without faith; in yourself, in others, and in the world.

Faith, unlike hope, has not yet been developed by psychological science. This is unfortunate, because I believe faith is a central part of our driving forces toward change. As I see it, you can't fully hope—yearning for good things and moving toward them despite difficult odds and an unknown future—without the implicit confidence of faith. To say to yourself "I can do it," and to feel like you can influence your world, requires the kind of trust in yourself that isn't only based on facts, but on belief.

Like hope, when you act on faith you risk; you leap. When you take a leap of faith you risk that your confidence is misplaced or just plain wrong.

Law Three of Personal Change: The Driving Force of Faith and the Restraining Power of Helplessness

If hope is the yearning for something you've appointed as important that you feel you lack, then faith is the message that you have the ability to attain this important thing. It's difficult, if not impossible, to move on your hope without also having faith.

We tend to talk about hope and faith as if they are interchangeable concepts. But they aren't. They are, in fact, very different from each other, even though each is also a part of the other.

Here's a story form my own practice that I think illustrates the difference between hope and faith, and how these different experiences are intricately entwined. It's about Bridget and her parents, a remarkable trio with an uncanny ability to keep their confidence intact no matter their disappointments.

"I WOULD TRUST HER WITH MY LIFE"

Twenty-five and really smart, Bridget was also remarkably creative. She designed her own clothing, made short documentary films, and threw lavish, whimsical parties with her many friends. Diagnosed with bipolar disorder, she also experienced long periods of acute mania, a symptom of the disorder marked by high exuberance and a delusory sense of invincibility. When manic, Bridget often behaved in ways that put her at significant risk, such as sleeping with strangers, traveling long distances in her car while drinking, and once trespassing into an amusement park. She was in and out of psychiatric hospitals during these manic phases, and was unable to hold down a job or finish college. But somehow Bridget kept moving ahead, never stopping her creative endeavors, the results of which were often brilliant.

Unlike a lot of people I work with who have been in and out of treatment facilities, Bridget didn't take a negative view of her mood-related problems. It wasn't that she was cavalier about the risks she would take when she was manic. But she also felt that her moods "gave [her] clear messages about life," and, while extreme at times, were "always on target regarding reality." She wanted help managing her moods, but she also told anyone who would listen that she "wouldn't give up being bipolar for anything in the world."

I met regularly with Bridget's parents as they dealt with her almost persistent state of crisis. Her parents were a lot like Bridget. They never seemed too upset when she went back into the hospital, and they always looked to the next day as another chance to set things straight. When things looked bad, they energetically looked for solutions and new ideas. Her mom's mantra was "There's always a way."

Bridget's parents did not kowtow to my expertise. They treated me as an equal, finding some of my ideas good but also telling me when they thought I was off the mark. They were friendly and affable, but had little time for anything they felt wasn't useful.

I met with them over a span of three years, and during that time Bridget was able to build a much better life, going back to college, never returning to the hospital, and continuing with her creative pursuits. I knew her future would be remarkable, exceptional, and exciting. In fact, part of me felt a little envious of Bridget's passion and willingness to try new things and approach life with such creativity.

I requested that Bridget join us for my last meeting with her parents.

"I have to ask," I said near the end of our session. "What kept you all going? I've been amazed by how positive and energized you all remained."

"It's Bridget," her mother replied. "I know all parents say this, but she's truly amazing. We were just convinced she would be okay. Knowing her as we do, it was obvious things were finally going to work out. We never lost hope—ever."

"She's strong as hell," her father said. "I would trust her with my life more than almost anyone. It's obvious to us that she will always do fine."

"Aw, shucks," said Bridget, bringing a little humor into the room to lighten the weight of her parent's compliments. "Here's the deal: My parents totally believe in me. I've definitely scared them with my behavior, but they have this real confidence that I'll be okay. I guess the best way to put it is: They have faith in me."

Bridget was right. Her parents did have tremendous faith in her and her ability to keep going no matter what. Their faith gave them hope regarding her future. To put it another way, they couldn't really hope she would be okay without having faith she would.

The simplest way of thinking about the difference between hope and faith starts with two seemingly insignificant words: *for* (implying action toward something) and *in* (implying something that exists within something else). Just like Bridget and her parents regarding her ability to finally reach a more stable state in her life, when you hope, you are hoping *for* something to happen. Like their belief in her abilities, when you have faith, you are trusting *in* something that you believe is already occurring that can get you to the place you hope *for*. When Bridget's mom spoke her mantra of "There's always a way," she was talking about alternative pathways toward something they all wanted, and were moving *for*ward to. When her father said, "I would trust her with my life," he was stating his confident belief *in* Bridget, as she was in the present.

When I think about Bridget's experience in her family, my heart breaks for Mark. Where Bridget had everything she needed to keep her head up and stay confident, Mark had tragically little, if any, resources to do so. When, like Mark, you lose hope, you lose a sense of a future, which is always a *toward*. When you lose faith, you lose trust in yourself, in others, and in the established order. When your faith is injured, it slows or stops the otherwise forward motion of hope. You can't follow through on a hopeful future without having faith you'll get there.

The Gut Information of Faith

Martin Luther King[12] joins Churchill in the pantheon of the great orators of hope. In his most famous speech, he beautifully captures the relationship between the tenacity of this emotion and the confidence of faith.

"I am not unmindful that some of you have come here out of great trials and tribulations," said King in his "I Have a Dream" speech,

> Some of you have come fresh from narrow jail cells. Some of you have come from areas where your quest for freedom left you battered by the storms of persecution and staggered by the winds of police brutality. You have been the veterans of creative suffering. Continue to work with the faith that unearned suffering is redemptive.

Transforming "unearned suffering" into something "redemptive"— that's the tallest of orders. By imploring people to engage in this unfathomably vulnerable act, he's asking them to take a giant leap of faith, and he's expressing his own faith that they can do it.

The words "faith" and "trust" share a lexical parent. Their common Latin root is *fid* (meaning "trust"), as in fidelity and bona fide (not to mention Fido, the name we give our most trusted— and trusting—animal companion). Faith is trust with no affidavit of proof. When you say to someone, "I believe in you," you are expressing a faith-based confidence in them. When you say to them, "You can do it," you are doing the same. You are agency thinking, in Snyder's terms, acting on your sense of self-efficacy in Bandura's.

You're climbing toward the goal you set for yourself, every step raising the importance of the goal and making more salient its absence in your life. You are fortified by the hope that your efforts

will succeed. But what validates your hope is your confidence—one of those *fid* words, meaning "with trust"—that you can keep climbing, and that you'll be able to pick yourself up if you fall.

So what informs this confidence, telling you it's okay to follow hope up that mountain? Where do you get enough good information that the chances of making it are good, that the risk is worth it, and that you'll be okay if you fall? Part of the confidence comes from verifiable, external facts: You've achieved many observable things in your life, so you know you're capable, and as you worked to achieve these things, you've discovered the environment around you is benign enough to give you room to achieve them. As Bandura puts it, "A resilient sense of efficacy requires experience in overcoming obstacles through perseverant effort. After people become convinced they have what it takes to succeed, they persevere in the face of adversity and quickly rebound from setbacks. By sticking it out through tough times, they emerge stronger from adversity."[13] In other words, the more data you collect on your ability to achieve things, the more your sense of efficacy grows, since your head is full of proof that you can accomplish things.

Facts, data: These are very important things that add a lot to your ability to decide, then act. However, they aren't enough.

When you move toward a goal, you also rely on other, less objective, less logically derived information to give you this confidence to make a decision and go. That information comes from your *feelings*. Even when all the facts are in, and you lean a certain way toward a decision, the decision you choose and then your next step to act on that decision come from a combination of your logic and your emotions.

Think about a decision you made regarding your future: what college to go to, what job to accept, whom to marry, what house to buy or apartment to rent. You probably thought of all the pros and cons, perhaps even made lists of them. But when it came down to finally deciding, didn't it come down to how you felt? Wasn't it the strength of positive emotion—like excitement, longing, anticipation, desire—that drove you head-on toward the final decision? Or, when you chose against the power of negative emotions—like fear, anxiety, disgust?

That's what the affect-as-information[14,15] approach in social psychology posits: that we use our emotions as important information when we deliberate on our next move.

AFFECT AS INFORMATION. Research on affect as information shows that emotions help you with more creative and flexible planning (the result of emotional intelligence), distinguishing things as good or bad, and deciding on the attitude to take and how quickly to respond in the face of a significant event.[16] A lot of what we do when we make decisions, in other words, depends on a gut response.

And by "gut" we may not be talking metaphorically.

As neuroscientist Antonio Damasio describes in his research, we depend on "somatic markers" to make decisions. These are bodily sensations—a rising heartbeat, sweaty palms, and a nauseated stomach—that are tied to emotions. Research on somatic markers[17] shows evidence that people who rely on these markers make decisions quicker and their decisions more often lead to positive outcomes than individuals who are unable to access these somatic markers (e.g., brain-injured subjects). In fact, people who have suffered damage to emotional centers in the brain, such as the amygdala, can spin out countless reasons why they should and should not take a certain course of action without being able to finally settle on a resolution.

So what is it about emotions that make them especially important sources of information in our decision making, and different from a Vulcan reliance only on logic? The affect-as-information theorists, Gerald Clore and Stanley Colcombe, write that "the information from feelings is convincing because it is experienced as arising spontaneously from within [ourselves]," and coming from within gives this information special validity since we "find ourselves to be particularly credible sources."[18]

Great point, but not always true.

We have to first see ourselves as credible—*have faith that the source of our emotions is trustworthy*, in other words—in order to believe emotions hold important information.

The results from research by social psychologist Kent Harber (who is also the lead researcher on the fear of hope project), points us in that direction. His work shows that people with a lower sense of their own self-worth are less likely to use their emotions when making decisions than are people with more self-worth.[19] Harber agrees wholeheartedly with the affect-as-information group, that better and quicker decisions are made when people depend on their emotions as signals. But people first have to "trust and respect the source of these signals, that is, themselves." In other words, you have to have faith in yourself in order to have faith in your emotions, in order to use these emotions to make decisions and then act on them.[20]

How we deliberate over a decision is a lot like reading a

newspaper. You read some piece of information, stated as fact. You accept this information as fact, however, because you *feel* the newspaper is credible. And if someone—let's say, for the sake of argument, the leader of the free world—doesn't like the facts in the article, and also doesn't want to put in the hard work of doing their own research, they might try to persuade you that the newspaper isn't credible, that maybe it is even FAKE NEWS. If you don't trust the newspaper, you won't believe in the facts it contains. Discredit the messenger, and all its messages are themselves discredited.

Let's go back to that list of important decisions: job, marriage, and house. According to Harber, you were not simply able to make the decisions in these areas because your emotions were strong: You were able to do so because you believed in them; you had faith in them, and this was probably because you had faith in yourself. Think of these same kinds of decisions in a situation where you couldn't make up your mind. You may have had the same amount of positive emotions, and the same absence of negative ones, or vice versa, but you didn't feel you could depend on your gut because you didn't trust yourself.

That's how it works for all of us when we're about to change or engaged in change. You have some valid facts that support an affirmative choice. But in the end, you also rely on how you feel about the decision, and that reliance on feelings relies on your faith in yourself. It probably also requires faith that the world around you will let you forge forward to what you want. Without that faith—in yourself, in the world—data will always feel insufficient, and the feelings needed to act on them will be regarded as fake news: as untrustworthy sources of information.

Let me go back to Bridget and her parents to clarify this important point about emotions and faith.

I've worked with hundreds of people in my career who, like

Bridget, have experienced manic events and the depressions that follow. Every one of them has been smart, and many of them have had the same creative spirit and innovative, spontaneous approach to life as does Bridget. Like a lot of people, I'm convinced that there is something that connects mania to genius and to creativity. From Vincent van Gogh to Virginia Woolf, Winston Churchill, Vivien Leigh, Buzz Aldrin, Ernest Hemingway, Graham Green, Lou Reed, and many others, history is filled with famous leaders and creative people diagnosed (often, mind you, from armchairs) as having bipolar experiences. I've also seen, however, a particularly poignant result of having these emotional swings: a loss of faith in one's emotions. *Am I happy right now, or is that a mania coming on? Did that good-bye to my beloved make me sad, or am I heading toward a deep depression?* And if so on both counts, *Are my emotions taking me toward danger and risk again?* That loss of faith in one's emotions, as I see it, often leads to a person unable to tap into his or her own significant talents. Bridget's parents' faith in her, and her own stalwart faith in herself, protected her from the potential trauma of her emotional swings, since this faith carried the message that she was always credible no matter where her emotions took her, and that her emotions themselves were credible too. As she told me, emotions "give me clear messages about life" and are "always on target regarding reality." They are extreme, but accurate.

The same kind of relationship with emotions absolutely can't be said for Mark. Mark learned not to trust important, positive, and primal emotions related to spontaneity and joy, because in his situation these emotions betrayed him more often than not, leading him to punishment whenever he acted on them. And that distrust in his emotions caused him to lack faith in himself, the source of these feelings, and thus the source of the very things that got him in trouble. Seeing positive feelings as leading to bad results caused him to severely constrict his personal growth and experience himself as splintered into pieces. He led a life in which he couldn't follow any inner compass, because following it in his family meant going astray into very painful experiences.

There's a sort of sequence to Harber's idea in which lack of faith in yourself leads to lack of faith in your emotions, which leads to difficulty in making a decision and then acting. I think the injury to your faith can work in the opposite direction. Something bad happens to you because of a decision you made and an action you took based on this decision. You then see your emotions, which are information that come from within you, as taking you on a path toward disappointment. From there, you lose faith in yourself, the generator of these emotions.

Let me recap Mark's story with the record player, when he first danced joyfully and then was derided for being joyful, to make this point. Mark used that episode as a metaphor to describe a repeated pattern of interactions in his family and their effect on him. It offers a full picture of the interplay among all the elements in the force field of change, and a narrative about how disappointment can lead to lack of faith in yourself.

When Mark began to dance, he was acting on information from his emotions. And that required a lot of faith, since he had plenty of data that things would not end well if he did let his emotions guide him. So in that moment, he invested a significant amount of credibility into himself as the source of this information. Some part of him must have known the dangers of dancing, and the fact that his risk to nakedly express his full autonomy in the world—his lone capacity to spontaneously and joyously move to the music—could end up in catastrophe. But he hoped for a minute or so of joy in a joyless life, his yearning for fun outweighing his concerns about the likely punishment over his autonomous gesture. Because he was hoping, it felt right in the moment to dance—more right than his typical denial of his own autonomy.

But again, Mark couldn't have acted on his hope if he didn't have faith that his emotions held valid information from a person whom he could trust (that is, himself). Each move he made, each one relying on his credible source that it was okay to make, was a climb up that aspirational hill, from which the fall into disappointment grew deeper the higher he climbed. His father's harsh response pushed him off that hill. And when he experienced the profound disappointment from his fall, he learned a couple of crippling lessons: that it's best to distrust the person sending those emotional signals to act (his own self, in other words), and that it's dangerous to be an autonomous, spontaneous, hopeful, faithful person. He learned that staying still was much safer than dancing. Like tonic immobility, that frozen pose animals take to escape danger, staying the same, rigid and in place, was Mark's haven.

R. D. Laing, an important and controversial psychiatrist, had a term for this frozen position Mark assumed: petrification. For Laing, petrification, the result of profound insecurity, is a "general law that at some point those very dangers most dreaded can be encompassed to forestall their actual occurrence. Thus to forgo one's autonomy becomes the means of secretly safeguarding it; to play possum, to feign death becomes a means to preserving one's aliveness."[21]

Petrification: Does that sound a lot like sameness to you?

It is.

PETRIFICATION AND STAYING THE SAME

The act of petrification that Laing describes can be tracked all the way back to the crib, tangled up, I believe, in hoping for sustenance and warmth and the terror of not being fed. Every time an infant wails she's acting on her gut (feelings of hunger, the need for warmth). She is also acting on hope, calling for what she needs and crying out with the pain of not having it. When psychologists first studied the bonding relationship between children and their mothers (only mothers back then), they had a name for a kind of depression that happened when the infant's needs were regularly not met: anaclitic depression[22]—"anaclitic" meaning the yearning for nurturance from a caretaker (rooted in the Greek word for "leaning," as in "lean on me"— "depending," in other words). Anaclitic depression is marked by a severe resignation.

Babies who have suffered absent parents, who receive all their physical needs—food, clothing, medical attention—but not reliable emotional connections, look grief stricken. In the late 1940s, the psychologist René Spitz visited a foundling home, an orphanage for infants whose parents were in prison or otherwise unable to care for them.[23] The staff were responsible and conscientious, but could not provide each baby the dedicated emotional response that each baby called for. Photos and films that Spitz made are devastating to see, even today. Many infants appear inconsolable in their desolation, crying in a manner resembling an adult grief reaction. And perhaps worse still were those displaying a listless resignation. Often, this inability to have emotional needs met, to be disappointed in their calls for connection, depresses physical growth—a condition called deprivation dwarfism, as well as illness and even, tragically, death.

Related work[24,25] on attachment styles shows, in less dire but still dramatic fashion, what happens to babies who's unverbalized hope for connection is not reliably realized. In fact, you can observe this resignation directly, in the behavior of infants and babies who have been deprived of warmth and nourishment—a tragic ballet of giving up, as they *lean away* from their parents when their parents enter a room, and will often refuse their emotional nourishment (also called avoidant attachment). In severe cases, these infants and babies become completely resigned, moving little, responding to nothing. "Failure to thrive" is the label aptly applied to them when this happens.

While the typical disappointments you might feel when you try to make personal change are hardly as traumatic as the devastating experience of deprived children, you still engage in a version of this ballet when you risk hoping, depend on your faith to act, and potentially discover that you can't get what you believe you need. And when you do take the risk of reaching out and try to get your needs met, and things don't turn out the way you had hoped, your tendency is to aim toward something similar to anaclitic and avoidant stances: sameness—not moving. Turning away from the nourishment of faith in order to avoid the pain of disappointment, you freeze.

Let's say you yearn to find a mate. It's been a year since a really bad breakup, and you've been timid about trying again. But you finally join a dating website and discover someone interesting. You go out on a first date with this person and come home excited about the possibility of a relationship. You feel like this person is just the right one for you; you just know it in your gut. And you allow yourself to hope, letting your enthusiasm spool out imagined romantic scenarios. But then this person doesn't return your calls or texts. You are crushed; the depth of your disappointment matches the height of your hope. If you hadn't trusted your emotions in the first place, you wouldn't have enthusiastically appointed this person as someone you wanted and needed in your life. But now that you have made this person important, the failure to get a relationship makes your desire for a mate even more stark and more pressing. *Why*, you ask yourself, *did I let my emotions get the better of me?*

Even though this is only your first attempt, you can't help questioning your own ability ever to find someone. You do keep trying, however. The next time you get on the web and meet someone with real prospects, your gut tells you this person seems right. But you also tell yourself to *take it slow; don't jump into it.* You go on a few dates with this person. But lacking confidence regarding what your emotions tell you, and worried about feeling that awful sense of letdown you did last time, you're reticent, distant. In fact, every time you feel a little excited about this new prospect, you start shutting down emotionally. Your emotions got the better of you last time; this time they won't.

Your open hand of hope is now a tight fist. And because you are more held back, so is the person you are dating, and so is any feeling of connection you might have from which a relationship can grow. You decide "things just don't click," and you move on. However, once you end things with this person, you see them in the same light you did at the beginning: your gut telling you they are a real prospect. You feel a little like they might be exactly what you need. You text them about giving it another try, but they've moved on. You think, *Why didn't I listen to my gut?!*

You now feel disappointed in yourself, and you question where your squeamishness regarding your feelings got you. You begin to lose faith in yourself, wondering if you're *just no good at commitment.* You also lose faith that the world is bountiful enough to offer you more options, doubtful that there is anyone actually out there who will draw your interest and affection. You had really strong feelings about that person at one point. What if they were "the One"? The next time you get on the dating site and find a possible match, you immediately close your laptop. You don't want to follow your feelings again, because they will lead you to hope again that a person out there might make you feel more complete, with all the possibility that you will end up feeling more lost if things turn to disappointment. Datingwise, your life is frozen.

In this example, petrification is specific to dating, not an overall stance toward life like with Mark. And it doesn't leave you curled up in your bed, unwilling to respond to any of the ways life can entice risk, in a truly anaclitic kind of way, but it does hold you in place in your particular force field of change regarding dating.

While there can be all kinds of areas in your life where you move forward with gusto, there may be other places where you play possum because you can't stand the idea of hoping for something you feel you need and then not getting it.

Take a second and list all the things you're doing right now that have to do with improving something about yourself that you really yearn to improve, things you feel strongly are missing in your life. If I gave you a little possum ink stamp, I bet you could easily find those places on the list where it should be applied. Yoga: no stamp; eating healthy: possum stamp; calling your mother more regularly: no stamp; working on the promotion: no stamp; getting back into playing racquetball: possum stamp. Each of those places marked with the stamp represents petrified states, in which your struggle with faith outweighs the strength of your hope, weakening the ability of your driving force to move you forward.

This loss of faith also strengthens the restraining forces that hold you back. When you lose faith in yourself and the world, the anxiety fostered by your awareness of your existential accountability and aloneness can become unbearable.

LOST FAITH AND HELPLESSNESS: THE SCAR OF DISAPPOINTMENT

You've been given the exhilarating, challenging purple crayon of human agency, the capacity to decide on things and choose. That capacity offers you great opportunity, but it also makes you anxious. You're anxious because with this ability to decide comes the awareness that you are alone in your decisions and accountable for their results, and that these results matter a lot since you don't live forever.

The dual anxieties of aloneness and accountability become most evident when *you decide on something*. And you can dampen this awareness by finding ways *not to decide*. Personal change is a decision, and a particularly important one, because you are making a choice about changing something about yourself. And that kind of decision tends to expose your accountability even further. So what happens if you begin to suspect that the purple crayon of personal agency isn't reliable, or worse yet, defective? When that happens you feel accountable for your life yet lacking the wherewithal to make it work. What does that feel like? What's the result of the dastardly arithmetic of existential accountability + lack of faith?

I think it's the experience of extreme helplessness in getting your needs met.

I think that experience of helplessness is what shackled Mark, trapping him in a vice of unmet but essential needs and his felt inability to meet these needs. And while babies do not have to deal with the adult experiences of accountability and mortality, I do think this same extreme sense of helplessness in getting their needs met is at the root of their anaclitic and avoidant behavior. It's this same helplessness, too, that causes the resignation among the would-be daters, whose initial disappointment leads to a wariness that dampens the spark needed to ignite a new romance. In this way, hopelessness becomes a self-fulfilling prophecy.

It causes you enough anxiety already that you carry the awesome responsibility to navigate your life. Helplessness—this diminishment of agency thinking and self-efficacy—says that you'll be perpetually lost, even if you're able to muster the courage to take on this responsibility. Whether you experience yourself as a leaky, broken vessel in general, incapable of arriving at destinations without sinking, or as the sailor approaching a whirlpool of impossible deprivation, or both, I believe the message in helplessness is that you can't possibly attain what you're accountable for attaining. That's an unbearable experience, and the indescribable distress articulated in an infant's scream. It intensifies your existential anxiety by telling you that you can't author your life, even if you want to do so.

In this situation, bad faith looks quite attractive. *Just tell me what to do!* your mind pleads to the world, since you no longer trust yourself to take hold and guide the ship that is your life.

A scene in the BBC show *Fleabag* captures this stance perfectly. The heroine, Fleabag, is always making mistakes, and is regularly disappointed by herself and by the behavior of others. But she keeps going; keeps her head up, always remaining courageously authentic. She never stops being herself, unwilling to become petrified. (Fleabag is truly heroic in this regard, and I think of the show as being about existential courage.) The temptation to stop and just hand herself over to a bad faith stance is always there, however. In one scene, after a series of painful disappointments, she yearns to give in and just act as if life were without choice. She's in a confessional with a priest she's befriended (and in her tendency toward catastrophe, wants to sleep with). He asks her what she wants from life. Here's her reply:

> *I want someone to tell me what to wear in the morning. I want someone to tell me what to wear every morning. I want someone to tell me what to eat. What to like, what to hate, what to rage about, what to listen to, what band to like, what to buy tickets for, what to joke about, what not to joke about. I want someone to tell me what to believe in, who to vote for, who to love and how to tell them.*
>
> *I just think I want someone to tell me how to live my life, Father, because so far I think I've been getting it wrong, and I know that's why people want people like you in their lives, because you just tell*

them how to do it. You just tell them what to do and what they'll get out at the end of it, and even though I don't believe your bull-shit, and I know that scientifically nothing I do makes any differ-ence in the end anyway, I'm still scared. Why am I still scared?[26]

Just brilliant. Perfect. That's exactly it: When you lack faith in your own agency due to disappointments in your life, your accountability and aloneness—those things we all try to keep out of our awareness, but that personal change inevitably *bring into awareness*—now feel scarier than scary. And so playing possum begins to make some sense. It protects you from the awful expe-rience that you are alone, accountable, yet not a credible source for getting from here to there. And so you begin to look outside yourself for the answers. Not because those answers are really out there, but because you can no longer stand the idea that you are the source of all answers regarding your existence.

The policeman pointed the way Harold was
going anyway. But Harold thanked him.

I just think I want someone to tell me how to live my life.

It's singularly unbearable to view yourself as helpless—to be too broken to get on that road that you, alone, are accountable to walk. And when you are in this state, worried about any messages that you might not be able to actually master your own life, there is one experience out there that threatens to cajole you out of your petrified state and get you moving down that frightening road: hope.

When you lose faith in yourself and in the world, you see hope as your greatest threat, because it tempts you into having aspirations, ones you are afraid you can't meet, and conveys a brokenness if you don't meet them.

FEAR OF HOPE

Let's recall the complex anatomy of hope. Hope requires identifying an important goal, charting a pathway to that goal, and feeling confident in your ability to successfully follow that path. What happens when agency is missing? When you know what you want, you can see how to get there, but you lack faith in yourself as an agent? When you lack that crucial belief in your efficacy—the element in you that is about your faith in your capacity to actually pull the whole thing off, or pick yourself up if you don't—you won't move forward.

Hope that's empty of faith is an awful, agitated experience. You designate something as important, you see you lack it, and you don't believe you are capable of getting it, or able to build a strong enough boat to keep you afloat if you don't. You yearn to get home, and you're terrified to draw the next step there.

Think of a personal change you want to make right now. It can be small and simple, or large and complex. It doesn't matter. What's in the way? *I've failed at this a million times; this time will be no different,* Or, *I really don't want to feel awful about myself if I fail.*

That's your lack of faith talking, and it eats at you because you've appointed the thing in front of you as important by hoping for it. Part of you then tries to smother the hope by denigrating what you seek. *It's not that important to do. I can wait on it. There are more important things to achieve in my life.*

At this point your relationship with hope becomes conflicted. Hope moves you forward toward things you want. And when you move toward things you want, you also face the anxiety that you are on your own in doing so. When you don't have faith that you can reach the thing you want, or don't recover from failing to reach it, hope becomes scary. It scares you because it turns aspiration and desire into disappointment and frustration. And because it threatens to make you lose faith in yourself and in the world.

In this situation, hope—the emotion that drives you forward toward your goal, and thus challenges your confidence every step of the way—appears dangerous: a tempter that seems to coax you along a doomed path. Lacking faith in hope, and thus terrified of the next step, you reject it—the guiding and goading you need to move forward. I call this cramped, defensive attitude fear of hope.

Fear of hope strengthens the restraining force of existential anxiety by causing you to worry about failing to meet the goals you are accountable for attaining. Fear of hope also weakens your driving forces by spoiling your ability to drink from the well of change. No matter your situation, whether you have been injured by debilitating setbacks like Mark, or less catastrophic ones, I believe that when you face personal change your ability to reach your goal is determined in large part by how much or how little you fear hope.

In the next chapter you'll read about the surprising, complex, and difficult relationship between having hope and fearing hope, and the way faith plays into how you keep moving forward.

CHAPTER 4

FEAR OF HOPE

Anyone whose goal is "something higher" must expect
someday to suffer vertigo. What is vertigo? Fear of falling? No, vertigo
is something other than fear of falling. It is the voice of the emptiness
below us which tempts and lures us, it is the desire to fall,
against which, terrified, we defend ourselves.

—Milan Kundera

Mary and the Don't-Get-Your-Hopes-Up Wall

It's 2006. Mary is thirty-five years old. She comes to see me after
years of therapeutic work with other clinicians. Diagnosed by her
previous therapists with a severe and intractable depression, combined with an anxiety disorder, Mary lives with her mother, has
few friends, and spends most of her days traveling as a sales rep for
a software company. Mary has a history of suicide attempts, and
has been admitted to psychiatric facilities a few times in the last
year by her prior psychiatrist.

She tells me her story.

Her life was not always like this. In fact, she was once the very embodiment of someone with strong driving forces, acting, often with great courage, on her hope. She was the very picture of a person who could face, and even appreciate, the potentially restraining experience of her own accountability to take hold of her life.

In 1994, her senior year in high school, she was a state-ranked soccer player and at the top of her class academically. She was energetic, popular, with lots of close friends from the soccer team.

Mary's soccer coach always exhorted the team to "go bold or go home." Like her teammates, Mary cringed at those words, their corniness. But secretly she knew what her coach meant. Life was about putting in your all, pushing the limits, taking risks. In her classes, Mary came up with solutions to problems that were unique, sometimes quirky, always a new take on things, and they gained her significant validation from teachers, who commented more than once that she was "brilliant." On the soccer field, she was famous for her finely tuned execution of a left-side tackle, a risky move in soccer that can lead to both injury and fouls. For Mary, boldness almost always equaled success. She never really experienced a downside to "going bold."

But then Mary met with a long series of setbacks. It began with a bad case of mononucleosis her senior year of high school, which meant she couldn't play soccer at the start of the fall semester. Then she ruptured her spleen, after secretly practicing her soccer moves at a local park, against the advice of her doctor. Lying in the grass, knowing immediately that she was painfully experiencing the results of her own willingness to risk, she felt a hint of despair, knowing that she was now off the field for the entire year.

For the first time in her life, Mary understood what it was like to watch rather than be watched; to be part of the crowd, not its focus. As she sat on the bench during games, her despair took on a more complex shape and color: a slight sense that things might *not* work out for her, a vague experience of helplessness she had never felt before, and a burgeoning anger at herself for taking things too far that day at the park. But she also knew she had to keep pushing herself forward. She had entrance exams coming up, and a GPA to maintain, which mattered more now that soccer would no longer boost her application. This was not a time to dwell on unwanted feelings. Her driving forces brought her back to the scholastic tasks at hand.

Spring came, as did the rejection letters from most of the best colleges. That new sense that things might not work out for her, and that anger at herself, grew bigger—dark clouds in an otherwise productive life. Mary kept her hopes up for one more letter. One of the better universities—a rather large institution in California—still hadn't gotten back to her, and she looked for their reply every day, hoping that somehow there was still a chance. It finally came, and in a big, thick acceptance envelope. Everything was going to be okay. She was energized: all systems go.

The next fall, Mary entered the university with gusto. Getting into one of her top schools without the persuasion of their soccer coaches, she had dodged a bullet, and she was going to take full advantage of this gift. She enjoyed dorm life, the parties, the camaraderie, and she loved her classes and the challenges they posed.

Mary particularly liked her sports psychology class, and was especially enthralled with the research and writing on teamwork. The professor, the head of the department, was well known in this particular field of study, and kind and thoughtful with the students. It seemed to Mary, however, that he took a special interest in her work, calling her ideas "innovative," "creative," and "thought provoking," words she had heard in high school about her way of looking at the world. At the end of the semester, he pulled Mary aside and asked if she would like to join his lab as an assistant. Mary was flabbergasted. This was a position typically held by grad students and the occasional senior. Her hopes for the future had never been higher. She knew that she wanted to make sports psychology her major, and she could see this important decision as propelling her to a life that would be fulfilling and exciting. She felt the irresistible pull of a winning goal.

But one night in the lab changed all that. Working late by herself, the professor stopped at the door to say goodnight. He asked what Mary was working on, and when she told him he came over to take a look, sitting down next to her. He began asking questions and making suggestions, sounding surprised and excited by her insights. As they talked eagerly about the data, he placed his hand on her knee. Mary started and pushed him away. He quickly got up and, somewhat awkwardly, said he realized he had an appointment and left.

Mary didn't know whom to tell about the incident. She felt embarrassed by it and confused about what it meant. She felt trapped, unable to make a decisive move.

Mary quit her position at the lab, leaving a curt note for the professor with an envelope of unfinished work. Her professor's prominence in mind, Mary knew she was at a crossroads. She couldn't bear the idea of coming forward with what happened and she also couldn't imagine ever working with the professor again. She would either need to change her major in sports psychology or transfer to another school. Mary met with her adviser and quit her major, focusing on the general field of clinical psychology.

That night, she tossed in bed, lamenting her future. Nothing seemed solid; she no longer saw a clear road to success. She doubted her ability to captain her existence and make it work. And she felt anxious about this: That once proud ability to take her existence into her hands and boldly move forward was now filled with insecurity. The downward force of helplessness was entering her perspective.

Over the summer and back at home, Mary thought a lot about how to prepare better for the next semester. She kicked herself a bit for responding so dramatically to the professor's advances. *Life isn't over because of some jerk*, she thought. Not that she felt comfortable exposing the professor, or that she could resume her original major. But *college is for exploring; I jumped into what was familiar too fast. I should look around a bit while I can. Besides*, she thought, *I can always get a degree in sports psychology in grad school*. Mary actually got excited again about the next semester. She was going to try new things, get out of her comfort zone. All she had to do was avoid the building that housed the sports psychology lab and she would be fine. Her driving forces had taken hold again.

Mary's goal of academic exploration didn't really come to fruition, however. She was bored with her classes, and met each challenge as a burden. Everything she did academically was rote. Her curiosity and imagination, once steady and strong, were shut down. She felt a barrier in her way every time she started to formulate an interesting answer, as if such answers held risks that weren't worth taking.

Mary got a C in her class on psychopathology, Bs in the rest of her courses. *How could this be?* she thought. *A bad grade in the one important class, and nothing great in the fun classes? Ridiculous!* During the winter break, Mary evaluated her plans to explore things academically. She realized she needed to get her act together, filling her schedule with psychology courses and heading into the second semester with a renewed sense of purpose.

But psychology bored her, and she quickly realized that it was really not for her. She loved teamwork and camaraderie. These were her interests, not the intricacies of individual psyches. That anger she felt toward herself when she ruptured her spleen grew more prominent. Her mind was filled with questions about her ability to manage her life: *What am I doing with myself? Why can't I get it together?*

Mary had a foreboding sense of being lost and disconnected. But she also felt something new: an inability to generate excitement about the future. Not only was the road ahead something to fear, but she also didn't really want to get on it at all. She felt shut down and slowed down, cautiously holding herself back from the spontaneous curious self that once made her life so lively.

Then she met Mike at a party.

A senior, Mike had played baseball in high school. He was fun and adored Mary. A high achiever himself, he saw that same tendency in her, and loved her unique and intelligent take on the world. His interest in her was like a spark that ignited her old gifts, and as he delighted in how she looked at the world, her quirky take on things emerged again, and Mary applied her unique worldview to her coursework. Mary felt a new excitement about life, again feeling a deep and energized sense of possibility. Not only did school and her future career stir in her a sense of bright expectation, but she could also see a life with Mike.

Mike was a business major. As he listened to Mary question whether a psychology degree really matched her interests, he suggested she try a business class.

Maybe she could apply her interest in teamwork to something in business. She signed up for an organizational behavior class for the fall semester.

Mary loved that class and excelled in it. Her mind was working again; she came up with ideas and insights that excited the whole class. She was the star. This is what she was meant to do. And it wasn't too late to change majors. A couple of summer-school classes and a full load of business classes, and she would be fine. Just in the nick of time, and with Mike's help, she was back on track.

Mary didn't go home that summer. She stayed in her apartment, took classes, and hung out with Mike. It was a lovely time. Mike would be heading to Tokyo in the fall for a coveted internship at a corporate headquarters. He would then return to the college town, take a break, figure out his next steps, and spend time with Mary. The couple felt secure in their relationship and they would only be apart for six months. Besides, Mary really needed to focus if she was going to finish that major.

She was ready for the challenge, and headed into her junior year ready for action.

That October, Mary received an alarming phone call from her mother. Her father had had a heart attack. Against her mother's request that she "stay put and keep working at school," Mary got a plane ticket home. She had a paper to finish, so she waited a day, but then she was off to see her dad.

When Mary's plane landed, she checked her cell phone for messages, finding one from her mother: "Mary, please call me as soon as you can." Mary immediately called home. Her mother picked up on the first ring: "Honey, your father died last night. Something went wrong after the surgery." Stunned, numb, Mary rushed through the airport and took the first cab home.

After arranging matters with the university, Mary planned to stay home another two weeks following her father's funeral. But she couldn't keep up with the coursework, couldn't concentrate, and couldn't comprehend the material. The only choice, she felt, was to take a semester's leave from school.

The upcoming months were predictably painful, and very lonely. Mary didn't have any friends left in her old town, and Mike was hard to reach, busy as he was, and living in another time zone.

Mary didn't do much with her days; mostly she read magazines or watched TV, interspersed with walking the dog. Most evenings she ate dinner with her mom. Three months and she would be back in school and reunited with Mike. This was a horrible period, but she also knew she would recuperate at some point.

One day while grocery shopping, she ran into Dan, an acquaintance from high school. He had heard about Mary's father dying, and hugged Mary, telling her how sorry he was and offering support. A third-string player for the men's soccer team in high school, and two years her senior, Dan remembered her and her reputation as a fierce player. "You were a legend, even in your freshman year, Mary," he told her as they exchanged phone numbers.

Dan worked at a local software development business, which had its own company indoor soccer team. One day, Dan called Mary and asked if she would join. Mary accepted the invitation and Dan and his colleagues snuck her in as a member of their squad. Soccer again, and as a ringer! She loved it, and she was a star. Her sense of self-efficacy bolstered by the successful use of her own skills, her sense of hope about the future increased.

I could play intramural soccer when I get back to school, Mary thought. *It will be my medicine.*

By late December, Mary was feeling ready to return to school. She was looking forward to more purpose and structure in her life. And the prospect of living with Mike excited her. As she completed the lease on their new apartment, she could taste it, the new sense of adulthood that would come when she lived with her mate. One night, Mike called with news.

"Mary, I know this is so late in the game, but something amazing has happened. I've been offered an executive-track position in the company. They're moving me to New York City."

"What about the apartment?" she cried. "What about you and me? We had plans." They argued late into the night.

Mary was devastated. She kicked herself hard for staying away from college so long, thinking over and over again about what could have been if she had taken a different route. Waking the next morning from a fitful sleep, her immediate future seemed unmanageably uncertain. *What am I returning to,* she thought, *an apartment by myself? I can't bear that right now; I'm not ready for that.* Her grief for her father returned full force. So did that loneliness she felt so harshly on that airport floor after hearing of her father's death.

That night she slept with Dan.

That was the beginning of a very quick end for her and Mike. He moved to New York, and Mary decided to take some more time off from school, settle in at her mom's, and regroup. She took her time with Dan, worried about her own stability and scared about more heartache. But over time, they fell in love. Dan helped her get a job at his company, nothing great, just inputting data, but it gave her something to do and brought in a little money.

Mary planned to return to university that fall, and Dan was going to join her. He would find some work in California for sure. But Mary kept putting aside the tasks she needed to achieve to come back, like reenrolling and getting a place to live. And every time she did postpone her return she would question herself, deliberating about all the chances she was missing by her decisions. And that thinking ate at her, digging deeper into her past: *Why didn't I stand up for myself and confront that professor? I would still be on course for a degree in sports psychology!* And *My life would be so much different now if I had just gone back to school earlier and finished up—I would have my degree in hand.* And *If I wasn't so serious about getting that paper finished, I would have made it home in time, to say good-bye to dad.* These were the thoughts that filled her head. Spreading doubt about her decisions, they further eroded her faith in herself. The idea that she could take hold of her life and make it worth living felt like a distant dream.

Dan and Mary moved in together. She postponed her return to

the university again that spring. That fall, she changed her mind again and withdrew from school altogether.

Mary felt a growing sense of emptiness in her, a feeling that her activities weren't connected to her talents. But she also saw no path back to her previous life, so full of hope and vivid expectations. She saw herself as broken and unfixable, and she saw the world outside her as unmanageable, an impossible place in which her needs would never be met. In her head, she kept ruminating about a person and a world that could have been, if only she had made different decisions. Even in her happiest moments, a sense of empty regret remained, nagging at her, preoccupying her thoughts. She talked a lot about "what could have been" with Dan. It became a central topic for her when they were out on a date, lying around in bed, at meals. The one future she could hold on to was with Dan. When Dan and Mary began their relationship, it was as if Mary were the attracting force; Dan was the lucky one. But now things felt reversed, as if Mary needed Dan more than he needed her.

Dan was, in fact, having doubts. This lovely and talented star from high school now seemed broken, obsessed with past decisions, and never satisfied. Every time Mary brought up her sense of failure and her belief that she should be further along in life, Dan felt insulted. Not only was the life she wanted far beyond what Dan expected of himself, but he also felt inadequate whenever he heard about her painful feelings of being unfulfilled. Was she blind to the message she was sending to him? Then there was the way she always wanted his attention when they were out with friends. Before, she would pick up a conversation with anyone at the table. Now she would close down and mope when Dan paid attention to anyone else. Increasingly, Mary planned their weekends around dates for the two of them. Dan started to dread it when Mary came home from work, and he hated the weekend plans. Mary felt clingy, insecure, and a burden. Finally, Dan broke up with her and soon accepted a transfer to a job in another state.

Mary was devastated, of course. That desperate and painful feeling of being completely alone and lost was back. Her regretful ruminations increased. She moved back in with her mother and started seeing a therapist. Mary stayed with her job, but her performance reviews became increasingly negative. She was demoted to a sales position, with bonuses based on commission, and a poor salary. She traveled a lot, and was sometimes on the road more than at home. She kept planning to transfer her university credits to the local state college, but never got around to it. She drank a lot. She was alone a lot. She hated her life and couldn't stand what she had become. This was not the life she was meant to have, Mary increasingly felt. Ending it, at times, made sense to her, and she made attempts to kill herself. She landed in psychiatric hospitals a couple of times, ashamed of her behavior. Soon after her most recent stint in the hospital, Mary started seeing me for therapy.

At this point in our interview, I asked Mary about her past treatments. She told me that she'd seen a few therapists and psychiatrists. Concerned about her pessimistic ruminations about her situation, some of her therapists diagnosed her as severely depressed. But Mary's chief complaint was about a constant agitation and fear, so others saw her as suffering from an anxiety disorder. Her last psychiatrist thought she fit the diagnostic categories for both depression and anxiety. None of the interventions by her treaters really worked, however, and so most of them believed her mental illnesses were resistant to treatment. Some called her problem "treatment refectory," or "non-responsive" to treatment. Their prognosticating made Mary feel even more hopelessly broken.

After hearing her story, I asked Mary to explain why she came to see me. "I don't like my life," she replied. "I'm far from what makes me happy and I'm not meeting my potential. I've been told my depression and anxiety get in the way of me getting to where I thought I would be. Nothing ever seems to work out."

Often in my work, I like to use a technique called externalization. This is a way for a person to contemplate a problem as outside themselves, something they can see at a distance. The first step in externalizing an issue is to give it a name, something different from a diagnosis; something that expresses the person's own relationship to this experience, rather than a label applied by an expert. I ask Mary to name the thing that "keeps you far from what makes you happy, and away from meeting your potential."

"Depression," she said.

"Yeah, but what does that word mean? How would you name these feelings?"

"Sadness, I guess. Grief too. And just being scared to try anything all the time."

"So you would name these things 'sadness and grief,' and being 'scared' of trying? These are the things that keep you from happiness and your potential?"

"Well, sort of. It's more like they are the result of something, rather than the cause."

"They are the results. So what would you name the cause? What would you call it?"

"I don't know. It's hard to explain. Something about holding back and not taking any risks. But it's not quite that. Every time I try to do something to get back on track, I just get overwhelmed. It's like I'm at this door but no one will let me in."

"So, a door and no one will let you in?"

"Well, I guess. I don't know. It's also like I'm not *able to go in*. Like I'm just too stupid to know how to turn the knob. It's just really hard to explain."

"Try again, take your time."

"It's . . . it's . . . it's the opposite of bold, but I can't explain it. It's like this wall I hit when I try to take a few steps forward. It's this weird thing that just stops me in my tracks. It's like I don't want to get excited about anything because it feels too risky to do so."

"Okay. Can you name that wall? Take a risk right now and just name it."

Mary thought for a minute or two. "It's um . . . it's um . . . hmm . . . It's the wall of 'don't get your hopes up.'" She laughed a little at the awkwardness of the phrase, then repeated, "I name it the don't-get-your-hopes-up wall."

The "don't-get-your-hopes-up wall": that's a perfect way of describing fear of hope. While most of us may not have gone through the kinds of disappointments Mary endured, I believe most of us face different intensities of this fear when we head toward personal change.

As with Mary, fear of hope causes you to experience as dangerous the forces that are essential to pushing you forward toward change. Here's how it works:

Hope—that experience of moving toward something you have appointed as important, while knowing you lack it—takes you on a route in which you acknowledge your accountability to make your life as deep and rich as possible. It is a great privilege of being a free human to chart your own path upward toward deeper, better experiences. But if your ascent is blocked—by kicking a ball when too sick to do so, by the trespassing hand of a person in whom you've placed trust—then the fall can produce profound disappointment in yourself and in the world. And that disappointment can cause you to lose faith in yourself and in that world. Now, with less faith that you can be efficacious, and worried about experiencing another blow to your confidence in your ability to make your life work, you're fearful of hoping again, since hope is the only route to this experience.

We call disappointment "crushing" for a reason. At its root, the word "disappointment" means to fail ("dis") to reach an "appointed" goal, i.e., a goal you're "pointing to" as desirable. You hope for something, and by hoping for it you appoint it as something you need and want, but don't have. When you are disappointed because you can't attain it, you face the painful experience of losing something you've identified as important and needed.

Of course, most of the disappointments you experience in your life don't bring you to your knees, like Hamlet. If fact, we often apply the word "disappointment" to everyday situations: "That movie was a disappointment!" "I'm disappointed by your behavior, young man!" And rightly so. Disappointment is the rule, not the exception, every day of our lives. From "My iced chai latte doesn't have enough ice" to "I didn't like the way things went in my discussion with my boss," disappointments are as reliable as the rising sun.

While disappointment is regular and expected, when you hope for something that you know you lack *in yourself* and are disappointed because you didn't get it, the result is often rotten: the despairing experience of your failed attempt to act accountable and take the responsibility to make your life better, and the resulting recognition that something you see as valuably life-giving is missing in you.

That's why you risk despair when you move toward a personal goal and are disappointed: you experience the helpless, anaclitic feeling of not getting what you believe you need that is missing in you.

The fact that hope is the main route to possible disappointment means that the more you are propelled by this driving force, the stronger the chances that the restraining one of increasing anxiety about your accountability will grow. If, like Mary, you are worried about experiencing your accountability and aloneness and are concerned about another disappointment and the resulting helplessness, the thing you fear is the very thing that got you on the road in the first place: hope—that feeling of yearning for something important that you lack.

All along, you are avoiding one thing: a moment when you recognize that you are accountable to make your life work, and that you lack faith that you can make that happen. *I'm given this one finite existence, I'm in charge of finding depth, connection, and meaning, and I'm incompetent to do so, or the world is just not bountiful enough to fulfill my needs*: That is an existentially horrific moment, an adult version of infant deprivation. It causes you to want to protect what you can of your own autonomy—by petrifying.

When you bound toward the threats and challenges of change with hope, you are in the best position to alter your behaviors. If, on the other hand, you see hope as the warm woolen coat that conceals a merciless wolf of disappointing helplessness, the threats will seem too scary and the challenges insurmountable. Overwhelmed with doubt, you will stop in your tracks.

That was Mary's experience, I think. Not that her mind literally froze. In fact it would not go silent. Instead, her mental energy and imaginative skills took a direction that effectively kept her tethered to the past. Rather than thinking about where next to go in her growth and how to get there, Mary was obsessed with what she'd done wrong, how the world had failed her, and how her life would be otherwise if only . . . If only she had stayed in sports psychology or if only Mike had not gotten that New York position or if only she had gone back to school after her father died. If only . . . If only . . . If only. Those thoughts kept her neither here nor there, but frozen.

Social psychologists call these "if-onlys" "counterfactuals"[1] (because they are thoughts about a wished-for past that counter the facts of what actually occurred). They're thoughts like "If only A had happened, B wouldn't have occurred," or "If only A didn't happen, B would have." In our research at Rutgers on fear of hope, counterfactuals—these second-guesses and remorseful experiences of missed alternative futures—provide an important clue to how fear of hope affects the tension between where you are and where you want to be.

A Science of Fear of Hope

The Rutgers group has been able to show that fear of hope can be reliably measured, using a brief (six-item) measurement called, appropriately, the Fear of Hope (FOH) Scale (fig. 7). Turns out that fear of hope is not a lot of other things: it's not fear of success, nor fear of failure, not anxiety, nor depression, although it is closely related to them. Most important, fear of hope is *not* the experience of having less hope. In fact, hope and fear of hope are so weakly connected that a person can simultaneously have hope and fear hope. That's a very important concept to understand as we go along and you'll see why very shortly.

We first used the measure to test whether counterfactual thinking is a common feature of fear of hope. It is. In several studies

Fear of Hope Measure

		Not At All	Very Little	Some-what	A Lot	A Great Degree
1.	It is unwise to have faith in one's future	1	2	3	4	5
2.	Being hopeful scares me	1	2	3	4	5
3.	I feel safer not placing faith in the future	1	2	3	4	5
4.	It is very hard for me to just accept feeling hopeful	1	2	3	4	5
5.	I feel it is unsafe to be hopeful	1	2	3	4	5
6.	I'm setting myself up for a fall when I'm hopeful	1	2	3	4	5

Fig. 7

done with the general public we found that those who report greater fear of hope also are more likely to engage in the same demoralizing counterfactuals that Mary did.

There is a surprising twist to this connection between fear of hope and obsessions with "should haves" and "could haves" that has to do with that interesting difference between hopelessness and FOH. The people who are most likely to punish themselves with these thoughts *fear hope the most* while at the same time *being the most hopeful*! In other words, fear of hope plus hope leads to more obsessions with how life could have turned out better—if only A had happened or if only B had not happened.

Here's another startling fact regarding the combustible tension between high hope and high fear of hope. When research subjects (college undergraduates) were given the opportunity to list potentially positive events in their future, those who experienced both high hope and high fear of hope listed fewer such positive upcoming events than did other subjects. They even listed fewer positive events than did people who had low hope.

Yes: When you have high hope, but are afraid of that hope, you don't envision as many positive things coming up as when you're less hopeful about your future.[2]

Did you just do a double-take and reread that last sentence? I know I did when I first perused the finding. In reality, though, this result is rather understandable as long as you understand the mechanisms of hope and disappointment. Remember, when you fear hope, you fear where hope might take you. And the place you fear it will take you is devastating disappointment as well as resulting experiences in which you are helpless to get your needs met.

Positive events are events to hope for, and so they are also events that might lead to the negative and painful consequences of hoping. So, like a grueling oral surgery appointment in the month ahead, you put these scary, anxiety-generating events to the side of your consciousness until you have to face them. When you have less hope, and less fear of hope, you don't need to ignore these events, since you don't appoint much value to them and you don't really care that they are missing in your life: they are just positive events without any pull to reach them. Your graduation? *Whatever.* A job promotion? *What else is new.* An upcoming vacation? *Yeah, well, we'll see how that goes.*

The results about positive events in the future, and how they relate to people who both fear hope and have high hope, were part of a larger set of questions we were pursuing about the relationship between FOH and a person's overall outlook on time, both past and future. This is the "time perspective" I mentioned earlier, which Lewin[3] saw as central to hope.

To study time perspective in regard to fear of hope, we gave each subject a simple graph and asked them to rate the "time point where you focus most." We then asked that they place brackets around these scores that "best fits your mind-set"—their time perspective, in other words (fig. 8).

Tellingly, those individuals who scored high in both hope and fear of hope produced the narrowest of brackets. The breadth of their time perspective was the smallest, their focus most limited to the very recent past and the very near future.

The fact that these individuals were more focused on the present absolutely does not mean they were "be here now" Zen masters. Far from it. The way my FOH collaborators and I see it, this narrow bracketing of past and future is the furthest thing from a meditative practice: the exact opposite, actually, since filling the space between those brackets is the "monkey brain" ruminations of what "could have" and what "should have," and an aching attempt to restrict any expectations about the future.

Social science research is often a practice of looking for phe-

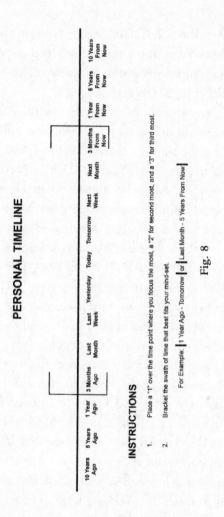

PERSONAL TIMELINE

10 Years Ago · 5 Years Ago · 1 Year Ago · 3 Months Ago · Last Month · Last Week · Yesterday · Today · Tomorrow · Next Week · Next Month · 3 Months From Now · 1 Year From Now · 5 Years From Now · 10 Years From Now

INSTRUCTIONS

1. Place a "1" over the time point where you focus the most, a "2" for second most, and a "3" for third most.

2. Bracket the swath of time that best fits your mind-set.

For Example: [1 Year Ago - Tomorrow] or [Last Month - 5 Years From Now]

Fig. 8

nomena that are not immediately obvious, but detectable in patterns and relationships. I think that when you combine our FOH findings regarding counterfactuals, anticipated future positive events, and timeline-based visions of the future, an image of that petrification Laing[4] describes begins to become clear. We see a person anxious about looking too closely at their aloneness and accountability, who is thus afraid of their hope, and hence restricts any movement forward through counterfactuals, a sweeping away of the explosive mines of hopeful future events, and a limiting of their thoughts of past or future.

Mary is an example of this restricting inward. The way I see it, she faced the awful discrepancy between powerfully hoping for something that she felt she needed and just as powerfully fearing that she wouldn't (or couldn't) get it. That's a horrible, agitated, unbearably anaclitic state—the ultimate point of existential crisis. To relieve herself of the tension brought on by this discrepancy, Mary created little and inevitably dissatisfying gestalts of meaning through counterfactuals, either blaming herself ("If I could have just returned to college earlier") or her fate ("Life didn't go the way I wanted because of that pervert professor"). These counterfactuals kept her in place, since they weren't really about future action, just a ruminative attempt to understand the past. And in regard to time, her ruminations also kept her eyes off the future.

The FOH research (and there are more findings ahead) paints a picture of someone tightly closing inward in a petrified state. What is it like to live this way? I imagine a person in a chair that faces forward toward the light of their future. They are bound to the chair, unable to shield themselves completely from the glare. So they bend downward as far as they can go. Their forehead is close to their stomach and their knees are raised and pointing to the top of their head; their body—meant to be erect—is formed into an uneven circle, averting their gaze and their heart from what's ahead. They ache with the strain of contorting themselves away from the destined growth of all living creatures. But painfully bend they do, in order to avoid what terrifies them most:

The light of hope.

I want you to remember this image as you read on about fear of hope, because I believe the posture toward hope it represents is the central factor in our tendency to stay the same. Like Mary, when you fear hope, you fear the very thing that counters your existential anxiety. That means that your main driving force, hope, is weakened when you assume this position. It also means your central restraining force, existential anxiety, is strengthened if you fear hope. Between the two arrows in the force field of personal change, it places you closer to sameness and further from the change you want. And that's true in all situations when you're trying to change something or to grow.

Think of a time when you achieved some important goal. You likely felt good; you successfully achieved something that took effort, and reached it despite the fact that failure and disappointment were always a possibility. I'm betting you felt a sense of your own efficacy, too, your own capacity to make things happen for yourself. But did you also feel a counterpressure, a craving to sabotage this experience? You're on a diet, for example. You step on the scale and discover that you've lost a few pounds. As you step off, does your mind turn—in a whisper or a yell—to celebrating, and does it offer up the idea a big bowl of ice cream to do so? Your mind here is looking to put a lid on your elation, to firmly cover some of your budding feelings of hope. And it's playing a trick on you, trying to get you to trip up in order to dampen this hope.

That's fear of hope talking. It's bending the posture of your mind downward and away from a vast future of hoped-for possibilities, and toward short-term issues (*Will I, or will I not, eat that ice cream?*). It does this because you lack faith that you will reach your targeted weight, and you fear the sense of helplessness that will come if you don't reach it. You're not thinking of positive things that can happen anymore, just the present experience of *Should I or shouldn't I?*

And if you eat that ice cream? What typically happens after that last spoonful? *Why did I do that? What was I thinking? If I had resisted that bowl of ice cream I would be further along in the diet!* It's counter-factuals moving those brackets even closer to the place where fear of hope wanted to hold you back, once it saw you heading toward that scary proposition of advancing further on your diet and rais-ing your hopes to scarier levels. You are now anchored from the dizziness of your freedom, with all the unlimited possibilities of both hope and disappointment it portends.

Whenever you feel the pull toward sameness it's because you are simultaneously feeling hopeful and fearing that hope. This means that your hope isn't necessarily injured or depleted when you stick to staying the same; rather, it is there, chugging along, yearning for things it appoints as important that are lacking in your life. It's just that this hope also worries you, so you restrict its ability to move you forward. Fearing hope, you put a lid on it, because you are so anxious about that always-present problem of your possible disappointment, and the resulting sense that you are helpless in getting your needs met.

When it comes to hoping for personal change, disappointment—the injuries from it, the fears of it—is a big deal. But fear of hope doesn't always injure your hope; sometimes it just makes you want to hide it from yourself. Your faith in yourself, and in the benign nature of the world around you, is a different story.

INJURED FAITH

Counterfactual thinking can sometimes be sensible. After all, those after-the-fact what-ifs get you to review your own bad de-cisions and induce you to consider how you could have done things better. In fact, in relatively small doses, counterfactuals do serve this corrective purpose. The problem is when counterfactu-als occur in big doses, when people seem addicted to them.

Why would anyone want to perpetually punish themselves with damning thoughts of *If only I had done this!* or *If only I hadn't done that!*? We get a clue from the third president of the United States, Thomas Jefferson.[5] Jefferson wrote a remarkable love letter to his paramour Maria Cosway that conveyed a conversation between "my Head and my Heart." In it, Jefferson's Head and Heart go after each other. The Head berates the Heart with a slew of counterfactuals regarding the doomed romance with Mrs. Cosway (there was that awkward issue of Mr. Cosway, after all). *Why'd you get us involved? You knew this was going to happen, so why didn't you think about consequence?* are part of the Head's onslaught of the Heart. The Heart writhes in contrition, until the Head says, *The secret of life is the avoidance of pain.* At this the Heart roars back: Crucial life decisions, it says, are *too important to leave to the* "uncertain combinations of the head."

"The uncertain combinations of the head." What an apt phrase for those who spin out endless streams of self-punishing counterfactuals. What makes the head, so clever at coming up with new ideas, new approaches, and alternative perspectives, "uncertain"? Simply that, by itself, it lacks that warm moment of emotional signaling; the "Go/Don't Go" messages of emotions—of the Heart in Jefferson's parable. These emotional messages provide the resolving "click" that stops the head from its endless spinning, and directs the whole person, head and heart, toward an actionable decision.

So what does all this have to do with fear of hope and counterfactuals? Recall that people who both have hope and fear of hope are those most likely to engage in prolonged counterfactual thinking. Maybe the problem is that for these high hope/high fear of hope people, the head is spinning out uncertain combinations because the heart, which dictates the emotions, is not being heeded.

To see if this was so, we included a measure of emotional intelligence called the Trait Meta–Mood Scale (TMMS)[6] in our FOH research. The TMMS measured three things—awareness of emotions, clarity of emotions, and ability to repair emotions. People who both have and fear hope—the ones who spin out the most counterfactuals—showed a marked deficit in emotional clarity. They know they're getting an emotional signal, but have a hard time tuning into it: Are they feeling sad, melancholy, depressed, dejected? They're not sure. If you can't properly identify your emotions, it's going to be hard to act on them. You can't collaborate with your heart if you can't make out what it is telling you.

Making good use of emotional messages does not necessarily mean becoming overly emotionally aroused—often just the opposite. We want the heart to counsel the head, not deafen it. It turns out that those who have and fear hope have the most difficulty controlling their emotions; anger, sadness, depression, anxiety, even joy, seem to overwhelm them.

In sum, people who have and fear hope are not collaborating well with their heart; they can't effectively detect what it's saying or control the heart when it is engaged. The heart, that vital, final judge of what is good or bad, of whether to approach or avoid, seems to become less credible for hopeful people who also fear hope.

Less credible. Get it?

Remember, faith has a close relationship to making decisions and taking action based on emotions. When you use your emotions to make a decision and then act, you're acting on the information that your emotions convey, because you see yourself—the source of your emotional messages—*as credible.*

What we think this route toward counterfactuals tells us is that when you fear hope and have high hope, your trust in yourself as the producer of emotional information—and thus your ability to act on faith—has taken a hit. Your hope in this situation is still strong, yearning for something you appointed as important, and aching over the fact that you lack it. But your faith might be injured.

More results from the FOH research support this point about injured faith. As you'll remember, I see Bandura's concept of self-efficacy—the belief in one's own ability to successfully complete tasks—as a scientific sister to faith. We measured general self-efficacy in our research. People who have a lot of hope also have greater self-efficacy—unless they also fear hope, which causes their self-efficacy to plummet.

The findings from this part of our research accords with our earlier discussion of the ensuing loss of faith. You're hit with disappointments. The disappointments make you distrust your emotions, since they were major players in your decisions to take the risks that ended in these disappointments. And once you distrust your emotions, seeing the information they produce as fake news, you begin to lose faith in their source—you. Once you no longer trust yourself, you are perpetually threatened with that unbearable feeling of helplessness in getting your needs met.

In light of all this thinking and research, I believe now that Mary may have been misdiagnosed as suffering from a distinct psychiatric malady, something wrong with her brain that required a medical intervention to fix. In fact, I don't think she was suffering from something *wrong* with her. Instead, I believe she was suffering as a result of something that *happened* and was *happening to* her—a series of awful disappointments that caused her to fear hope, even though she was still hoping, because she lost faith in her ability to attain what she was hoping for.

What looked to the medically trained eye like an anxiety disorder was Mary's anxious experience of worrying about her high hopes being crushed again, her lack of faith that she could pick herself up if they were crushed, and her terror that she could not handle another experience of acute helplessness. And the "symptoms" that a clinician might check off as clear criteria for depression—her depressive-seeming "ruminations" and her bleak view of the future? These were Mary's focus on counterfactuals, caused by her loss of faith and her limiting of possible positive events coming up as a means to avoid the crush of disappointment.

No, not mental illness. Mary's problem was the "don't-get-your-hopes-up wall," a difficult conundrum that would daunt even the sanest person. Mary was hopeful, but acting on this hope was precisely what scared her most. She had lost faith in herself and faith that the world around her would be generous enough to allow her to put her hopes into action. So she doubted that she could reach the goals that her hope would cajole her into pursuing. And what most scared Mary was what would happen to her if she failed to realize her hope—not just failing to obtain a desired goal, not just the loss of time and effort, not even the social embarrassment. Instead, it was the perception of herself as utterly helpless because she was defective in her ability to manage her life.

Once you see yourself as unable to captain your existence, despair wins its perpetual wrestling match with hope. Mary didn't want to lose that match, so she stayed the same.

And that means Mary wasn't just afraid of hope, she was protecting it—that evolutionary force in all our lives that always needs protection.

THE HOPEFUL ACTION OF SAMENESS

All of Mary's experiences in relationship to her fear of hope were both a guarding against hope and a means to protect it.

Yes, another paradox: Staying the same is the result of fearing the possible results of hoping, and it's also an act of preserving hope. When you petrify, you're playing dead in order to protect the very thing that makes your life *lively*. Mary, in this light, wasn't simply resisting hope; she was holding tightly to it. Like a parent holds a child, she wrapped herself around hope to shield it from unpredictable circumstances, and she also constrained hope from its own wild and unpredictable nature, it's tendency to move on faith and take risky leaps with potentially dangerous falls.

That's why Mary was anxious—she was hoping and protecting this hope from the destructive force of helplessness. That's why she limited her future—she was holding hope back from the dangerous light of a failed attempt at agency. That's why she engaged in counterfactuals—they kept her wandering in search of a faultlessly safe strategy out, while holding her back from action. And through all these processes and more, that's why she stayed the same.

Mary's sameness was the very thing she needed at that time.

It saved her.

A BATTERY DOCK WITH NO INDICATOR LIGHT

Mary continued in therapy with me. And while the months ahead were far from optimal, Mary's life did become more stable. She requested and was granted a job in the company that didn't require travel. The salary was worse than the low-paying sales position, and the actual work bored her no end, but it kept her safely at home, where she felt her mother needed her. The stability seemed to help a lot: she made no more attempts at suicide and she stopped drinking. She also got involved in some regular social activities, like going to church each Sunday, playing in a soccer league a couple of nights a week, and after some wheedling from her cousin and pressure from her mom, joining her cousin's book club. Mary didn't have any close friends, and she rarely engaged in any after-work social gatherings, but her life had a rhythm to it, its ups and downs neither precipitously high nor miserably low.

About a year into our therapy, Mary said to me:

"I feel like I'm one of those rechargeable batteries, recharging. If you take me out of the charger right now, I'll be, like, really low in energy. But if I stay docked for a while longer, I'll get fully charged. At least I think so: I don't know."

"That's a remarkable way to put it, Mary," I said to her.

"Well, yeah, but there's actually no indicator light."

"Indicator light?"

"Yeah, the little light on the side of the charger that tells you when the batteries are fully charged. I don't actually know if the power is low right now or high. I have no idea when it will be time to get undocked. That light was broken when I busted my spleen."

"I think I get that."

"And I'm afraid that if I get undocked now, I won't be strong enough to get over or through that wall, and I'll have lost a lot of energy doing so. But the other half of the problem is that maybe I *am* ready, full of as much energy as I'm going to get, and just wasting more really valuable time."

Lord, was Mary smart! *Man*, could she come up with the best, most eloquent analogies. Here's how I see it. The docking port is staying the same and supplies the stability of her life at this point. The battery is hope, safeguarded in that dock, and building energy. The indicator light is the unachievable wish for something or someone to tell her that all is safe, and she should move ahead (like Fleabag's cry for "someone to tell me how to live my life," and Harold's request for directions from the police officer, even though Harold knew exactly where he was going).

Mary was traumatized by disappointments and she was terrified of experiencing any further events that would leave her feeling helpless. These events would be most likely, and their disruptive power would be most potent, the more she hoped. She was able to hold on to a hoped-for someday, but she didn't feel she could trust herself to act on this hope. And that meant that her ambitious aspirations were deflated by her profound lack of faith in herself. She felt anxious, fearing hope would entice her into a risky situation that would inevitably end with her seeing herself as a poor steward of the life she was accountable for. It thus makes a lot of sense that she wanted some indisputable proof that she was fully charged before she tried again: a confirmation that it was safe to move ahead.

But for Mary, like all of us, there's no indicator light . . . ever. That's why we need faith—that gut response, coming from a self we trust—and faith is what Mary was lacking, not an external indicator blinking from orange to green.

I believe that's another reason why Mary engaged so ruminatively in counterfactuals: Her mind was trying to find a rational solution that would indisputably indicate that it was time; some hidden, logical strategy she missed last time she failed. If she could just dig into the past and unearth new data on what would work, she would have enough information to move forward. But, of course, this spinning for the right combination got Mary nowhere, because she was unable to rely on her emotions to formulate the next leap.

I didn't have all these ideas perfectly worked out in my head at that time (just the Ten Reasons Not to Change—and a vague understanding of fear of hope). But I did have a gut sense that waiting for the indicator light was a mistake. I pushed a little further:

"Mary, what if that light stays broken. What will you do?" I asked.

"I don't want to think about that. That's way too scary."

"Well, please, give it a second. What would you need to do?"

"I don't want to think about it. Can we talk about something else?"

I let it go.

Again, Mary deeply hoped for a better life, saw that she lacked the life she wanted, and felt she couldn't have it because she didn't trust herself to get it. So the only positive future she could imagine was one in which her safety was guaranteed by something more credible than her own self, something that operated independent of human error and provided that most reassuring of messages: *All's okay. You can come out now.*

I was right to point out that such infallible signals are rarely if ever available, but I was wrong to state this so blithely. As I sat there in my favorite well-worn chair, sipping my satisfying and steaming tea in my own professional office, the thermostat set to 72, doing the work I felt competent at, in a settled career, with a family I would return to that evening in the neighborhood we loved, sheltered within deeper experiences of continuity and security, I took for granted what the prospect of an endlessly broken indicator light would mean.

I was also following Mary's lead away from hope's vastness to a more constricted experience a little too much. Like Mary, my focus on the issue of that indicator light kept my gaze off of something very important. Mary wasn't sitting still; she wasn't really docked. She was moving slowly forward. No more suicidal behavior, no more drinking; church on Sunday, the book group and the soccer league. These were very big deals—they were a source of stability and safety and social engagement that Mary herself had created. Her life might have achieved some calmness, but that didn't make it static. In these different ways, Mary was testing her faith while rebuilding her own gut-level green light.

Mary was docked for good reason. And while she was uncertain if she would ever be able to leave this static-seeming state, her staying still for a while did end up working for her. Her steps were real during this docking period; they were gradual and small steps that allowed her wounds to heal, her strength to recover. And perhaps, though she and I did not pursue this any further, her internal docking light was beginning ever-so-faintly to flicker.

CHAPTER 5

THE INGENIOUS PRESERVATION OF THE POSSUM'S POSE

And the day came when the risk to remain tight in a bud was more
painful than the risk it took to blossom.

—Anaïs Nin

Recovery

A year or so after Mary described her experience of being in the
battery dock with no indicator light, she took a large step out
of her comfort zone. Things were going really well in her reading group. Even though Mary would decline the offers of other
members to go out for drinks or dinner after meetings, she sensed
a slight whiff of camaraderie, a scent of that experience of a team
she'd felt on the high school soccer team and in her college dorm.

She especially liked Holly, a convivial and energetic woman her
age. Holly worked at a local outdoor store, often leading group
outings for the customers. When it was Holly's turn to pick a book,

she chose Jon Krakauer's *Into Thin Air*, a harrowing tale of a climb up Mount Everest that went tragically wrong. Mary was enthralled with the book, finishing it in two nights. Something about the guts and, yes, boldness of the climbing party, and the interdependence of that team, reminded her of certain feelings she'd left behind: the exciting power of a clear goal, the pristine sense of unburdened action when reaching that goal with a group of skilled others, and the experience of freedom that comes from acting boldly.

When the book group met again, Mary was the first to talk, a change from her habit of waiting to hear what others said before she spoke.

"I loved it," Mary said. "First off, it was so exciting. More important, it made me amazed and sort of jazzed about that group and what they did."

Most of her fellow readers began to laugh affectionately, finding Mary's joy about the book ill-matched to the devastatingly sad story within its covers. Holly, however, nodded, replying, "I know exactly what she means."

Holly called Mary that week, inviting her to one of her excursions at work: rock climbing. Mary felt it: the point of decision— *go bold or go home*. She went bold.

As Mary expected, it felt awkward getting together with this group of strangers, and she felt a pang of envy mixed with shame, comparing herself to Holly, with her athletic confidence and clear sense of pride. But once she was climbing with a partner who was belaying her from below, she felt it: like a perfect pass from a midfielder hitting her cleat just where it should—the pure joy of teamwork, competence, and shared risk.

Mary soon joined a rock-climbing gym and took every class she could. She learned quickly as she developed new calluses on her hands. Her friendship with Holly blossomed, and the two headed for the mountains every chance they got.

She told me one session around that time, "It's like I've been recuperating from some really bad sprain. I've been through such hell in my life: I couldn't see that when I was in the middle of it, but now I do."

"Like you're rehabbing?"

"Yeah, that's it: Like I'm in rehab for some injury, and I'm not supposed to do too much or I'll reinjure myself. I was sidelined, but in a good way."

"That sounds so right, Mary."

"It's sort of like that mistake with the mono. I should have done what the doctor told me, but I didn't, and ended up ruining a lot of stuff. I mean, this time it's not physical, but I took my time and rehabbed it."

"I get that."

"And you're like my physical therapist. You're helping me heal, but it's totally up to me what I do when I leave the office. Am I going to take big or little moves forward? That's up to me. Too big a move, and I'm injured again; too small a one and nothing changes. But now I'm ready to get back out there fully, I think."

"I think so too."

"You do?"

"Yeah, I do."

"I'm recharged."

"You're recharged."

Mary continued in therapy with me for another year, then returned to college in another state, where she pursued a business degree and then an MBA. She entered therapy there, with a new therapist.

I lost track of Mary until just recently, when she emailed me to fill me in on her life.

After graduating with her master's degree, she continued to work in software development, now as a project manager. Teamwork is back in Mary's life. She loves her job, all the challenges, the fact that her brain is always "switched to on," as she puts it, creative, ready for the next puzzle to solve. She's married now. She and her husband spend a lot of their free time scaling the boulders and cliffs near their home. They save up every year for some sort of adventurous travel—white-water kayaking on the Kaituna River, paragliding in Torrey Pines. She coaches soccer on the weekends.

When I finished reading Mary's email, and I thought of that long trek to recovery, from a person bound by problems and failure, to someone reengaged with the daring, creative existence she was born to live, a movie played in my head. It's Mary, lying still and sideways on the dewy grass. She's been there for years, playing possum with hope, ever since that fall that burst her spleen. But now—like a light blinking to green—she opens her eyes a sliver. Mary then surveys the landscape for threat, and then tests for detection by cautiously wiggling her toes. She then slowly, stealthily gets up on one knee, then carefully stands on her own two feet, gently stretches her legs in a lunge, then lightly jogs in place, fills her lungs with air, hears a voice say "Go!" then boldly sprints through the wet, green turf toward that glorious netted goal across the field.

Her faith healed, her hope engaged, Mary's back.

The Preservation in Sameness

Like Mary, when you stay the same, you're not only stuck in place because you're pushing up against powerful restraining forces; *you are also trying to preserve your driving forces.* Staying the same, in other words, isn't just the negative result of your existential anxiety. It's also an act of hope and faith in that it protects the very thing that makes you anxious: your ability to purple-crayon your existence. That logic might sound a little pretzel-like, but bear with me. It's important to understand.

When you choose sameness, you're choosing to shelter your hope from disappointment. That's an *act*, not a state of passivity or inertness, as so often assumed. It is a strategic retreat, not a surrender. A big part of the motivation for choosing sameness is to preserve hope and protect the part of you that authors your life. Sameness, in this light, is an expression of self-care, perhaps as protest, and definitely an action—as it was for Mary—of rehabilitation: a way to restore the resources you need to return to the challenge.

The location between where you are now and where you want to be is dynamic, a site of behavior and experience right at the point where your restraining and driving forces meet. That means that even when you might seem as immobile as a rock in your resistance to change, you're actually in an active state. Something continues to push upward; that proverbial weed pointing toward the sun through a crack of restraining pavement.

In the force field of change, in other words, there is rarely a point when it's all restraint, no drive. As with all living things, it's our nature to grow, and it takes an atom bomb of despair to stop this tendency completely. In most situations—even in those situations when you might be acting as if you are hopeless, hope is still pushing upward, sometimes powerfully.

But let's not get too Hallmark-y about the idea that hope springs eternal. Just because hope is almost always present doesn't mean rainbows and unicorns are too. Sure, in some shape or form, hope is perennial. But the hope you feel at certain points may be enfeebled, pushing up against a powerful despair, or it may be very strong, but no match for your fear of it, and it may remain in these positions for long periods of time. It's important to find hope in the places where it's most concealed precisely *because* of the ever-present despair and fear of hope, not despite them.

LOCATING HOPE WHERE IT'S LEAST EXPECTED

Think about existential anxiety. You feel it when your hope is pushing upward against the restraining force of your awareness of your accountability. That means anxiety is the product of your attempt to move ahead, despite hope's tendency to expose your accountability and disappointment's threat of exposing you as not only accountable, but helpless. Anxiety, in other words, is a sign of your fortitude and effort. You don't feel it when you don't hope, just like you don't build muscle without feeling the ache of strain.

Don't get me wrong: your anxiety about your accountability, especially when compounded by helplessness, can flatten you. You feel your anxiety approach the red line when the restraining forces are winning, filling most of the force field of change. Still, anxiety is *not* the result of hopelessness. Instead, it's the effect of both your driving force of hope and restraining awareness of your accountability and aloneness, caused by hoping. This same kind of both-and relationship is true of your experience of helplessness.

If you feel helpless about getting what you need, part of you is still willing to reach out and try to meet those needs. True, you might feel stymied, but this is because you're still aspiring to change: you're not giving up. You feel helpless, in other words, not because you've completely given up on hope, but because you've lost faith in your ability to realize your hope. Helplessness enters your experience because you're still trying to move ahead despite the powerful force of disappointment. That's better than withdrawing into the total apathy of nothingness. The great Russian composer and dissident Dmitri Shostakovich captured this idea when he wrote, "When a man is in despair, it means that he still believes in something."[1]

This idea that sameness is an active state in which hope is being preserved brings us back to those nagging counterfactuals.

When you think about what-ifs, you're imagining alternative pathways to better futures, which sounds an awful lot like hope. In fact, you're generating a sort of contained, protected hope when you think in this way, holding yourself in one place because you're injured in the other half of hope—the agency-thinking half, the part that depends on faith.

Two types of counterfactuals are especially relevant. One type involves blaming yourself (*If I had just had the guts to talk to my boss, I would have that promotion by now*). The other kind occurs when you blame someone else or some circumstance outside your control (*If my boss wasn't such a jerk, that promotion would have been mine*).

When you focus on what you could have done differently, you're also not focusing as much or at all on the possibility that the world is capricious, malevolent, and depriving, unresponsive to your efforts to make meaningful, satisfying changes. Thus blaming yourself offers an alternative pathway to an intolerable and hopeless point of view. Thinking "what if" about your behaviors, searching for the thing you could have done "right," you preserve the hope that someday you'll be able to change *yourself*, which can be an easier thing to envision than changing the whole world outside you. This is a classic position for children: they tend to choose shame over the intolerable thought that their parents aren't protecting them or worse. But I believe we also turn to this same position when we are adults, after facing damaging disappointments, and I'm convinced this is one main reason Mary engaged in what-if thinking about herself: It would have caused her profound despair to manage the idea that all her disappointments came from sources outside her control, since clustered together they formed an inaccessibly dense and poisonous jungle out there.

On the other hand, engaging in counterfactuals that assign

cause to a dangerous and chaotic wilderness can also act as an alternative pathway. In doing so, you turn away from shamefully believing that the problem is all you, and thus reach the same hope-preserving benefit as turning inward. If the problem isn't you, you might be strong enough to endure, despite what little the world around you has to offer. I think this is likely the reason Mary also saw the world outside her as depriving. By offering an explanation for her helplessness, it counterbalanced her shame, lifting some of the existential burden off her shoulders.

Like most of us, Mary balanced one kind of counterfactual against the other, and I think that's one reason she became so ruminative: If she stayed in one mode, it would lead her slowly toward helplessness (*I totally ruined my life!*), so she would counterfactualize in the opposite direction when deep helplessness loomed in front of her (*The world is never going to change!*), then change direction again when that mode took her down that same road, then again change direction once *that* road became too painful, and on and on. Her counterfactual rumination, in other words, was also protective.

So was Mary's constricted time perspective and her nearsightedness about a positive future. When you move those time perspective brackets closer together, you're also protecting yourself from this threat. And when you limit your view of potential positive events in your future, you limit the chance of getting your hopes up only to be disappointed. So when you constrain time, you're holding hope, protecting yourself from feeling helpless about not getting your needs met.

It's time to recall that image I asked you to remember in the previous chapter: a person in a chair, painfully curled downward, unable to totally avoid the glare of the future in front of them, but doing everything possible to shield themselves from its rays. The pain they feel is excruciating, but they stay in that contorted position because looking forward is terrifying. Now picture one addition to this image, something you didn't notice before: The person is tightly holding something in their arms that glows with the same hue and brightness of the glare in front of them, wrapping their body around this thing, protecting it with all their might. Painfully bending from their rightful stature, they protect what they cherish most and need for their survival—hope—from the hope-destroying force of anaclitic helplessness.

The experiences you have when you bend downward from hope—ruminating questions that tempt with helplessness, a sense of deep shame, worry about an unforgiving universe, great anxiety about the project that is your life, pessimistic and limiting views of the future—can painfully bend the vertebrae of your soul. But part of the reason you suffer from these experiences is that you're assuming a hunched position to protect something very important. You're trying your best to care for yourself, even comfort yourself, *even love yourself,* in situations where there seem to be few other options for doing so.

That means that the greatest feelings of existential anxiety and helplessness only enter your existence when you are hoping for something of great personal value, and a lot of what you do or feel that you might interpret as signs of hopelessness are also attempts at preserving hope and autonomy.

That also means we've reached another paradox: The restraining forces keeping you the same aren't all bad, and they aren't always merely restraining you. In fact, they are signs that you're still caring for yourself in the worst of times.

These are both-and ideas, seeing causes as effects and effects as causes, and you and I live with brains that like nothing more than a good map between cause and effect, and in a culture of gadgets and sales pitches that feeds off our minds' preference for a single cause that leads in one direction only to a single effect (*Step right up! Easy change in five steps, a magic pill for what ails you, a proven technique that will scrub away any psychological blemish!*). So I have to admit, I'm feeling a little helpless myself right now about reaching you with my words, my own faith in my ability to do so a little weak. But this idea that hope exists—protected and preserved—within the restraining forces of change gets us to a completely different attitude about sameness than the one put forth by the purveyors of the easy fix, and by our judgmental culture at large based on supposed dichotomies of sick/well and failed/successful. And I believe this attitude makes change a whole lot easier (but please, only *easier*, not easy: there are no free rides to a more hopeful existence, and hope itself is a painful, turbulent experience).

The attitude I'm writing about is one in which you honor the forces of sameness.

The Preservation in Sameness

When you set out to make a change in your life, I bet you do an excellent job criticizing yourself for your failures, and I'm guessing even the most modest of you recognize your part in your successes. But do you also see staying the same as a choice—something you may want and even yearn for? I'm guessing you don't. I suspect you view sameness as the logical outcome of poor choices and failures; something thrust upon you—an unwanted coat you're forced to wear—rather than a destination you were plotting all along in the deepest core of your being.

That was Sartre's point about bad faith. Bad faith—the mode of experience in which you see yourself as choiceless—is a choice. (We don't see it as a choice because that would defeat the purpose of acting in bad faith: *to believe we don't have choice!*)

Sameness is a kind of bad faith, since by staying the same, we are typically trying to avoid feeling accountable. However, there are ways to contemplate sameness as an action, to see it within the force field of personal change, and to understand it as an act of preservation, even self-love.

Paradoxically, and luckily for all of us, when we're able to view sameness as a choice, and one based on self-protective reasons, it can lose some of its power to keep us the same.

To illustrate this point, let's go back to the example of you, your diet, and the big bowl of ice cream described in the previous chapter. Let's say you made it through the challenge of resisting the ice cream. It's a new day, and you feel really good about your success. You go to the office, and a new challenge comes with this new day: your boss's birthday celebration in the conference room, and that flourless chocolate cake—your favorite.

You go to the celebration, and they're passing around slices of cake. When a plate is passed to you, you demur. But despite your outer self-control, your mind is fighting with all its might to resist the impulse to have a piece (make that a *big* piece). Meanwhile, your mind is racing: *What's wrong with me? How could I even be thinking about this? I'm such a self-sabotager!* You make it through the celebration, but the cake sits in the conference room all day, tempting you every time you pass by. As you feel the inner struggle starting up, more negative thoughts enter your brain: *I'm a sugar addict! I've worked so hard on this diet, and here I am thinking about cake again!*

At the end of your day, you grab a giant wedge of the damn cake and eat it in your car on the way home.

Your mind stops while you enjoy the fudgelike, sugary delight; the tension regarding whether or not to eat the cake is gone. But your satisfaction is fleeting. As soon as you take your second bite, your mind shifts gears to counterfactual thinking: Chew. *I would have felt so much better about myself if I wasn't doing this.* Chew. *If I'd just eaten those almonds I brought along today I wouldn't be stuffing myself with cake right now.* Chew. *Why did Barb have to bring a flourless chocolate cake, of all choices?*

Here's the thing: You're smart. Your brain works. You likely have some familiarity with Pavlov. When you picked up that slice of cake you knew you would feel more punishingly lousy for a much longer period than you would feel the satisfying reward of eating cake. So why did you do it? Why did you choose the one-second pleasure of that first sweet mouthful, followed by hours of bitter remorse?

Here's why: Unbeknownst to you as you casually lifted the paper plate off the conference room table, you were seeking a different goal at that moment than dieting. While you might have appeared to the casual Lewinian observer to be a person *failing* in their pursuit of the goal to lose weight due to powerful restraining forces, you were actually someone *succeeding* in a completely different force field: one in which the goal was to put a lid on hope. Hope—not shame of eating the cake—was the "aversive stimuli," as behavioral psychologists would call it. And the reward you were looking for? No, not the pleasure of that first bite, but rather the turning away from hope—was what you truly wanted.

The cake story captures the twisting paradox Laing describes in regard to petrification: that you do the thing that keeps you where you are in order to safeguard some inner sense of your own autonomy. In other words, sameness, and even helplessness, are not always things we try to avoid. We sometimes head straight toward them when we are concerned about our accountability. And we do this in big ways, like complete lethargy; and in little ones, like eating cake in our car when we're dieting. No matter how painful and counterproductive this act of petrification is, its intention is benign: to safeguard your hope.

How perverse and abnormal is this choice? It's not. For Sartre, bad faith (hiding your accountability from yourself and others) is the norm, and good faith is the exception, and that's why sameness, too, is the direction we typically go, and why real personal change is hard to do.

When you approach sameness as a negative force, you are like Harold at his most anxious moments, forgetting that the monster he now confronts is the result of his own creative decision. But, like Harold, you do have some control over this predicament. If you can accept that sameness is drawn from the very same purple crayon you grip in your hand—a choice, a decision—there is always a means to draw your way out. The opposite is also true. If you remain in a state of forgetting, the monster takes on a life of its own.

I suggest that it's more empowering to acknowledge sameness as a choice rather than to deny even a nodding acquaintance with it, and to understand *why* you made that particular choice. It's even more empowering to see that sameness can result from understandable, even reasonable, choices. Now here's the paradox: *When you can contemplate sameness as a choice, and understand why you made it, the odds of your changing go up.* This is the turning point in understanding your resistance to change. When you embrace this choice, it puts you back in charge.

Let's perform our own counterfactual regarding you and that cake, the what-if being your willingness to accept sameness as a force with good intentions.

You attend the birthday party in the conference room. They pass around the cake, and you feel the urge to accept the piece handed to you. In this scenario, however, you identify the urge not as sugar addiction or lack of self-discipline; instead, you see it as a retreat from hope. With gentleness toward yourself, you think, *There I go again, scared of where this diet might take me.* You return to your office with a new appreciation of the diet's importance based on how it's raising your hope enough to frighten you. You feel proud that you stayed the course. Throughout the day, you pass the cake in the conference room and it beckons to you. Feeling the pull, you think to yourself: *If I eat that cake, I'll reach that safe place of feeling lousy. Do I really want to do that?*

It's the end of the day, no one is around, and the cake is still sitting there, a little stale, but promising a luscious chocolaty moment. Here are three reactions that could happen if you approach sameness with respect, each reaction more positively supporting your driving forces than approaching eating the cake as a bad and unreasonable act:

1. You walk right past the conference room and to the parking garage: *I can handle my authorship of my own life today*, you think. *I don't need to put a lid on hope.*

2. You pick up a piece of cake and head to the garage. When you take that second bite and counterfactuals begin to set in, you notice them and recognize their intent. *Wow, that was fast*, you think. *I'm protecting myself from hoping with these lousy feelings. It's not really the cake I want at all.* You pull up to the nearest trash container in the garage and throw the plate of cake away.

3. You eat the damn cake. And on the way home, you think, *I'm putting the brakes on hope for some reason; some part of me needed the safety of feeling lousy.* You're annoyed with yourself, but you don't experience yourself as broken or a failure, nor do you see your behavior as caused by outside forces, like the allure of chocolate or your addictions to sugar.

In all three scenarios, you see yourself as active, heading toward a choice, or making one, that is about your own wish to protect yourself. You see your agency, and you see it as coming from a good place, even though it might lead to some not-so-good results. *That stance helps feed your driving force of hope by strengthening your sense that you are in control, and thus buttressing your faith.* The other stance, that you're a pathetic failure in resisting cake, only strengthens your restraining force by mirroring to you that you are helpless at dieting.

When you understand that the reason you resist change has partly to do with something protective, you see your sameness (and even your sense of brokenness and your belief that the world won't meet your needs) as something you're doing to take care of yourself as best you can. Thus, you see your impulse to sameness as active rather than passive. Detecting the agency and hope in sameness, your shameful worries about your broken ability to attain goals will likely diminish (though anxiety about your own accountability and aloneness might also go up—sorry!).

You are now in a place to more dispassionately contemplate your next step.

You are also now in a place to bring about the change you want.

That's how I see things working for Mary. In Mary's prior treatments, her therapists and doctors saw the symptoms of her depression and anxiety as the sites for intervention. In a way, they were approaching her as if she were a surgery patient who required aggressive intervention. Mary was participating in this approach, experiencing herself as a person with major depression and an anxiety disorder who needed to be fixed through the interventions of an expert. Metaphorically, she was anesthetized, passive, lacking any agency in her recovery. As she said to me that first session, "My depression and anxiety get in the way of me getting to where I thought I would be." These diseases, in other words, gave her no choice. In this way, she lowered her expectations about self-efficacy, approaching herself as not accountable—a person with issues that took away her control, handing whatever faith she might have over to the experts. This was an understandable maneuver of bad faith, an intentional act of petrification designed to protect her hope.

However, when Mary was able to see her problem as one involving the "don't-get-your-hopes-up wall," that ushered in an important new perspective in our therapeutic work. Her fear of hope was the problem. No longer was her lack of motivation a static psychiatric *trait*, rather it was an existential and dynamic *state*: a site in her life where she confronted the dangers of hoping. It was *her* facing that wall, and *her* making decisions about what to do with this barrier in her life.[2] Maybe it was even *her*—far from listless, doing the best possible job of protecting her hope. Mary was, in other words, being successfully efficacious. And that small sense of success had the potential to raise her faith in herself.

As Mary increasingly built her faith, the idea about this barrier took on a whole new metaphor—the docked battery. This metaphor was about building energy and taking a more measured approach to her recovery, while also heading toward a greater acceptance of herself as a decision maker. She was beginning to see more clearly that her lack of motivation was itself a kind of action, something she was *doing*; not something thrust upon her by chemicals in her brain or a malign fate. And once she could see that staying still was an action, she could also discern how this action was actually protective, even caring—just about the opposite of being broken. She wasn't helpless, she was "rehabbing."

Of course, coming up with a good metaphor is hardly the only thing that helped Mary. The reasons she changed are "multidetermined": armies of positive arrows driving upward, likely against an opposing army of restraining arrows (including all the complex neurotic stuff of therapy), that became enfeebled. But what she achieved by engaging in these metaphors was to strengthen her hope, the one particularly important driving force that's always baked into personal change. She also weakened the baked-in restraining force of existential anxiety by increasing her faith in herself. So what she did was very important psychologically. But it was also countercultural. Mary was fighting against destructive ways of looking at change that are pervasive in our culture: big restraining arrows disguised as driving ones.

The Danger of a Magic Bullet

Turn on your TV and watch the commercials. From bumpy dry skin on the back of your arm and restless legs, to addictive habits and difficult experiences with mood, there's a cure for whatever ails you, each as simple as swallowing a pill or following instructions. We live in an age of what narrative therapists call "problem saturation,"[3] in which we buy into stories about ourselves that are about eradicating problems through the intervention of experts, instead of crafting stories about what drives us forward on the power of our own hope and courage. The problem-saturated stories always hold sameness as a problem, never as a rightful solution. They thus denigrate and disrespect sameness, and in doing so, ignore the places where we're strong in the face of significant challenges.

By painting an idealized portrait of what it looks like to be fixed, fix-it approaches simultaneously create a silent, ugly shadow portrait of sameness. Every instruction for fixing, every pill, every technique branded as the newest, shiniest "best practice" is a stroke added to a rendering of a failed person: fat, dumb, disorganized, addicted, unhealthy, a bad partner, a failing parent, a lazy, distracted soul who can't live in the "now." Fix-it approaches tell you that the path to an ideal is well marked and direct, and that only damaged people refuse to take it.

"Those who do not recover are people who cannot or will not completely give themselves to this simple program."[4] So it says in *The Big Book of Alcoholics Anonymous* (the AA bible). Those poor folks who can't follow the twelve steps? Well, they are "usually men and women who are constitutionally incapable of being honest with themselves." *Wow!* That's harsh. But that's the message in most approaches to change these days. They imply or say outright that by being unwilling to unwrap the gift of an easily reached potential, you're a failed person exhibiting behavior that borders on immoral.

Helplessness and anxiety: These experiences may hold some hope within them, but that doesn't mean we should be prescribing them as a means toward change. Yet that's exactly what magic bullets and miracle cures do, by making sameness a shameful mark of your brokenness. That scarlet mark then impedes the very process that leads toward change: contemplation.

Instructing you to relegate the part of you that doesn't want to change to the stinking box of ugly malfunction, these approaches tell you to avert your eyes from its presence, ignoring its worth and its eternal connection to your life. They thus hamper your ability to contemplate the role of remaining the same in making the change you want to make, since the message is that there is nothing to contemplate.

The more you mistake sameness for something so repugnant that you can't look at it, the more you are likely to resist change. Averting your eyes, you don't see the logic of sameness, think about its place in your life, find where it's preserving hope, and perhaps even appreciate it.

In this light, I believe that when Mary first came to me, she wasn't only suffering from all the disappointments in her life: she was iatrogenically injured—that is, hurt by her cures. Mary started treatment because she felt helplessly broken as a person. In our age, when you feel broken, you seek out the mechanics for personal issues: therapists and psychiatrists. The experts she turned to, however, only confirmed that her view of herself was accurate. By focusing only on the virtues of change, and ignoring the saving grace of sameness, they made her feel saturated with problems. For them, there was only the arrow of restraint in her life—no hopeful Mary pushing upward.

Were these therapists and psychiatrists bad? No. Were they awful people, set to destroy Mary? Absolutely not. In fact, they were likely doing their best, most compassionate job within a framework that allows little room for sameness as an acceptable choice. Their intentions were good. Yet we know which road is often paved with such intentions.

When Mary took the opposite route, veering off the superhighway of easy fixes to the potholed lanes of hope and fear of hope, and thus came to see her sameness as rooted in self-protective motives, she broke from our current culture's pervasive approach to change. And good for her, since this approach to change— perhaps inadvertently, perhaps not—*keeps us the same* by viewing change as the only logical solution when it is not.

Honoring Sameness

The Hindu religion assigns a god to protection: Vishnu, god of maintenance and preservation. He sits alongside Shiva, the god of destruction and change, and Brahman, the originator of the world. Vishnu is equal to the other two, and painted blue as the vast and reliable sky. His actions are always balanced by the actions of the others, just as his own always balance their actions.

The force that propels you toward sameness is the Vishnu in all of us. It is your self-protective mechanism, the force that ensures your security and safety, and it can save your very life, whether physical or psychological. While this force may lead you to less-exciting endeavors than the energy that inspires you toward originality and creativity, and while it can often stop you from the growth you are entitled to, it's a part of you that deserves to be honored.

This perspective on sameness is hard to hold. Based on faith, it can feel like a weak argument in the face of the certainty of simple solutions and easy fixes. What's more, when you take a stand for sameness, you're honoring something that can lead you down the wrong path. In other words, just because sameness is protective doesn't mean staying the same is a good thing.

The impulse toward sameness comes from the most well-meaning part of you: your self-love. And like all love, it's quite fallible.

THE BUMBLING NATURE OF RESTRAINT

Imagine you're on the curb at a busy intersection. You're in a rush and distracted. You step off the curb, unaware of oncoming traffic. A hand comes from behind, landing on your shoulder, holding you back. The forces for staying the same are a lot like that hand keeping you safe, protecting you from the oncoming traffic of frightening helplessness. They come from the same part of you that wants you to be secure in other areas of your life. It's the part tasked with the thankless jobs of keeping you clothed, fed, and sheltered. It cleans your room, keeps your office organized, maintains your budget, and hits the turn signal every time you change lanes. It doesn't like to see you hurt, and so it steps in.

This force behind sameness makes a lot of mistakes, tending to clamp down on your shoulder too soon, or responding disproportionately to risk. It tends to be cautious when it doesn't need to be, often telling you to run when it sees a hint of disappointment or anxiety on the horizon.

For me, this excessive caution, this wish to paralyze action out of an exaggerated fear for safety, is easier to understand if I see it as similar to the way I try to protect the people I love. When I observe the mistakes I make with them, anxiously intervening to secure their safety, I see a mirror image of the mistakes I make when I resist changing. Love is love, I guess. It bumbles in the same way, whether it's directed at the people I cherish or at myself.

My son, Max, now nineteen and the draftsman of his own expanding Crayola story, sent me a cell phone photo of him, his girlfriend, and their dog driving in his truck across the California desert. His girlfriend is holding the phone outside the passenger window and all three of them are looking up into the camera and grinning. It's a portrait of freedom and bountiful happiness. I texted back: "Her seat belt isn't on, and your eyes aren't on the road." I'm sure my son took this text as a bit of a blow, a tone-deaf response to what he wanted. But all I saw in the photo was danger.

Like most parents, I'm built to protect my child. This also means that my protectiveness often goes too far, and it's not calibrated to his level of independence. All these mistakes I make, these little disappointments that can end up hurting his pride, come from love. The restraining forces against change are like the parents in us. They are protective and don't want us to feel any agony. Sometimes we're hurt by this protection. Other times, we're saved by it.

As in kintsugi, the Japanese art form in which ceramics are repaired but the cracks are left to be clearly seen, held together with gold and silver, the residue of love is found at the site of our preservation, even if it's also the site of brokenness. Or, better yet, *because* it is the site of our brokenness.

Here's another reason texting Max might have been a mistake: He probably read it while driving in the car with his two grinning companions, his eyes diverted by my text from the very place I wanted them to be. Helping your child is never perfect. Neither is helping yourself. Things can look more dangerous than they are; sometimes they're more dangerous than you think; many times you see achievable challenges as unachievable; and sometimes things are just too challenging. Keeping yourself secure in the face of uncertainty is a practice of "good enough." In no way does this practice ever reach perfection. But that's okay. Love isn't perfect. It often comes in forms that are jagged and cracked.

For all of us there are two columns: one for our self-dislike, the other for our self-love. It's very hard, if not impossible, to rid ourselves of all the criticism—that unbending experience of shame in your consciousness no matter how small or large. But if you can recognize that some of the things that you dislike about yourself actually come from the often-blundering anxiety of your self-love, you have the chance to move these behaviors from the former column to the latter. The more you can do that, the more you add to the driving forces of hope and faith in yourself, and the more you decrease the power of the restraining force that comes with a message that you are too broken to be left accountable to make your life work.

Imagine again that you're on that curb. This time, you're looking up at the traffic light. It's about to turn green. Watching it, you are fully synchronized with the traffic, knowing it's coming to a stop. You take a step into the street. But a hand on your shoulder yanks you back. "Why'd you do that?!" you yell. "I knew what I was doing!" At that moment, you resent the force that restrains you. Its intrusions seem to deny how competent you are, obstructing your desire to journey forth. You had everything in control, and its pull only slowed you down. You shrug off the hand and quickly walk ahead, fuming at the restraining force and leaving it well behind. A few blocks later, you calm down and start to think about the intent behind that yank, rather than its result. "Did it really want to quash my independence?" you ponder. "Wasn't it just afraid, concerned for my safety? In another situation it might well have saved my life!" You slow down, hoping it will catch up. You have no illusions. You know it's going to do something that irritates you again. But what are you going to do? You need it.

When you decide to make a change, to make the jump from where you are to where you want to be, you step closer to an abyss of uncertainty, looking down into the real risk of disappointment and debilitating experiences of helplessness. The protective parent in you doesn't want you too close to the edge of that abyss. It's afraid for you, doesn't want you to get hurt. Worry causes it to make mistakes: It slows you down, stifles your movement toward change. But, again, you need it.

You can't surgically remove just the blunders restraint makes without banishing all the ways a restraining force keeps you safe. Without this force, you would live with no warnings of danger and would move through your existence incurring injury after injury. Your Vishnu makes mistakes, for sure. But these blunders are dwarfed by the catastrophes of a life with no restraint.

When the restraining force of sameness overwhelms the driving force of change—causing you to stop dieting, cancel your gym membership, put off that course in Italian, or give yourself a pass on smoking—you're often in danger of losing mastery over your life. But there are also beautiful, self-loving reasons why you protect yourself by not changing, and these are very much worth your contemplation.

I would now like to help you contemplate ten of them.

As you read the chapters in the next section, I ask that you go gently, viewing the part of you that wants to snuggle into the high-thread-count security of sameness without too much negative judgment, maybe with some humor, and perhaps even a bit of forgiveness. Remember to listen for the *intent* of the restraining force rather than focusing only on its often-destructive effects. See a bit of gold in the scar it leaves behind, or marvel at its sky-blue hue. Taking this approach might cause you to consider changing, or it might lead to more sameness for now. Whether you change or not this time around, I promise you that understanding, and maybe even appreciating, the hand pulling you back puts you in the best place to take a risk and step forward.

THE TEN REASONS NOT TO CHANGE

CHAPTER 6

NO CHANGE, NO PAIN

The frightened individual . . . cannot bear to be his own individual self
any longer, and he tries frantically to get rid of it and to feel security
again by the elimination of this burden: the self.

—Erich Fromm

- #1: Staying the same protects you from your aloneness
  and accountability.
- #2: Staying the same protects you from the
  accountability of "what's next."
- #3: Staying the same protects you from the unknown.

I woke up in the dark this morning, around 5:00 a.m., with the
intention of writing what you're now reading. The chimes, preset
on my cell phone, woke me. But then I had to actually get myself out of bed. I knew I wasn't going back to sleep, but I stayed
there. I checked the news on my phone, scrolled through emails,
and then told myself to get up. I didn't. I went back to the phone,
checking my bank account, rechecking a hotel reservation for
an upcoming vacation, reading a bit from Politico, reviewing an

email I'd sent the day before. Now I was truly ready. But I still didn't get up. Something caught my eye: a story on *BuzzFeed* about Bill O'Reilly. After reading it, I noticed a recipe for a fondue bread boat. How could I pass *that* up? Perusing the article, I felt a growing pang of shame, telling myself I'd hit the rock bottom of distractions. I was no longer comfortable lying in bed. I felt agitated and bored. I *had* to get up. But I didn't. It was now 5:45.

Finally, my wife, irritated by the glare of the phone, mumbled, "Please do that somewhere else." I got up, went into the kitchen and made myself a cup of coffee, turned on the computer, started searching for a pet sitter for our dog, downloaded some music that I thought would help with my writing, checked the news again, again reviewed my emails, then wrote a few more. I left the computer to make myself breakfast. At 6:45, I sat down to eat breakfast and watch the news on TV. Breakfast completed, I looked behind me to the kitchen clock. It was now 7:30. I had until 8:15 to write before I needed to get ready for my day. I finally started, over two hours after I awoke, and with only forty-five minutes left for my writing. I was able to finish this paragraph and just a little more.

Writing, like all expressive forms, is a highly existential act, since when we write we are literally giving voice to our unique inner life, "putting it out there," as they say. To write requires a lot of grit in the face of aloneness and accountability, of which I had little this morning. Personal change requires this same kind of grit. As I noted in the previous chapter, it's an important existential moment when you head toward change, and your ability to actually make the change happen depends on your capacity to see yourself as the master of your fate.

Change, in other words, forces you to confront the discomfort and even terror of your freedom. If you had no other choice than to look your aloneness and accountability right in the eye, you might muster everything you've got to do so. What other choice would you have? But an exit door with easy access is almost always available to escape your freedom.

Escape from Freedom

You've likely experienced or witnessed in others my process this morning of procrastination in regard to writing. The "avoidant writer" is a bit clichéd. But it's actually not only a story about procrastination, since I *did* end up writing and getting something done. On a deeper level, it's a story about the dance between the pain of recognizing my accountability and thus aloneness, and my attempts at a psychological cover-up regarding this accountability.

What kept me in bed, other than the comfort of a cotton duvet and the wish for more sleep? It was my reluctance to witness myself as accountable for creating something on paper. I struggled to hold at arm's length the feelings that accountability stirred up: that blank white page, or actually that blank gray screen, reflecting back to me the aloneness, loneliness, and always-present possibility of failing in the goal I'd assigned myself. What finally forced me out of bed? My wife. My resistance to start writing, however, remained, once I was in the cold of our living room and kitchen. So what propelled me to finally write? The clock. In other words, the two points when I moved toward my goal were external: parental nags rather than adult choices. Getting out of bed wasn't my choice; then I was forced to start writing, since time was running out. I was concealing my own agency during a task highly charged with signals about the fact that I was accountable: my chosen aim to express my own unique views in writing with no boss threatening me with external consequences.

These often subtle deceptions, these quiet little fantasies, in which I'm propelled and compelled into action—a top spun by some outside force—are a part of a play I'm always performing for myself.

That's how life works for most of us most of the time: we authentically take control of our existence only sparingly, and mainly pretend we're not in control when we actually are. All the theatrics stop, however, when we head toward personal change.

You really can't achieve the change you want without also looking—sometimes only partially, often with blinders on to larger issues in your periphery—at your accountability and aloneness. Thus, personal change always requires the courage to act with more good faith than bad, and to do so even though bad faith always seductively offers you an easy way out.

Take a step toward change, and bad faith is always right at your side, tempting you, whispering things like *You're just too tired to go to the gym*, *You can't possibly practice guitar until you've cleaned the kitchen*, *Everyone else is having a cookie*—all positions that deceptively portray you as compelled to act, all aimed at keeping you from seeing that you are in charge, and thus all stopping you, or slowing you down, from reaching the change you want.

Sartre came up with a really evocative term for the attitude you take when you assume these positions of bad faith: a "spirit of seriousness."[1] Assuming the spirit of seriousness, you invest the world *outside* you with powers that actually belong *in you*. Biblically, it's a golden-calf approach to life, diverting one's own agency to the mysterious whims of another being. In Walt Disney's world, it's the Sorcerer's Apprentice; the brooms and candlesticks take a life of their own. I think of the spirit of seriousness as the attitude of waiting in line . . . and waiting . . . and waiting . . . for something to happen *to* you. When you tell yourself "I'll wait until tomorrow," your spirit is serious ("All good things come to those who wait," is its motto). And the job of this spirit of seriousness is to keep you in bad faith, and thus keep you the same—one person in an infinite line of other people—all for the cause of concealing your agency.

The difficult fork between the straight and well-paved boulevard of bad faith on which you travel in a seriously spirited self-driving car; and the Baja 1000 of authenticity, where you off-road it, gripping the wheel, shifting the gears, and hitting the gas in good faith, influences all Ten Reasons Not to Change. But concerns about your existential freedom are especially prevalent in the first three of these reasons.

Reason Not to Change #1:
Staying the same protects you from your aloneness and accountability.

Change always makes you face your aloneness and accountability. That's an unavoidable fact about change: on the road from where you are to where you want to be, it's you—no one else—putting one foot in front of the other.

That fact, in itself, is a damn good reason not to change.

Think of a time in your own life when you wanted to complete something, and you were certain that completing it would make things better for you. Did you sense that you were pushing up against an opposing energy that felt almost physical, like one of those half-dome, transparent, and bubblelike force fields in science fiction, where Kurt Lewin meets Captain Kirk? That's how I feel when I push myself to write. On the inside of this bubble (scrolling the Web, rechecking my email), I'm safe from the dangers of accountability and aloneness. But to get to my writing, I have to exit the bubble's safe barrier of sameness and enter the raw alien atmosphere where things are less safe, venturing toward a new frontier in which I'm accountable.

Inside the bubble of sameness life is scripted, predictable, and compulsory. Dull; stifling maybe. But safe from the risks of accountability. Outside this bubble is freedom, and the demand for good faith acceptance that I'm in charge. The bubble has its seductive comforts. It's *serious*, regimented, and knowable. The only problem is that change never happens inside it. Neither does creative action, invention, play, fun, love, passion, connection. You can dream about these things on the inside—lullabies of maybes and somedays inside the no-risk bubble—but you can't act on them.

How do we get in those bubbles, and what keeps us there? To some degree, it's learned from experience. That restraining force around us is like those invisible electric fences for dogs, who get small but painful shocks when they cross the front yard boundary. You, too, can be trained (and restrained) by the repeated shocks of anxious helplessness caused by disappointments. You are less likely to leave the safe parameter of bad faith if you've been shocked in this way when you've tried to go outside.

As we learned in the first part of the book, too much disappointment can lead you to lose faith in your own abilities to handle challenges. Lacking a sense of self-efficacy, you find confronting your own authorship singularly unbearable. You thus see making efforts toward the change you desire as a frightening prospect, the chance for another jolt of shame signifying that you are broken; another attack on your security; another experience of helplessness. And in this state, there is one emotion that lures you toward the risk of another disappointment: hope. Yet you need hope—that energy that keeps you going despite hardship and uncertainty—to force yourself outside the parameters of safety, to face the anxiety of your accountability.

Here is an extreme example of how existential anxiety can be the main motivator for staying the same when disappointment has dramatically entered the scene.

CHECKING IN WITH JIM

We had a client in my program who suffered from severe anxiety and panic. I'll call him Jim. Jim was once quite successful and, despite some general anxiety in his life, attained a good amount of contentment, in part due to a great marriage with a loving wife. But Jim later suffered a series of serious losses that sent him into a tailspin. They started when Jim was driving his son to soccer practice and got in a car accident that permanently injured his child. As his son recovered in the hospital, Jim spent most of his time, along with his wife, at the child's bedside. Jim worked as a computer programmer on a contract basis with a large software company. All that time he was visiting his son, he was not getting paid. And when Jim did go to the office, he was useless, his guilt and worry so great that he couldn't concentrate. The company finally ended his contract. Once his son came home and things settled into a routine, Jim found it difficult to take the steps to find work. He became obsessed with his son's safety and the safety of his entire family. Jim felt that if he left the house, he was putting his family at risk. So he rarely left. Six months of mortgage payments behind, the house was finally foreclosed on and put up for auction.

Jim was missing on the day of the family's move to a small apartment in town. The police had caught him trying to kill himself, and he was locked in a psychiatric facility. His wife, who had tried to hide her fury regarding the accident, now couldn't see past it, nor could she see past the fact that Jim was not behaving like a responsible partner in their marriage. She met Jim on the unit and asked for a separation. When Jim left the hospital, a referral to my program in hand, he moved into his parents' house.

We provided many treatments for Jim's excessive anxiety. Aside from his pharmacological care, we offered cognitive behavioral treatment, psychotherapy, art therapy, meditation, and vocational help. Jim would listen to our suggestions during his treatment hours, but during the day, when he felt most anxious, he would rarely apply the skills he learned. He proposed a different technique to alleviate his symptoms: that we call him at scheduled times to provide him support. Our program offers twenty-four-hour phone access. Therefore, we explained to Jim, he did not need to reserve his calls for crises; he could just call anytime if he needed to talk to someone. But this provision of impromptu support didn't satisfy Jim. He argued that *scheduled* calls during the day—at times when he was most likely to panic—would be more helpful.

Jim claimed that his worst times of anxiety were in the evening, and he especially wanted us to call then. When Jim suggested this plan, we recommended that we help him apply the skills he was learning in his treatments when we called. But Jim declined this offer. "All I need is just a little reminder that I'm okay at the end of the day," he told us.

Here's what I think was happening for Jim: To use his learned psychological skills on his own and ask for help when he needed it (rather than setting up scheduled calls) would feel as if he were exposing himself as an accountable individual. If he used the skills, he would see himself doing something on his own. And Jim had no faith in himself as a good steward of his actions. Following the accident and the subsequent decline in his functioning, he felt an intense helplessness. If Jim asked for help, he would witness himself requesting it as an independent and accountable person. This would also be an intolerable reminder that he was accountable for having devastatingly injured his child. Jim couldn't bear the experience of accountability that came with these gestures. The scheduled calls were his way of having contact with us without experiencing his existential aloneness, his need and ability to author his life. As long as we called him at particular times, he could feel *acted upon*, rather than a person *taking action*. He was soothed, in other words, by a play he secretly directed, in which his character was the passive recipient of others' decisions.

I call this kind of behavior effective ineffectualness.[2] While Jim set up a scenario in which he appeared passive, he was actually quite an effective advocate for himself. However, what he advocated for was rather perverse: an interaction that treated him as if he were ineffective, lacking any agency. In addition, Jim was so scared about accountability that he couldn't process his treatment. He would go to sessions, but he wouldn't use what he learned, since his ability to use new skills and insights meant recognizing that he was in charge of his change, inevitably alone and accountable. Jim, in other words, wanted to be fed, but he didn't want to eat. While his plan offered safety, it also led to an empty existence.

Jim's predicament—and his seriously spirited solution—is an extreme illustration of the Reason Not to Change #1. But Jim's attempts to deny his accountability are hardly unique. When faced with the prospect of change, we all struggle in the tug-of-war between the allure of bad faith and the dangers of authenticity.

I have a messy office that always causes me some shame. I perpetually plan to clean it up. But I rarely do. Cleaning the office would make me feel so much better about myself, lifting my shame at being disorganized. And, surely, knowing where to find the phone charger, the ink cartridge, my favorite pen would make my life a whole lot easier. One reason I don't tidy it up makes me similar to Jim: If it's messy, I'm passive. Like Jim, if I stay passive, I can wait for someone to intervene. Somehow—and I know this must sound strange—I find a perverse comfort in hoping someone will help me with the mess. It's an act of what psychologists might call wish fulfillment—a moment in which I feel some level of satisfaction that a wish is coming true, and the wish is of someone serving me, caring for me, while I sit passively. Aside from divine intervention, this will never happen. But the waiting is nice. If, on the other hand, I clean my office, I break the spell of waiting and recognize my accountability and aloneness.

It's just a messy office. What's with all the existential angst? you might be thinking. And if you are thinking this, I have to admit that telling you this scenario does feel a little embarrassing, in a mountain/molehill kind of way. But the fact is, I really want a neat and clean office and something's getting in the way of that. And if I stop and just let my curiosity run regarding what it is, my mind settles on that invisible but very real barrier, wrapped up in issues of aloneness. Besides, you don't know enough about me (yet) to understand how my own experiences of disappointment are entwined with issues of disorganization and order. In fact, there is even more to be garnered from the office scenario in the pages to come.

A messy office doesn't only make me feel less alone, it anchors me in bad faith, keeping me steady in the face of the dizziness of freedom in other areas of my life. Even when I'm successful in other tasks, the cluttered office remains one of a host of unfinished things in my life, a burden of my own making that keeps me from feeling too free and unencumbered. Offering a self-manufactured sense that I am constrained, it provides me a kind of ballast to the weighty awareness that I'm in charge of my own life and accountable to make it work.

In the larger scheme of things, is this all bad? It depends.

Sometimes the mess is a perfect foil. I enter my office to write, but see the mess as an obligation I must meet before I can do that. I then set out to clean it, but get distracted by the discovery of a book I thought was long gone, or a folder with my son's art projects from grade school. Time flies by, little is finished in my task, and—*quelle surprise!*—I have no time left for writing! I've also neglected to clean the office. Distracted by all the shiny objects around me, and never actually getting to the mess, I set up a sort of *Groundhog Day* scenario, in which I return, in perpetuity, to the same messy office. It's as if the bad faith part of me has created an elaborate maze, keeping me from venturing along paths of my own choosing.

Sometimes, however, the messy office, along with all my other unfinished tasks, holds my feet firmly on the ground as I take on riskier tasks. I have a book to write, a talk to give, a wife to enjoy time with. If my cluttered office provides a smidgen of burden—because, let's face it, a messy office isn't exactly a catastrophe—I can experience my freedom in these other situations without feeling the anxiety of being *too free*. I can get excited and engaged, while knowing there is always that weight on my back of a messy office slowing me down from the prospect of too much anxiety.

Persian rug makers always intentionally weave an imperfection into their creations. This tradition of "perfectly imperfect, precisely imprecise" is rooted in the belief that only God is perfect. Sometimes my office keeps me off track, an imperfection that draws my attention away from creating more meaningful patterns in my life. But other times it keeps me humble, grounded, a reminder that even though I'm capable and have met some important goals, I can also be that schlub with the messy office.

It's a good thing to recognize that sameness in one task might offer you the safety to take a risk in others. You're imperfect, and—

it's okay, I promise you—you can't completely master a good faith existence. A smidgen of bad faith isn't going to destroy you. It might even be there for a good reason—perhaps an anchor that steadies you enough to risk a move forward.

That's how it seems to work in my life at least.

I believe you're going to need that anchor of bad faith handy if you really want to change. Heading toward change, you'll think there will be some final port of arrival, a moment when you break that habit, lose that weight, reach that new point in your career, and rock softly there in calm, shallow waters, docked in achievement, satisfied and safe, no other challenges to confront. But that's not how it works. I hate to drill some very big holes in the boat you float, but every time you change, you actually raise the prospect of new, more challenging voyages. It's inevitable that change now creates greater accountability later.

This fact leads to Reason Not to Change #2.

Reason Not to Change #2:
Staying the same protects you from the accountability of "what's next."

Each change you make testifies that you are accountable for the life that lies ahead. The more you change, in other words, the more you see that future change is within your power.

Change is rabbitlike—exponentially reproductive. Never stopping at one achievement, change will always inspire you to deliver a litter of other proposed changes, and it will always increase your expectations about what you can do next. Every time you change, the cautious, sameness-oriented part of you sees this coming: *If I lose a couple of pounds, I know I'm going to want to lose more. If I finally get to my ideal weight, I'll be energized to pursue other goals. If I achieve these goals, my confidence will grow, and I'll want to take greater risks. At some point, I'm going to end up disappointing myself. And everything will come crashing down.* The fear that one change will beget others of increasing risk is not irrational. The odds are that as you attempt more changes you will be at greater risk of hitting an iceberg of disappointment than if you stayed moored to the pier of sameness.

You begin a new job in the career of your dreams. You do well in this job. You're competent and responsible. Your confidence grows with every excellent performance review. That confidence opens you up to the possibility that you might want to move up the ladder from your current position. It also opens your eyes to other risks you might want to take in your life. You've now multiplied the possibilities of failure and of being held accountable for these failures.

When you started out getting that first position in your chosen career, you saw this all coming. You knew the question would always be "what's next?" repeated again and again. From the vantage of that entry-level job, you had no evidence that you could meet all the future challenges in the career, and you felt scared of the possibility of an expanded sense of freedom. So that first day when you embarked on your career took a lot of chutzpah. You knew you would be headed toward a lot of questions about what's next.

Your concern about the question of what's next doesn't only affect you when you're looking at something as arduous as plotting out a career. It's often there in even the smallest of changes. My friend Ann is a case in point.

ONE THING, AND THAT'S IT

Over coffee the other day, Ann mentioned that she wanted to learn Spanish for a trip she was planning to Mexico.

"But I can't get myself to take a step in that direction," she tells me.

"Why do you think?"

"I don't know. I really want to be able to do it, and then I just stop myself."

"I know that feeling. What's stopping you?

"If I knew, I'd be speaking Spanish by now! But it's something about actually doing it. I mean, I don't mind learning it, but if I do get good at it, I'll be actually using it on my trip and that somehow feels scary."

"Right."

"I wish I were in college and it was a prerequisite," she said. "Then I would just have to do it, and it wouldn't be about actually using what I learned. I know that sounds weird, but that's how it feels: I don't want the pressure to try to use it when I'm on my trip. Why can't learning Spanish be just one thing and that's it."

Ann has two things going on that are stopping her from learning Spanish. The first, obviously, is her struggle over freedom. She wants someone to demand that she learn Spanish (that wish for a college prerequisite), because she can't stand the idea that she's *choosing* to learn it. But something else is going on here: Ann doesn't want to learn Spanish because she fears that learning it raises the possibility of another goal, with other possibilities of failure: actually speaking Spanish to someone in a country where this language is the native tongue.

Stepping on a path toward change always means a process of future challenges in front of you, ones that increasingly test your abilities. That path is not only riddled with the likelihood that you'll continue to be accountable for reaching a warren of other goals, it also threatens you with uncertainty. Step on it, and you don't know where you'll end up. This idea that change always delivers you to more unknown experiences leads to Reason Not to Change #3.

Reason Not to Change #3:
Staying the same protects you from the unknown.

By enacting change in your life, you face the unknown possibilities of a life that is in your hands. You thus must contend not only with exponential challenges, but also with an unpredictable world with a multitude of unpredictable potential experiences of disappointment.

There are two fundamental and related risks regarding change in the face of uncertainty. The first has to do with the challenge of simply leaving the safety of predictability and entering a world of the unknown. The second has to do with larger existential issues related to our purpose and meaning in life.

THE INEVITABLE ILL-PREPAREDNESS OF FACING THE UNKNOWN

Adventure and venture are two words that sound like they mean the same thing. But they are actually slightly opposed to each other, forming a yin-yang regarding change. Adventure is about an "advent": something added to your world when you step into the unknown. Venture is about the possibility of losing something when you take the same step. When you head toward change you are on an adventure toward a novel, not fully predictable, change in your life, and you are also venturing, risking the unknown and the real possibility that you will end your adventure with more loss than gain. The problem is that you can't know if you will get what you want until you either get it or don't. That's just a fact: You will not know the result of any adventure into change, until you've ventured through on the plan.

I was reminded of this fact the other day, helping my son, Max, prepare for his college semester abroad.

NOT READY

"I'm not ready for this, Dad," Max tells me, just two days before he heads off to Europe.

"Sure you are," I tell him. "You're totally ready for this."

"No, really, I'm not. I'm telling you, I'm not ready to do this."

"You're gonna love it. You'll be fine."

"Dad, you're not getting it: I'm not ready."

We return to this conversation intermittently during the two days of waiting and getting organized for his trip, Max telling me he isn't ready for this next challenge and me assuring him that he is well prepared and perfectly equipped to handle it. I want badly for him to feel that I have confidence in him, and to see that the people who love him believe in him, have faith in him. But the unsaid, elephant-size fact in the room is that I don't know if he *is* ready. How can I be sure he can handle this next step? Most of the evidence I've gathered the last few years gives me confidence that he does have the capacities to leave his girlfriend, his parents, his dog, and his country for a new challenge. But the only way I will actually know if he is prepared enough for this *adventure* will come after he returns from *venturing* forth.

"I'm really not ready, Dad," he says to me as we sit on a bench near ticketing at the airport, backpack and suitcase at our feet, his mom and his girlfriend off getting him a coffee. I don't know what else to tell him, so I tell him the truth:

"You aren't."

"What?!"

"No one is."

"You're telling me this now!"

"No one is, Max. Not a single kid heading out today is ready."

"You're scaring me. What are you trying to tell me?"

"I guess that the feeling of being 'not ready' is exactly what you should be feeling right now."

"Great! You're really not helping, Dad."

"Look, all I'm trying to say is that 'not ready' is what it feels like whenever you do something new and challenging. No one ever feels not-not ready when they take a risk."

Max calms down somewhat, looking a little less irritated with me. But that's as far as we get. As his girlfriend hands him a coffee, and she and my wife sit on either side of him, jostling me to the outskirts of our little clan and comforting him in ways I never can, my comment—in my mind, a gold star on my parent chart—floats off into the conditioned air of the departure floor. As we wait silently to say good-bye, I feel a pang of regret that I hadn't been more honest with my son from the start. All that assurance was really useless. Again, Max has all the right in the world to feel not ready.

His complaints about not being ready expressed his lack of faith that he could risk venturing, and his preoccupation with this complaint meant he was losing sight of the adventure he was about to take. By telling Max, somewhat disingenuously, that he was ready, I thought I was being encouraging, as though my stated faith in him was fuel that could take his tank of confidence from empty to full. But my protests meant little to him, since he had every right to his feeling. In fact, they only added to his anxieties: one of his two main caretakers acting cavalierly about a real dilemma. Max didn't need encouraging words from me. He needed words in action. If I had told him from the start that *feeling "not ready" is exactly the feeling you should have right now*, I would have been sending the authentic message that I believed he could handle such news, and deal with the fact that feeling *not ready* was inescapable. Instead, I wanted to tightly—even painfully—grab his arm and run to the closest exit, fleeing from the frightening sense of uncertainty we both faced, my reassurances as much for me as they were for him.

My love, in other words, was bumbling and insecure: Frantic in my wish to protect him, I wanted to magically remove Max's anxiety with the abracadabra of *You're totally ready for this*. Like all magic, my attempts to make Max feel safe were fake. Worse, they were an expression of my momentary crisis of faith about both of us, as we both faced the unknown.

The unknown can't be known. That's what makes it unknown! Everything that has to do with your freedom is unknown. If you assume a spirit of seriousness, your future will look as systematic as that queue at that deli, ad infinitum. You'll never place your order, but you'll attain the safety of *being ordered*. Your ticket to this endless line is sameness. You'll lose your place in line if you change.

Remember, when you fear hope, it's because you're struggling with your faith in yourself and in the world around you. And, as our research shows, the more you find hope scary, the more you want to both block out too many possible good events immediately in front of you, and constrict your overall time perspective, a sort of nearsightedness about the past and future. The line-waiting of a spirit of seriousness places you exactly in this limited and containing experience of time. You're stuck between past and future, and you don't know what will happen next, while assuming that *what will happen* will occur because of forces outside your control. And those counterfactuals, those ruminative what-if's that FOH ignites in you? They keep you there too. Focused on that agitated experience between past and future, you think about all kinds of events, caused by you or by others, that would have made life different. And even though you may blame yourself for missed opportunities, the lost results of these missed chances for a better now float there as ways of describing why you're standing in line instead of heading into the future: *If I had done (this or that) I would be free right now, but I'm not.*

"You won't know until you try": That adage can sound cheery, like a happy-go-lucky inducement for you to "just do it!" But the idea that you can't know if you made the right decision until you actually act on this decision can make you feel very conflicted about changing. It means that there are no guarantees in the changes you plan, and it hints at the fact that planning and predicting alone won't get you anywhere—that these are often a clever way of postponing what might happen if you take a breath, then leap into uncertainty. Your faith—that force that moves you forward despite unknown results—is what propels you into this leap. Faith gives you the strength to commit in the face of the risk that what you'll *know* after you *tried* is that you made the wrong decision.

To commit is to pledge, to make a promise you won't break. Change always demands that you commit to getting from one place to another. But it doesn't reciprocate with a promise that you will achieve anything worth that effort. Thus change is a rigged agreement: You sign a contract to take a new direction without any promise regarding where you'll end up.

The pledge to change—that fateful act of committing with no promise—is a moderately difficult one to make when you're planning on altering small behaviors, like losing weight or giving up some habit. It becomes more difficult and risky when the change is harder to reverse and involves serious adjustments, like heading off alone for a semester abroad. But this pledge is downright terrifying when the change you seek concerns issues of fulfillment and meaning, such as striking out on a career or entering a relationship; or quitting an unfulfilling job or ending an unsatisfying relationship. In these kinds of changes, when issues of meaning, purpose, and connection are at risk, the stakes are precariously high. Taking the deep plunge into endeavors such as love and work, the effort you put in is strenuous, the duration between "trying" and "finding out" is long, and the inevitable tension of hope—that feeling of not having what you need, and wanting it—takes hold in a powerful way.

The Unknown and the Risk of Committing to Depth

Back to the example of entering a career: You begin a new job in the career of your dreams. It's a small and mundane job, but it is a stepping-stone to the career you want. Even though it's hardly fulfilling, you stick to it and do well. From there, you move up to more challenging positions. You're still not where you envision yourself at the pinnacle of the career, the day-to-day work is still far from satisfying, but you're close to your goal. Then, you finally get that position that signals you've arrived. You are now fully at the top of your career, and . . . you hate it.

You've worked so hard to reach that large corner office, only to discover that it doesn't fit you. The actual day-to-day activities of this job don't satiate you in the way you had expected. They don't match your values, and don't offer you activities that feel gratifying.

When you started out, you couldn't know whether the career you chose would work for you or not. So it took a big *don't-know-until-you-try* kind of risk to commit at that point, and at every point when you kept pledging to continue to try, even though your jobs along the way felt empty of meaning and purpose. But now—after all these years, and all that hard labor—you're at the only place where you can get the answer to whether it was all worth it. And that answer is deeply disappointing.

Take the story above, play a kind of Mad Libs with it, replacing the career with a potential mate, and you'll end up with the same conclusion: You meet the person of your dreams. You start out dating them. Things aren't exciting, but they're okay. The relationship feels like it's working, there's enough there to make you want to take the next step, so you commit to being "exclusive." You hope that taking the risk of this new pledge will bring you and your mate closer, filling you with love and intimacy. You pour your heart and soul into the relationship. But still, when you're with your mate there's dull distance. You're afraid there might be a lack of actual connection between the two of you. On the other hand, things are good on the surface. You get along well. You do have fun. It feels like a good match, and there's so much potential. You make the ultimate pledge and get married. A decade in, you've got it all: an attentive partner, a house in the suburbs, the occasional vacation, lots of friends, and . . . you hate it.

After all these years, all these points of opening your heart and trying and trying again, you're at the only place where you can get the answer regarding whether your decision to commit was the right one to make. And it's deeply disappointing.

The risk of venturing on a path toward a summit that you'll know was worth the trek only when you reach it, is present in every choice, large or small. But this risk is especially difficult when the choice has to do with a life change that you make in order to reach a deeper experience, like career or love. The reason the commitment is more difficult to make depending on the depth of the experience the goal offers has to do as much with the time and effort you put into larger goals related to your fulfillment as it does with the problem of what you lose when you don't get what you want. The risk of your commitment has to do with the serious potential that you'll lose something you value. Your ability to handle that risk, and thus to step toward making changes in your life, has a lot to do with what is called your loss aversion.

LOSS AVERSION AND THE UNKNOWN OF ALTERNATIVE UNIVERSES

All commitments raise two questions: 1) *Is this choice the right one?* and 2) *What choices do I leave behind if I make it?* These questions are about loss.

You're at a restaurant like Chili's or TGI Fridays, perusing their giant menu, trying your best to pick the right meal. The waiter arrives and you feel an ever-so-slight sense of panic. You think you might want the fajitas, but you're worried that this will be the wrong choice and you predict that you might not be satisfied when the dish arrives and you finally bite in. The waiter, pen in hand, is poised to take your order, while two unanswerable questions swirl in your head: 1) *Are the fajitas really the right entrée for me tonight?* and 2) *If I choose the fajitas, what other entrées on the menu did I leave behind that might have been more satisfying?*

You're worried about loss: loss of a good meal and loss of all the other choices you could have made.

Paradoxically, what makes you so worried about these losses is the abundance of opportunities offered by that giant menu. The freedom of choice, in other words, constrains and upsets you. This fact isn't simply the product of existential philosophical musings; it's a property of every human psyche, and is definitively founded in math.

As animals, humans are more concerned with loss than gain. That's the conclusion of loss aversion theory, developed by Nobel laureates Daniel Kahneman and his collaborator Amos Tversky.[3] Their research shows that winning a hundred dollars is only half as appealing to us as losing a hundred dollars is unappealing. That feeling manifests itself in all kinds of situations. Your aversion to loss, and the fact that loss aversion is much stronger than your attraction to gain, is there for a good evolutionary reason: organisms that exert more energy protecting themselves from loss than they do seizing opportunities have a greater likelihood of survival.

Loss aversion explains the problem with that giant menu. The menu offers all kinds of opportunities, but just as many possibilities for loss. Here's where the math comes in: Let's say you're at dinner at a fancy place that only offers two items on the menu.

Choose one, and there's a 50 percent chance you made the wrong decision. Now, let's go back to Chili's or TGI Fridays with their giant menus offering a hundred choices. Freedom is at hand! However, with all those possibilities comes a 99 percent chance you'll make the wrong decision. Not only does your choice have the odds stacked against it as the *absolutely right choice*, but making any choice means you've lost the chance to taste all the other items on the menu.

Abundance of choice can cause you stress, because it presents you with both a higher probability of making the wrong and disappointing choice, and the increased risk that you'll miss more opportunities making any choice at all. That's why people flock to places like Chipotle, where they hedge their bets by picking exactly what they want in their burrito. That's why people like buffets—so they can miss no opportunity. They can have it all.

And that's very likely why we engage so ruminatively in counterfactuals, when our faith is injured: We're faced with our freedom, and we don't have faith in ourselves to pick the right choice, make the right decision, and then act.

Psychologist Barry Schwartz, in his book *The Paradox of Choice: Why More Is Less*, uses the idea of loss aversion to explain the seemingly conflicting facts that we're given innumerable choices as consumers in the United States, yet we perform quite poorly on scales for happiness compared to countries with fewer consumer choices. More important for our argument, Schwartz makes a telling observation about movements in the United States that try to counter this trend and help people increase their happiness by limiting choices and focusing on important issues related to individual values and purpose: "Taking care of our own 'wants' and focusing on what we 'want' to do," writes Schwartz, "does not strike me as a solution to the problem of too much choice."[4] In other words, ending your worry about whether you want fajitas or steak for dinner (or the steak fajitas!) and turning your thoughts to important choices about what you might find fulfilling doesn't decrease the anxiety of choice; it raises it.

No matter how large the menu, it's limited. On the other hand, the choices regarding what you'll find fulfilling in life—what will match your values, give you meaning, provide you purpose, deliver you to a sense of connection—are infinite. If you feel you've made a mistake in one of these choices about personal change, it thus makes sense that your mind will turn to reviewing all the other possible choices you could have made. Hence, counterfactuals. But it also makes sense that it will go haywire considering the choices in front of you—a sort of future counterfactualizing: a ruminating series of what-ifs regarding your next decision.

Think again about committing to a relationship. What holds you back? First is the question about whether your partner is really a good match. You see all their foibles, all the things that irritate you, and you wonder, *Is this person going to make my life better?* If you had just a few matrimonial choices—for example, if you lived in a small village, or candidates were provided by a matchmaker—these concerns about whether you've found the perfect fit wouldn't be that big a deal. But your choices in the world of internet dating are nearly unlimited and so you'll never know if you've made the right choice.

The second and related question is about all the missed opportunities around the corner. Someone else out there might be "the One." If you choose the person in front of you, you might miss out on the person you were destined to meet. Now here's the paradox: The amount of anxiety you experience about finding the singularly perfect match in career and love is directly related—as I'm sure you guessed—to the number of other choices in front of you.

Change is all about the game in your head about "alternative" universes, those parallel existences in science fiction where you live an infinitude of possible lives, each arising by a different choice at a different juncture. That game is no big deal when choosing a sizzling approximation of Mexican food. It's serious business when you choose a mate. The difference between an item on the menu at Chili's and the choice of change in a direction toward depth has to do with the stakes (not steaks) involved.

The stakes are very high when you make a commitment aimed at reaching a deeper and more meaningful existence. One way to address this situation is to play out possible scenarios: *What if my partner wants to move to another state? What if we don't agree on how to raise kids? What if they end up leaving me for someone they meet at the gym?* But this only takes you so far, and maybe nowhere useful at all. When you try to skip to the end of the story before you're willing to read it—obsessively tracking every possible scenario, listing the many possible alternative universes—you might find yourself in an endless orbit. You're never going to get all the data, never forecast all the outcomes, and at some point it's all going to be about gambling on your faith.

The more freedom, the less certain you can be about your decisions, and thus the more you have to rely on your gut, that emotional and bodily site of information I earlier tied to faith.

The term "fear of commitment" is thrown around a lot these days, most often used to describe a problem in relationships: "That Fred, he can't settle down because he has a fear of commitment." But we all fear commitment. And rightly so; commitment is scary. It's an act of making a significant investment in something you deeply yearn for, without knowing whether it's the right basket to toss all your eggs into. Your fear of making that pledge and taking that leap into the unknown increases the more choices you have and the greater you value what you want. For our gestalt-oriented brains (those problem solvers that like a lot of continuity), the discrepancy between a big investment and an unknowable outcome provokes a lot of anxiety. That anxiety isn't neurotic, it's the most accurate feeling we should have in such a predicament.

When you commit and do achieve what you want, it's great! Well worth the risk. But when your commitment ends in disappointment, you are faced with a new dilemma and a real challenge to your willingness to act in good faith: Do you try to recoup your loss by continuing in the direction you're going? Or do you drastically change course? It's a matter, in other words, of whether you want to continue to invest in a choice you made despite all the loss—to "throw good money after bad."

BIG DISAPPOINTMENT, THE UNKNOWN, AND SUNK COSTS

Combine your predetermined aversion to loss with the human brain's orientation to make things whole, and you get a tendency to invest more, the more you lose. When you stick to that job you hate, or that marriage that makes you miserable, you're trying to get your balance sheet out of the red and into the black. This tendency—called the "sunk-cost fallacy"[5] by economists, or "escalating commitment"[6] and "commitment bias"[7] by sociologists—is powerfully seductive when the problem has to do with failed attempts at making your life deep. When you've tried to make personal change in these areas and failed, one more factor causes your internal CPA to frantically try to salvage the loss: You are finite.

All that time spent following your heroic and vulnerable leap into commitment—that fruit of your faith and hope in the face of the unknown—can be felt as wasted. The time you spent pursuing your erstwhile dreams places you closer to the end of your existence than when you started out. Time is of the essence. The stakes are higher than they have ever been. It's literally do or die.

So what do you do? Once again, you stand poised before a choice that *might only possibly* bring you to the depth and meaning you seek. Your fear of this repeated leap into the unknown is, if anything, greater than before. You know you need to take a leap of faith and follow your gut once again, putting the failed produce of your last risk behind you. But you also know that your previous best effort ended up as a mistake, and that mistake cost you years. So your faith in your credibility as the source of information on how to navigate your life is injured, and it's limping along right at the point when you need it most: to daringly leap into a long-term investment on rebuilding, without a promise that you'll get a return on your investment of effort, emotion, and the ever-shortening supply of time. That can make the tension between where you are now and where you want to be excruciating.

Made anxious by this choice, you reach out to your old friends, Bad Faith and its agent the Spirit of Seriousness. They've always been there, waiting for your call, knowing you'll contact them once things got too tough out there in that scary world of ac-countability for your life. About your unhappy, exhausted mar-riage they tell you, "You're bound by 'I do'" and "Wait and see, it could get better"; about your dead-end career they urge you to "stick with it: all good things come to those who wait." They do solve your immediate problem—that anxiety that haunts you day and night. Calming you down, they hand you a lipstick for the pig of emptiness and routine, protecting you from the despair of sunk costs, and the painful experience of *try, try, try again.* Then they slowly lower a breathing mask, anesthetizing you from the unbearable pain of reality.

Of course, it doesn't have to be that way. But it takes a lot more fortitude and effort to leap into uncertainty than to just stay the same. Below is a story about someone I knew who found the right mantra to help him make that leap.

SAM AND YES-AND

I used to work with a guy named Sam. Sam was definitely some-one you would call commitment-phobic, going on dates every weekend, sleeping around a lot, but sprinting from relationships whenever things got serious. The fun of meeting a new woman and the excitement of the next sexual encounter worked for Sam when he was in his twenties. But now in his thirties, he found his encounters with women unsatisfying if not downright boring. He felt lonely and wanted more. Sam's concerns about finding a com-mitted relationship stuck with him through his days, sometimes a droning monologue of discomfort, often a cacophony of worry and frustration. He tried all kinds of gimmicks and approaches in his pursuit to meet his match, from dating apps and services to speed-dating and singles events.

Sam would often visit me in my office for a few stolen min-utes to tell me about his upcoming venture into the professional world of dating. Typically, he would express excitement about the next big thing he was going to try, then return disappointed that the newest tactic didn't work. To me, Sam seemed like someone who was frenetically trying to get help for something that needed deeper work, namely, his reluctance to become truly intimate with someone, which was the real barrier to his finding a match. But I didn't think it was my place to say anything. I kept my mouth mostly shut.

On the day Sam told me he was joining an improvisation class for singles, I did what I always did with Sam: nodded and provided some encouraging comments, even though my mind's eyes were actually rolling. I'd read about these classes, how they can be a lot of fun, but a little cultlike, and tend to drain pocket-books.

When it came to improv, however, Sam didn't return to my office with the same report of failure. He loved the class. During a break in our schedules, he plopped down on the couch in my office to tell me how it was going.

"It's all about yes-and," he told me.

Yes-and: that's the improv motto, its founding rule. You say to me, "I'm a giraffe," I agree with that new reality (the "yes"), but add an "and": "And I'm a Martian, meeting my first earth creature!" I understood how yes-and was an important part of actually performing improv, but as it applied to a philosophy on life, and as a strategy for overcoming Sam's commitment issues, it all sounded a little too pat—just another slogan in a long line of slogans about dating and commitment he would announce as we stole a few minutes during our workday. He had drunk the Second City Kool-Aid and he was now speaking the mantra.

As the weeks rolled by, Sam kept reporting back to me about the class. This was new: his sticking to one thing in the dating world. More important, he met a woman in the class, by the name of Lisa, whom he began to date.

In our future brief meetings in my office, Sam checked in with me about this relationship. When I asked him how it was going, his answers were always and irritatingly the same.

"Yes-and. It's going yes-and."

I can't stand slogans in general, and this one in particular grated at me. It just sounded like the worst possible way to think about commitment. Surely, I thought, commitment is the *yes* of a pledge. That's what makes it a commitment: there are no *ands*, *ifs*, or *buts* about it.

Sam found another job and moved on. A year or so later, I received an invitation to his wedding. He and Lisa were tying the knot.

I thought it would be nice to catch up a little. I gave Sam a call and we went out for drinks.

"So it all finally worked out for you," I said to Sam as we

settled in at the bar. "You were so sure you were never going to find someone and settle down."

"I know," Sam replied. "It's that improv class. It turned my head around."

"Really?"

"Yeah, that whole yes-and idea. I'm sure it was the right time for something to finally sink in, and that idea came at just that right time."

I felt my hand instinctively move up, aiming thumb and forefinger to clasp the bridge of my nose, my head ready to move back and forth. *He may never return from the Branch Davidian compound*, I thought. But I was polite.

Sam kept talking.

"You see, it's like this: I was afraid of committing because I saw a long-term relationship as sort of taking something away from me; mainly the part of me that likes a lot of freedom. But once I saw marriage as a yes-and proposition, the whole marriage thing seemed more like a contract Lisa and I agreed to sign, that we could then add a lot of *ands* to."

This sounded like the old commitment-fearing Sam to me. The way I saw it, Sam wanted the opportunity for amendments to his marriage contract, little escape clauses that could promise freedom when he needed it. As someone who couldn't fully commit to a mate, he was looking for a big compromise. *Yes*, he could have Lisa in his life, *and* do anything else he wanted.

I couldn't stand by and let this happen. Someone needed to pop Sam's balloon of denial, before it was too late.

"Sam, I'm sorry, but aren't you just talking about not really committing, with all this yes-and stuff?"

"What do you mean?"

"Like the *and* part; it's saying there's something other than the commitment. It's like you're saying '*Yes*, I'll take my vows, *and* I can quit the marriage any time I want.' Or even '*Yes*, I'm committed, *and* I can sleep around.'"

Surprisingly, Sam began to laugh, shaking his head a little. I could smell a hint of pity, and maybe just a smidgen of superiority in the air.

"Oh, man, you're not getting this at all. Dude, the *yes* is to the commitment, the *and* is to whatever Lisa and I want to do with that commitment. The *and* doesn't ruin anything about that. It makes it stronger."

"I really don't get it, Sam."

"Look, it's like 'Hey, we've decided to make a vow to each other, and now our lives can be a series of vows: travel, make our house really cool, have kids or don't, raise them in an interesting way that matches our values if we do, and maybe even decide how monogamous we want to be.'"

I was starting to get what he meant now, but—call me old-fashioned—the monogamy-by-choice part kept my suspicions going. "Sam, I get it. It's just that sleeping around . . ."

"I'm happy it's just the two of us. The relationship will likely be exclusive. But it's still a choice as long as we stick to the *yes*. We are a couple making decisions together."

"Okay, I think I'm getting this," I replied, dismounting my high horse.

"You see, I don't think I was ever really afraid of getting close to a woman. I was afraid a long-term relationship would restrict me. But now I see the whole thing as just a new way of being free, as long as she and I are both committed to yes-and."

"Right."

"When I was single I had to make decisions about my singlehood all the time, and singlehood had all kinds of restrictions. Now I have marriagehood, with its own decisions and drags on my independence, but it also has its own freedoms. Marriage is no less and no more creative a thing than singlehood, it's just that you're part of a project that involves another person."

"Okay, Sam. Now I get it."

The hard crust of my prejudices about slogans and gimmicks had dissolved; I could see somewhat clearly what Sam had been talking about all along. Yes-and helped Sam make a switch from a seriously spirited approach to commitment—in which he saw his marriage pledge as placing him on a conveyor belt of roles and rules, transporting him toward a future he could not control—to a view of marriage as a source of play. "Play" as in something having pliability or *give*: the ability to bend something solid into something your own.

"You don't play whatever you feel," writes jazz musician Branford Marsalis.[8] "The only freedom is in structure." Describing the elemental interplay between structure and improvisation, which is the very foundation of jazz music, Marsalis simultaneously articulates the intrinsic tension between something durable yet pliable, which you make your own through your creative approach. As my favorite psychoanalytic thinker, D. W. Winnicott, wrote, "It is not possible to be original except on the basis of tradition."[9] That's what Sam and Lisa were doing: being original within the tradition of marriage.

I now think of Sam's approach to his marriage, and how this marriage participated in his unknown future, as embodying a "spirit of playfulness," in which you imagine, invent, and create, yet always within the confines of a commitment, planted solidly in the ground by a "yes." Lisa was Sam's playmate in the best sense, and together they would take what seemed inert—marriage contracts, the social expectations of how a marriage works, the general expectations about adulthood—and animate it all, just like children do in their shared play, and fairy tales do with otherwise inanimate objects.

A spirit of playfulness turns your fears about your accountability for your life into an exciting appreciation of the gift of your life authorship. It makes the words "What's next?" the absolute best of questions, and it causes you to see an unknown future as abundant with meaningful choices.

Human life *is* improvisation, and improvisation is what makes you most human. Your giant neocortex—this newest invention in the animal kingdom—attests to this fact: It's there at the front of your skull for the purpose of imagining options, making something new out of something old, listening closely to others in a collaborative way, guessing at their experiences and accepting these experiences as valid, and innovating. That signature element of your humanity manifested itself the first time you gave the *yes* of a smile to your parents above you, *and* they smiled at this new reality. A yes-and spirit continues to animate your life. But it doesn't come as easily to you as when you were a kid. Far from it.

Unencumbered in your youth by the serious work of self-sufficiency, the knowledge of your accountability, and the ticking clock of your own demise, improvisation came naturally. Now that you're older, an improvisational approach takes work, requiring grit you didn't need then, pushing you to hope and have faith despite your concerns that you are accountable for the results of every *and*.

To improvise is to act on hope without too much fear—to say *yes* to a situation, *and* find alternative pathways. And it's to act out of faith—to believe that something good can come from your actions. You've already seen how difficult, if not painful, it is for us adults to enter into these modes of relating to the world.

Anxiety Is Your Frenemy

The "anxiety of life cannot be avoided except at the price of apathy or the numbing of one's sensibilities and imagination," wrote the great existential psychologist Rollo May.[10] No pain, no gain, in other words. The pain that comes with change always, ultimately, has to do with anguish over your accountability and aloneness. Often, as illustrated by the first three Reasons Not to Change, avoiding that pain is your central preoccupation. When you don't face that pain, you inevitably erase any chance of gain.

I have quite a few tattoos (as a matter of fact, Harold and his purple crayon are tattooed on my shin). For me, and like a lot of people, tattoos are like Pringles potato chips: "Once you pop, you can't stop." I knew the minute I got my first one that I would want more. Tattoos are also famously painful to imprint. Although I'm no masochist, and—as anyone who knows me will tell you—I'm hardly famous for my tolerance of pain, the pain of being inked is part of what attracts me to getting tattooed. It signifies that I'm doing something indelible, deeper than skin deep. In fact, if tattoos were painless, I doubt I would get them. But here's another important point about the pain of getting tattooed: If those needles were emptied of ink, puncturing my skin with no perceivable purpose, I would writhe in agony, a puddle of whining and complaint. If the needles were used for the intention of causing me pain, or—worse yet—applied against my will? Well, we have a word for that: torture.

That's a proven fact about physical pain: It's contextual, felt differently depending on its meaning and what's happening around you.[11,12] The same is true regarding the way you deal with the anguish of your aloneness. If you see it as only dangerous, only a threat—a flat, but terrifying prospect—you empty it of meaning. In that context, your anguish appears as alien to you, a monster attacking the shield of your bad faith. But if you can see it as an inevitable part of change, it's still painful and scary, but it's also an indicator that you're changing. Often, in fact, it's the only indicator that change is happening or on its way.

But don't forget: The risk you take, when you dare to feel your existential anxiety in order to change, is risky!

"Just do it!" "Just take the plunge!" "Just go for it!" When it comes to change—and especially when this change is in the service of deepening your life—such comments are just plain stupid. There is no "just" in any of this crazy, mixed-up world of change. When you head toward change, you face the real experience of your aloneness, the real chance that new and more difficult challenges will appear on the horizon, the real fact that you may leave a nugget of gold behind in all that sunk cost, the real possibility that the goal you want to reach will end up worthless, and the real potential that you will face significant disappointment. To dare to change in the face of your aloneness is to risk—and the risk is all real. In fact, making personal change is all about the risk of authentically approaching your life. The risk is real, because you're being at your most real.

We're offered a bum deal when it comes to personal change. Dare to change, and you feel the anxiety of risk. Don't change, and you feel like there is no risk, and therefore no anxiety. The whole scenario is rigged for sameness: When you change, you're consumed with the message anxiety is sent to deliver. "WARNING, WARNING, YOU ARE AT RISK!" it screams, imploring you to run. When you don't change, bad faith and a spirit of seriousness cocoon you from getting a similar message about the significant peril of sameness.

Anything but a Conclusion

I did it! Despite all the forces restraining me from completing chapter 6—the comfort of my bed, the allure of the bread boat recipe, the pain of facing my stark aloneness, the feeling that I'm not ready, the nerve-jabbing ache of what's next, and the struggle over committing to something without the promise that I'll gain more than lose—I finished; I made it to the other side.

Drop mic!

Not exactly. Tomorrow I'll wake in the dark of the morning, around 5:00 a.m., in order to write the next chapter. And I'll have no idea where I'll end up.

CHAPTER 7

"THERE'S NO REASON YOU CAN'T"

Blessed are they who expect nothing for they shall not be disappointed.

—Alexander Pope

- #4: Staying the same protects you from your own expectations.
- #5: Staying the same protects you from the expectations of others.

When Max calls from college to tell me about a good grade in a class, I always try to focus on this singular success. Yet somehow I end up talking to him about other possible successes ahead. "That's great about the A," I'll say, then a few minutes later, and against my better judgment, I'll add, "Just think, if you keep that up, you could get an A in the class!" His irritation is palpable from over three thousand miles of cell coverage. And I don't always stop here. Watching myself in slo-mo, alarms going off in my head telling me to STOP, LOOK, AND LISTEN! I'll ask, "And what about your other classes?"

In these all-too-frequent interactions, his comment about one success morphs into my push toward higher expectations. He wants to take a minute and be recognized by me for doing well at a particular task. But his success in this task only moves me to think about what else he can master. Well-calibrated but high expectations are a parent's prerogative (if my expectations stay the same, I'm slacking off in my job), so I don't feel too out of the norm when I make such comments. But for Max, I'm basically moving the goal post.

Well, actually I'm not moving it. Max is moving it by getting the good grade. It's his willingness to risk doing well that has caused this consequence of my tiresome raising of expectations. Some part of him knows that. I'm just the dad who can't keep his mouth shut about the obvious.

My son is a sturdy guy. While my goading irritates him, he can handle the idea that one positive change raises my expectations for him. I'm sure he's anxious about what these expectations might lead to, but I also know that his capacity to have hope and faith regarding his schoolwork outweighs this concern and allows him to be inspired rather than distressed when he gets that A. That's not always true for you or me, and I'm sure it's not true for Max all the time.

As expressed in the question "What's next?" in Reason Not to Change #2, if you improve yourself, your expectations for yourself and the expectations of others about you increase. That's just a fact: The more you're able to succeed at things, the more people, including you, will expect more things of you. Reason #2 is about staying the same in order to avoid the experience of your accountability. It's about you recognizing that you alone are in charge of what's next, and how that can send shivers of anxiety up your spine. Reasons Not to Change #4 and #5, on the other hand, are about how similar questions lead to fears about hope.

It's a subtle but important difference. Reasons #4 and #5 are not only about being accountable for something in the future; they are about your fear that by changing you generate greater expectations in yourself (from yourself and others), and how these expectations become new heights to hope for, and thus new, greater elevations of aspiration to risk falling from.

"There's No Reason You Can't" and the Fear of Hope

Expectations can grow outward. Blooming from the pistil of success, they remain even in challenge: *If I can decrease my caffeine intake, there's no reason I can't also stop eating so many carbs.* They can also grow upward, the seed of success branching toward the heights of greater challenges: *If I can lower my carb intake, there's no reason I can't cut carbs out completely.* Either way, there's that often irritating clause: *There's no reason I can't . . .* Success at one thing, in other words, is often evidence that any excuses you might have about dodging other reasonable challenges are bunk.

Self-efficacy,[1] Albert Bandura's concept that I tie to faith, has to do with your belief in your ability to master things. Your general experience of your self-efficacy increases when you get good at something specific. You probably know this in your own life: Mastery in one area makes you believe you can master something in another. In fact, your whole life can be tracked to such contagious moments of mastery. You learned how to ride a bike, got your first A, stood up to that bully. How did it feel? Was it only *I've mastered bikes* or *I've mastered spelling tests* or *I've mastered my fear of bullies*? Or was it instead the more general affirmation, *I'm masterful.* I'm betting it was the latter.

Lewin says something similar regarding hope. Hope increases every time you take an incremental step:

A successful individual typically sets his next goal somewhat but not too much above his last achievement. In this way he steadily raises his level of aspiration. Although, in the long run, he is guided by his ideal goal, which might be rather high, nevertheless his real goal is kept realistically close to his present position.[2]

For Lewin, you build motivation to achieve large goals by achieving small ones along the way. You want to bench-press 200 pounds. Today, you set your goal at 120. You're motivated to achieve this goal because it's doable, and because you know it's going to get you to your ultimate goal. Three sets of ten, pressing 120, and you're motivated now to go for 125 next time you come to the gym. Each small step motivates you for the next.

The motivating fuel to reach your goals is released from the cells of smaller changes. That's an exciting concept. It means that hope doesn't have to be a battery in a dock. Like a Prius, the more you move toward successfully reaching what you hope for, the more your hope is recharged. That's a good thing, made bad only by the possible trauma of deep disappointment and the resulting fear of hope.

When you head toward a change, you know from your own experience of mastering things that every change you make will likely lead you to take on other changes sitting on the shelf waiting for you to master them. If you're overly worried about disappointment, then you worry about taking all those changes off the shelf. If you're worried about taking them off the shelf, you worry that the one change in front of you might raise your expectations or the expectations of others that you can achieve other things.

The reason the "there's no reason you can't" clause so quickly comes to mind after you achieve something is because, as with Max, the achievement exposes you as an active agent.

And of all the achievements in your life, achieving personal change makes your accountability most visible.

Let's say you want to save money on home repairs. You find doing such repairs boring, and you don't get any real satisfaction out of doing them. But the amount of money you've spent over the years paying professionals on things you could fix is ridiculous.

Your bathroom faucet leaks. You've never done any plumbing in your life, so you go to an instructional YouTube channel on your cell phone. You fix the leak. You think, "If I can fix the faucet, *there's no reason I can't* patch that hole in the drywall." You're not thrilled with the idea of doing the next job, but you also don't have any excuse not to. Are you filled with existential angst? Maybe just a little, but likely not a lot. You learned to fix a faucet, *there's no reason you can't* learn how to fix other things, and that's going to help you save some cash.

Now let's say you've been a shy person all your life. Your shyness has always felt like a barrier, personally and professionally. This is especially true about speaking in public. You decide to take a public-speaking class. On the final night, you give a great speech. You leave the class with the skills and confidence to speak up more in public and effectively tackle those once-forbidding PowerPoint presentations at work. The "no reason you can't" clause is more profound here than when you fixed that faucet. It's about changing a fundamental part of yourself, and removing a major barrier to a better life. You did this, and the thing you fixed was yourself. In this situation, "there's no reason you can't" is not only about skills or motivation to complete something; it's about your willingness to author your life, to act on your hope and faith. That's scary. It's scary because it's inspiring. Inspiring for yourself, and inspiring for those people who root for you.

"Inspire" has the same source as the word Lewin used for the incremental growth of hope based on small successes: "aspire." Just like the word "spirit," these words are exquisitely rooted in the thing we do that proves we're alive: *to breathe*. When you're inspired by something you do that changes you, when you expand with hope and faith, you are also most exposed as alive and breathing.

The more your livingness is realized, and thus the more freedom you experience, the more you're caught, your accountability for your life naked and exposed, the expectations about what you can do with this accountability rising. When you're inspired by something you changed about yourself that previously made you feel stuck, you're inspired by the fact that you were willing to take a breath and move forward despite the gasp of existential anxiety. You're free to do more with your life. And since you successfully faced your accountability once, now there's no reason you can't face your accountability again.

Fear of hope is the fear of the helpless feeling that you didn't get something you saw as important and recognized that you lacked. When you hope for a change in yourself, you risk an injury to your faith in yourself and in the world if you don't reach your goal. That's why issues of failure and success, and concerns about the potential of "there's no reason you can't," don't worry you too much when you're working on your house to save money, yet feel quite threatening when you take that public-speaking class. In the first situation, the goal is mostly instrumental. It's about getting things done, and if you don't get things done, you might feel a tinge of the sense that you can't make your life work, but mostly you'll feel like you're just not good at something that doesn't really interest you. In the second situation, the goal is about making deep changes in who you are. In that situation, you risk feeling that the important thing you lack has to do with you and your ability to make your life work, so screwing up the task has much greater consequences regarding your hope and faith.

You and me both: We spend an inordinate amount of energy concealing our accountability from ourselves and from others, feigning through bad faith and a spirit of seriousness that we are petrified and lifeless. But when we do something to improve ourselves, it's like we're caught in the beam of a flashlight, exposed as the living authors of our experience. Once we're uncovered as master of our own fate, the jig is up, and all kinds of things are expected of us: "*If you can* muster the courage to face yourself and lose those ten pounds, *there's no reason you can't* take the same courage and start dating again."

While the feigned lifelessness of a possum is involuntary, it's still a performance, an act: the possum *plays* dead. The process of controlling expectations—the slowing and thinning of your breath to decrease the chance that your accountability will be detected—is also a kind of performance; part of a theater in which you are both the actor onstage and a member of the audience watching the show. It's like Jim in the previous chapter setting up those check-in calls in order to see himself as passive in his own eyes and in the eyes of his clinical team.

THE DRAMATURGY OF CONTROLLING EXPECTATIONS

As I write these words to you right now, I'm aware of you as an audience, and I think about how you are understanding what I have to say, whether I'm being clear, whether I'll be successful in getting my points across, and most important to me, whether I'll influence you to think in a different way about change. But while writing to you, I am also writing to myself, a "me" who I hope will understand my arguments and be influenced by them. So I'm putting on a sort of performance for you and me. We are both in the audience, awaiting what I'll do up there in the spotlight.

You may not notice it all the time, but you, too, are also always engaging in this kind of performance—a *dramaturgy*, as the great sociologist Erving Goffman[3] called it—in which you act for an audience that you are also a member of. We are all "looking-glass selves," as another prominent sociologist, Charles Cooley,[4] put it: knowing who we are based on reflections bounced back to us from others. Yet we aren't passive in front of this audience. We mold what they reflect back to us depending on the performance we give. That means our decisions to act in good or bad faith are not simply inner decisions; they are outer performances that you and others witness.

When you are performing in bad faith (hiding your accountability for your life), you play a puppet, your actions portrayed as if you're operated by control rods held in the hand of outside forces. Your toes barely touching the stage floor, your arms and hands awkwardly jerking to the pull of strings, you conceal from both yourself and the audience that you are actually the master of your existence. The strings, the control, the hand—all props:

Possum the Puppet: A Play in Three Acts

Act One

SETTING: A small cramped apartment. Evening.

YOU: *(Awaking from a nap, you sit up on the couch, stretch your arms above your head, and yawn.)* Oh, man! Look at the time. It's too late to work out now!

Act Two

SETTING: A drab break room in a large office floor filled with cubicles.

YOU: *(Turning to the coworker next to you)* I just can't find the time to exercise!

Act Three

SETTING: The interior of a compact car.

YOU: (*Whispering to yourself*) I need to work out tonight. But first I have to stop at the store.

Curtain, and your puppet feet have never set foot in the puppet gym.
THE END

In this kind of performance, your job is to keep everyone's expectations about your accountability as low as possible. Not only do you portray yourself as directed by an unseen master, but you also portray your inability to get to the gym as a matter of fate, not choice ("It's too late"; "I can't find the time"; "I have to stop at the store"). You don't want the audience to see you as accountable, because there is also *you* in the audience, who is afraid to seem capable, and also *them*—your family, friends, coworkers, therapist—who you don't want getting all inspired about you, only for you to disappoint them. If you can keep your performance as puppetlike as possible, the reflection of yourself you see in the mirror of the audience is of a wooden, inanimate thing. And no one hopes for the onward authorship of things, so no one is ever disappointed in things, as choosing, deciding entities.

Jim again: the performance of a hollow object, moving only through the control of my team.

When you act in good faith, acknowledging your authorship of your life and with a spirit of playfulness, the dramaturgy is just the opposite of a puppet show. This time it's a one-person performance, and there is no script. Like Sam in the previous chapter, who found marital success with his yes-and approach, it's just you up there onstage improvising. Everyone—including you, and sometimes only you—is watching and expecting you to make something happen. In this performance, you might be sweating it out on the StairMaster one night, pronouncing, "I planned to work out, and now I'm doing it!" On another night, you're on the couch binge-watching and binge-eating, whispering, "I planned to work out and I slacked off." In both of these performances, you're clearly accountable whether you succeed at the given task or fail. "That's me up there on the StairMaster, taking charge and working out," or "That's me up there on the couch, slacking off." There's no escaping the audience's expectations, and that means there's also no escaping the fact that their degree of hope for you will change depending on your performance. They will leave the theater either more inspired by what you can do next, or they'll leave despairing of your abilities.

When you risk raising expectations, your performance is often directed either more toward yourself or more toward others, depending on whom you most want to inspire by your change or most want to convince about your inability to change. Reason Not to Change #4 is about *your own expectations*, while Reason #5 is about the *expectations of others*.

Reason Not to Change #4:
Staying the same protects you from your own expectations.

When you raise your own expectations by making a change in your life, you always risk raising your faith in and hope for yourself. That means an increased risk for experiences of disappointment and loss of faith.

GUITAR LESSONS
After taking guitar lessons a million times and each time quitting after a few sessions, you want to make another attempt. But you can't stand the idea of people closest to you knowing you're trying again. Your friends and family have seen this show before. You don't need their doubt and cynicism dragging you down. So you

don't tell them. In fact, you're excited about the big reveal—when you get good enough to walk into the kitchen and play a song, proving them all wrong. "This will work," you tell yourself. "The problem before was all that pressure, that idea that everyone knew I was taking lessons and expected me to become good."

You take one or two lessons from your new teacher and discover that the pressure is still there. In fact, every time you get better and get a little more hopeful that this time will be different and you'll succeed, you get more worried that you'll give up. You find practicing more and more difficult; not the drills or scales per se, but the actual motivation to practice and stick with it. It's like there's a force keeping your fingers from touching the strings.

That's your fear of hope hitting up against your growing inspiration. Keeping your expectations low is a central means of calming this fear. If you don't have high expectations for yourself, there is less possibility you'll be recognized by yourself as an improviser—or imposter. In other words, your concerns about raising your own expectations about yourself are rarely about only one success in only one area. They typically relate to an overall growth of expectations in yourself. The more you fear hope, the more you're going to want to tamp down on these growing expectations.

Again, my office: Right now, I'm sitting in it and it's a bit disorganized. I know from my past failures that if I clean my office, it will quickly become messy again. But I also know that I can avoid the feeling of failure that comes when my clean office becomes messy by avoiding cleaning my office. If I keep my office messy, I live in one failure (the current state of messiness) instead of two (my habitual messiness plus another failure to keep it clean). At the same time, I trade the consistent background drone of Man with a Messy Office for the pain of making change, raising my expectations about myself, then watching myself fall from my new exalted status. In this situation, staying the same feels safer to me than change.

The problem is not, however, only my office. Instead, it's about how the clean office makes it less possible for me to conceal from myself the fact that I am able. If I can clean my office, *there's no reason I can't . . .*

Reason Not to Change #5:
Staying the same protects you from the expectations of others.

When you make positive change in your life, you inevitably raise the expectations of others. Doing so, you risk that others will witness you as the author of your life, and then expect more out of you.

GUITAR LESSONS REDUX

After starting to take guitar lessons a million times and quitting after a few lessons, you want to make another attempt. While you can't stand the idea that the people closest to you know you're trying again, you feel you need a trusted ally, a cheerleader who can keep you going. You know just the person for the job: your older brother. You look up to him, and he's always been there for you, willing to help out. He's very earnest and can be so upbeat at times that he irritates you, but you also feel these qualities will help you leap over the hurdle of trying again. He agrees to help.

"So you want me to check in with you, and give you a pep talk, right?"

"Yeah, something like that."

"And to push you when you start to slack off?'

"Sure."

"And you're not going to get pissed at me when I push?"

"No! Don't worry about it. I'll be good."

"Okay, 'cause this is my wheelhouse. My friends will tell you: I'm the go-to guy for motivation. You'll be playing like Jimmy Page in no time."

You call him after your first lesson.

"I feel this time is different; I really do," you tell him. "I'm just more mature about it."

"It sounds like this is your time!" he replies. "This will be the one. I feel it in my bones! Keep doing what you're doing, man! I can't wait to hear you play!"

You hang up, less certain than when you got on the phone, your brother's überenthusiasm a little ill-calibrated, considering it was just your first lesson. But he's doing you a favor. You're not going to coach him on how to coach you.

You succeed at a full week of practicing and your next lesson goes swimmingly.

You call your brother.

"Oh, man," he says. "This is great! You make me want to get out there and take lessons myself! Wow!"

It's just my second lesson, you think. *A little too many espressos in the old latte there.* But what are you going to do? He's a brother. The next week, you practice for four of the seven days. Your lesson goes well, but the instructor asks you to repeat a couple of pages from the practice book.

That night, you decide it might be better not to call your brother.

But he calls you.

"Hey, it's me, your coach. How'd it go?"

You tell him not as well this week, and you describe the missed practices and the fact that you had to redo some pages from your book.

"Oh, that's nothing! Don't get down! It's all good! Let me help you with a little visualization. You're at a party, no one knows you've been taking lessons. Mom and Dad are there. There's a guitar in the corner. You pick it up. People can't believe it. You're actually going to play a song. The room goes silent. Got that image in your head?"

"Um . . . yeah . . . sure."

"Okay. You strum a couple of chords. Nothing that great: basic 'Smoke on the Water.' But it's all a trick! You actually start playing like Kirk Hammett! It's crazy! Everyone is stunned. You finish the solo. It's silent in the room. Then one person, then two, then three, then everyone, starts to clap and cheer! It's mayhem, man. Mayhem, I tell you! Got it?"

"Yeah, yeah, I got it," you limply respond.

"Great! Now take that vision and go practice!" *Click*.

That week you practice only three times, and your lesson is a mess.

You avoid all the calls from your brother.

When you hear a knock at your apartment door, you immediately know who it is.

"Look," he says as he charges into your place, "you assigned me to keep you practicing. Did you think I was just going to give up on you?"

"Well, no."

"Then let me do my job."

"Okay, sorry."

He grabs you by the shoulders and looks you in the eye. "This isn't the time to give up! I'm positive you're going to get there; just absolutely positive! I know it: This time is different! And just think, if you get good at guitar, all the other doors will open up: that Toastmasters course you always talk about taking, that personal trainer you keep saying you want to call, that woman at work you're afraid to ask out. It's all there, man. It's at your fingertips. Now put down the remote and go practice!"

"Okay, I will."

"I'm waiting."

"Right now?"

"Yes, right now!"

You get your guitar and the lesson book and begin to strum.

"You see, you're doing it!" Grinning and walking backward as he watches you practice, he opens the door and lets himself out.

You practice for a few minutes, take a look through the blinds to be sure he's gone, then put down the guitar and pick up the remote.

The next day you call the instructor, leaving a voice mail that you are quitting lessons for now.

That's a rather cartoonish example of you raising someone else's expectations in a way that makes you just want to stay the same. But the issue of how you get others excited, then possibly let them down, is often a central concern when you set out to change.

Think about dieting in your own life. The first decision you have to make is which diet to go on: Atkins? South Beach? Paleo? Keto? If you're like me, you need to make another decision right after that: Do I tell people I'm on a diet or not? If you tell them, it might help, since they can keep you honest and might be helpful supporters. But they'll also notice you eating that cheeseburger when you fall off the diet. If you don't tell them, on the other hand, you won't raise their expectations. Any failure will happen in secret. Then again, if you keep it a secret and stick to the diet, they're going to notice you're losing weight at some point. And when they do, you'll face the challenge of continuing to diet, even though people might witness your waistline grow again if you fail.

The Man with the Clean Office again: If I clean it, I will not only raise my own expectations, I'll raise the expectations of my clients and staff too. They won't exactly be excited about the change, but they'll notice it. Then if I fail at keeping the office clean, they will witness this failure. That will feel bad. It will feel bad because of the ever-so-slight change in what my audience sees. When it's clean, they see someone who's competent, and taking control. When it's a mess, they see the opposite.

I believe this particular reason not to change is especially powerful in the lives of the people I work with professionally. For people who experience long periods of time identified as mentally ill, the risk of failing in the eyes of others equals or surpasses the risk of disappointing themselves. That's because for so much of their lives their only job—their career, actually—has been to change, and that change is the focus of all the people who help them.[5] Every day, they wake up and go to one or several therapeutic settings—their "workplace"—in order to get better. The people around them are focused on change, waiting for them to take the next step. Mental health professionals and family members develop treatment plans aimed at change, offer suggestions on what to do, and come up with the next intervention, the next treatment.

The recipients of all these plans for change know that any change will be detected and noted by others (in charts, treatment team meetings, calls to parents, and casual office chatter) as a positive sign of their overall recovery. But the opposite is also true: Any failure at even a small task will be viewed and recorded as a global step backward. The disappointment spreads like an oil slick, covering the patients, their therapy team, their family and friends. It's a madness-making system most of you will never experience. For someone stuck in this system, staying the same seems attractive precisely because of the combination of an all-hands-on-deck approach to their recovery—with so many people involved, watching and judging—and the trauma of their own significant disappointment regarding dreams of being self-sufficient and successful.

This is one reason I believe that issues of motivation and functioning are often misdiagnosed in my field. Though mainly identified as symptoms of mental illness, they are often—maybe most often—the effects of how we treat these behaviors.

I believe my clients are often far more preoccupied with controlling the expectations of others than are people who are not exposed to the often well-meaning surveillance these clients endure. Therapeutic settings, so focused on change, are fertile ground for a preoccupation with expectations. But none of us are immune to such concerns.

All of us, in different ways and to different degrees, try to control expectations as we set out toward personal change, shielding ourselves from the dangers of excessive expectations—whether our own, those of others, or both.

In fact, I believe that a lot of behaviors people exhibit when they are resisting a personal challenge, which we typically interpret as a matter of their innate character (they're lazy, depressed, anxious, obstinate, lack grit or resilience), are often the result of seriously spirited roles they're playing in order to control expectations.

I consider myself an expert on this phenomenon. Not because of research, my study of the literature, or my own professional observations, but because of my own formative personal experiences.

Lights, Camera, *In*action: Controlling Expectations

THE OUTSIDER

I grew up in the 1960s and '70s in a Southern California college town. The town had its proverbial "two sides," marked less by class than by lifestyle. One side of town was populated by professors and students, most of whom were part of the counterculture.

On the other side of town lived professionals who commuted into Los Angeles for work. I attended an experimental public grade school on the counterculture side of town, one in which teachers tried all kinds of creative ways to engage and teach kids, abandoned grades, and often taught in a democratic way that favored individual strengths. I attended junior high in the professionals part of town, a school like any suburban public school: hierarchical, teaching to the test, using the Scantron form and the dreaded Blue Book essay, all measured, of course, by grades.

I exceled in my grade school, exhibiting everything my experimental school cherished: creativity, outside-the-box thinking, eagerness to learn through new modes and methods. In fact, as I look back (lovingly, mostly) at this school, I can now perceive a hidden prejudice there. My guess is that the straitlaced students, the ones who wanted to just learn from the book, were probably ignored a bit, respected but not stars. I, on the other hand, was a star. I couldn't read well, nor could I spell worth a damn, and I found math impossible. I daydreamed a lot, and I couldn't seem to get my desk (turned, with the teacher's permission, into a fort) organized. But I handed in the best graphically creative book reports, took the leads in school plays, and even designed and built—with the help of my teacher and his hippie friends—a giant inflatable dragon large enough for people to walk inside. My feeling at that time was that life was literally in my hands. I felt almost magically self-efficacious. A flick of the wrist and everything was at my command. When I graduated to junior high, that feeling ended abruptly.

All the expectations at my new junior high played to my weaknesses. I was disoriented. It was culture shock. I cringe even today, remembering the first time I handed in a book report. I spent hours on a collage portrait of the book *The Outsiders*, only for the teacher to haul me aside after class and angrily ask, "What's *this*?"

It was a humiliating time, made more painful by being identified by school counselors as suffering from a learning disability. Deemed defective in learning at an age in life when learning was the central societal expectation for my cohorts, I felt like a broken piece of equipment on an assembly line of perfectly manufactured ones. Going to school each day was like being a visitor in a strange land, where I had no map and didn't speak the language. I felt helpless, lost. Shame set in. Since my sense of ostracism stung most when I was criticized for trying to learn or express myself the way I did so successfully in grade school, I put those seemingly childish things away and tried my best to color inside the lines. The problem was that I didn't have the brain for painting-by-numbers learning. I just wasn't wired that way. So even my attempts to keep my once-lauded talents in the shadows by conforming to a new culture of learning got me noticed in exactly the same negative light I was trying to avoid. I started giving up, before even trying, since I couldn't stand the idea that my best efforts would end in failure. And even though I was offered a significant amount of educational support from the school—like after-school tutoring and some special education classes in lieu of mainstream ones—my grades plummeted even further. I was caught in a vicious cycle: I wasn't trying to learn anymore, and so I appeared to my teacher and myself as someone more hopelessly disabled than I actually was.

With no perceivable way to win, I did what sociologists[6] tell us most people do when they are labeled an outsider: I internalized stigma. "I'm learning disabled" became a way to explain myself to myself and to others. My life ahead looked bleak, but at least I had a way to explain my poor performance as something other than such moral failings as a lack of discipline or laziness. And in some ways, the "learning disabled" role worked for me, lowering the expectations of my teachers and controlling my own aspirations with their potential for triggering another fall into failure. "Learning disabled" became part of my identity—but only part.

I started smoking pot. Even though I smoked weed minimally—maybe once or twice a week—I played the part of the stoner on campus. If I was going to feel like a loser, I might as well assume the persona of one who *chooses* not to try because it's cool. That persona added some balance of inclusion to an identity based on stigma. I wasn't just hopelessly broken, I was also opting out; the cool kid, hanging out with the other cool kids, snickering at all the squares.

Those were my ways of presenting myself in junior high, two "negative identities," in the words of the famous psychologist Erik Erikson.[7] Born from a lack of positive alternatives, I took on the negative ones of a disabled stoner, slipping into the costume of one or the other, depending on the immediate threat I faced.

Underneath all the cool, and behind my pronouncements about being disabled, was a morose sense that I was not capable of making my life work. I would lie in my bed at night staring into the dark, feeling a terrified sense of helplessness. I had once believed the world was in my hands. I could make my future what I wanted, just like when I made that dragon. I now felt that confident belief was seriously wrong. Meanwhile, I guarded against any further experiences of shameful disappointment by lowering my own expectations about myself as well as the expectations of the people around me. The way to do that was to portray myself—the stoner and the special-needs kid—as a buzzed and broken marionette with no ability or ambition of my own.

I'm sure that the effects of the social traumas from this time are why I grapple today with issues related to disorganization: both the shame of being disorganized, with its strong hint of being defective, and the struggle—caused by fear of hope, I'm sure—to get my act together and *just do it*, i.e., organize my office. I look at that office and my emotions flash back (subtly, mind you) to that sense of complete ineptitude and brokenness I felt in junior high. But still, even though it feels lousy to look at that office, I tend not to organize it, just like I didn't try to raise any expectations in myself and in others about my performance when I was twelve. Instead, I lay low.

I'm also convinced that my brush with stigma and ostracism, the wound of a spoiled and tainted conception of myself, and my resulting attempts to lower the expectations of others, informed my choice much later to work with people who have experienced these sorts of negative societal events and their injuries in ways much more extreme than my own. I'm positive it's the core reason I focus my work on helping people recover from the ravages of these experiences.

Like my clients, each day back then, when I was giving up before trying, playing roles that any success would expose as fraudulent, I missed out on the very thing that might have lifted my shame: small, incremental, inspiring successes, so important to building hope and faith. Using the supports from the school, I would have been a C student; in no way a star pupil, just average. But with those grades, I likely would have built confidence to aim higher and achieve more.

I was afraid, however, of taking the steps that would ultimately make me less fearful. Anxious about "there's no reason you can't," I was in a real conundrum: The action I needed to take in order to build my faith and then engage my motivation was also the action I most wanted to avoid.

When you attempt to direct expectations downward, you're caught in a catch-22. Every move that might help build your faith is also a move that makes your action appear less puppetlike, and more like an improvisational one-person show.

So how do you prime the pump? How do you create enough achievement to build aspiration and faith, when achievements inevitably make you anxious about overly raising expectations?

Sometimes it still takes a little theater, and maybe even a little espionage and manipulation to get there.

Look, here I am, writing these words right now, engaged in the very craft I'm supposedly defective in: the thing a stoner or dyslexic should never be expected to do.

I'm convinced now that my negative identities were my battery dock: a way to preserve my hope when faith was out of reach.

Sometimes you have to fake it 'til you make it.

THE REGENERATIVE ENERGY OF FAKING IT

"Do. Don't think, don't hope. Do . . . Do. Act. Don't think, act. Eye on the ball."[8] That's an excerpt from a speech by John Kennedy, not the U.S. president, but the Australian footballer and coach, as he famously pushed his team to focus only on their performance as players and not on the fact that they were miserably losing the game. In that speech, Kennedy perfectly captured the concept of "fake it 'til you make it," a term used in therapy and in general parlance for taking action toward a goal with blinders on regarding your distance to it. Another way to describe this concept is "acting as if," as the famous psychotherapeutic theorist Alfred Adler described it.[9] The idea is that action precedes motivation: The more you behave like you would if you were winning the game, the sooner your motivations will catch up.

As I look back at myself in junior high, I see how I was definitely "acting as if," but with a twist. In fact, I was doing just the opposite of acting like I was winning; I was "acting as if" I were broken and an intentional dropout in order to prime the pump of my motivation.

Remember Jim, who experienced a disabling anxiety after a

car accident involving his son? He ingeniously found a means to change while keeping the expectations of others low, by faking it.

"TWO"

Jim attended a group I ran in a day treatment program for people diagnosed with mood disorders. I would ask members to rate their mood on a scale from 1 to 10, 1 being utterly disabling depression and 10 being no depression. Each week, Jim would report his mood as a 2. Considering what Jim had been through—the accident, the loss of his home, marriage, and job—that low rating made sense. However, although he would report a 2 each week, I secretly knew a different story. I was the case manager for a couple of women in the program. Both women were members of a church Jim also attended. Both reported remarkable changes in Jim's behavior, things he didn't tell us in group. "Jim's running the coffee hour after services." "Jim asked us to help him decorate his new apartment." "Jim spoke in church today." "Jim got a job." "Jim and his wife might get back together." Jim was clearly improving. But in group, he continued to report that rating of 2. Finally, he stopped showing up, and he never returned. But I heard about him from my confidantes: he continued improving.

My guess is that Jim needed a way to improve without raising the expectations of the people most directly focused on him changing. He didn't want us to know he changed, because he didn't want us to see him taking charge and thus expect more out of him. So "my mood is at level 2" was a cover story that protected him while he made changes.

Smart move.

Jim was playing possum. He needed to lie low while nurturing and fortifying his driving forces of hope and faith in the face of a powerful restraining force about his accountability. If he boldly moved forward, his actions seen in the clear light of day, the restraining force of exposing himself as an accountable actor would overwhelm him. But if he could hide the fact that he was actually engaging his driving forces, he could build enough muscle to keep moving.

I'm actually ambivalent about the concept of "acting as if" as it is typically used: the variant that coaches you to act *as if* you're successful before you are. I'm not sure a lot of us can act as if we've already arrived at a goal when we haven't. For most of us, when we're not motivated, we're . . . um . . . *not motivated.* Acting as if we are motivated requires that we pretend there are no restraining forces holding us back, or that we are doing things to protect ourselves when we stay the same. That effort at pretending, the hiding who we are and where we are, seems like hiding sadness and fear behind a fake happy face.

On the other hand, sometimes you have to just do it.

Take my friends Susan and Jack. Susan is a psychotherapist, and Jack is a stand-up comedian who now dedicates his time to helping people in recovery from addictive habits. Both Susan and Jack are individuals in recovery who credit Alcoholics Anonymous as their central means of recovering. "Fake it 'til you make it" is a slogan used in AA. For Susan and Jack, this particular way of approaching change was the most helpful idea—in fact, a lifeline—when they first decided to get sober.

DON'T FUCKING DRINK

At their first meetings, they were desperate, disoriented, and needed direction. Says Susan, "The slogans 'One day at a time,' 'Think,' 'Easy does it,' 'Just for today'—along with posters of the twelve steps and the twelve traditions—were plastered all over the walls of the AA meetings. Honestly, I didn't pay them much mind at first. All I knew was that if I didn't drink, I would eventually feel better. I would be able to possibly refocus and maybe start over.

My life was a mess and instead of thinking about what a fuckup I was, I was told that if I didn't drink or drug today, I was a success. I was assured that if I worked with the program my life would get better. I was told that my best thinking is what landed me in a mess and that the steps would help to fix my thinking. I suppose that's why I followed what I was told: simply 'I'll feel and think better.'"

Jacks says something similar about his first days in AA: "My first sponsor was this really tough guy, a biker. His words were the ones that kept me from drinking at the beginning: *'Don't fucking drink.'* That was his answer to just about everything. Had a bad day? *Don't fucking drink.* Felt I deserved to take a break? *Don't fucking drink.* Wanted to let loose? *Don't . . . fucking . . . drink.* The solution was in there, a tiny bit more than I wanted to be drunk. *Don't fucking drink.* If you don't drink, you'll figure it out."

The path to Susan's and Jack's current and enduring sobriety, and very likely the reason they are still alive today, started with marching orders they followed as if they had no other choice. Once they got some time under their belts, however—incrementally raising their aspirations one day at a time—their commitment to sobriety became something they were authoring. "Once I was sober for a while," says Susan, "I started feeling and thinking better, albeit I was wobbly at first. Once my thinking cleared up I was able to plan ahead with more confidence." Says Jack, "I don't have cravings to use anymore: really, just fleeting thoughts. Over time I built a defense against the urges, and I didn't need to hear the slogans anymore. But it took following the ideas, over and over again—yeah, 'faking it'—to get me there."

Susan and Jack engaged in a spirit of seriousness—lowering expectations by playing possum—in order to reach a place in which they could assume accountability for their behavior. They temporarily postponed their recognition that they were deciders in their fate, in order to get to a point where they could accept this existential fact.

That's a kind of "fake it 'til you make it" I can get behind. When you follow orders, nothing is expected of you except following the orders. That's an awful approach to life in general—it's harmful for your own development—and we have irrefutable historical evidence that "just following orders" has horrific consequences for humanity. But "acting as if" you lack autonomy can be just the thing you need when you are insecure, want to move toward personal change, but need the incremental and inspiring small successes in order to build your sense of self-efficacy. When you're crushed by worry about disappointing yourself or others, it's not a bad thing to let yourself feel like you're controlled by an outside force. In fact, it may be your only way to prime the pump for action, from which you can then gain enough faith in yourself to look at your accountability head-on.

Sometimes you have to play the puppet in order to become more real.

CHAPTER 8

THE MIRROR OF CHANGING

Not everything that is faced can be changed, but nothing
can be changed until it is faced.

—James Baldwin

- #6: Staying the same protects you from seeing where
  you are.

Peter and the Undertow

The first time I meet Peter, on an overcast day at my office in
coastal Southern California, I like him immediately. A lanky,
good-looking kid in his midtwenties, he sits across from me in
my office wearing a surfer's tan, a tank top, checkered Quick-
silver shorts, and Birkenstocks. He's relaxed, friendly, exhibiting a
social ease I've never had and always coveted. In our first session,
Peter explains that he has come to therapy because "I just can't get
myself going in my life."

The story Peter tells me begins at a time in his life when his
passions and talents were aligned with what he did at work. In

fact, he was living a rather perfect work/life existence, one most people are rarely afforded. It was a time for him of significant faith in himself.

After high school, Peter spent a year traveling down to Central and South America to surf. He'd planned to go straight to college after his year abroad, but things were so much fun during his surfing trip that Peter didn't complete his applications. When he returned to the States, he was lucky enough to find a job at a nearby aquarium, giving tours to school groups. This was a coveted position most often filled by a recent college graduate.

Peter was as good with kids as he was with adults. His supervisor at the aquarium loved having Peter on board and took him under her wing, often inviting him to senior staff meetings, after-work parties, and even asking for his help with her research. Impressed by his abilities and confidence at such a young age, the staff at the aquarium dubbed him "the Boy Genius." Peter was in just the right place for that step-by-step fueling of inspiration described by Lewin and self-efficacy described by Bandura.

By the time college application deadlines loomed again, Peter decided to take another year off. He was now twenty, doing the work of someone beyond his years. He felt like he was further along in life than his friends in college. And his daily life felt deep and meaningful. "One more year" became one more. And then another.

The last delayed year became a tipping point for Peter, one during which the impressive heights he had reached as a teen working in the world of adult professionals would lead to a humiliating descent. Now twenty-two, Peter was losing the mantle of "Boy Genius." His performance with the occupational challenges he impressively mastered at nineteen now seemed age-appropriate.

His gang of friends from high school was now graduating college, and Peter felt uneasy about himself and his status in the world. He hated this new feeling of being sidelined and badly wanted to escape it. But he couldn't chart a plan that would diminish his sense of being inadequate, inferior to others, and even incapable of creating an adult life. He felt stuck, *incomplete*, and a fool for delaying his college applications. Counterfactuals set in: *Why didn't I just get those applications in? I would be so much further along if I did!* Peter began to wonder if the people around him were also noticing his lack of progress.

The aquarium had a supplementary tuition program, and his supervisor eagerly offered to help Peter access funds from the program so he could take classes in preparation for going back to college. Her offer stung a bit, however. Once able to handle the toughest feedback from others, Peter interpreted his supervisor's offer as a critical comment about his lack of professional progress. But he also knew that taking a class or two would show others that he was moving forward.

Although known for his efficiency and timeliness, Peter was noticeably hesitant to fill out the paperwork for tuition reimbursement. It consisted of only a few simple forms, but he approached it as a mark of his failure, a sign that he was well behind his friends. After considerable nudging by his supervisor, Peter finally completed the paperwork and enrolled in a college extension course, an introduction to marine biology.

In a class of retirees, high school students looking to burnish their transcripts, and hobbyists, Peter stood out. The professor turned to him often during class discussions, treating him almost like a peer, the one professional in a sea of amateurs. His success in the class bolstered Peter's confidence considerably. But he was on shaky ground, feeling on top of the world though winning at a game well below his talents and experience.

That fall, Peter requested applications from a few colleges. But he barely opened the envelopes that arrived. That feeling he'd had of a slow resistant slog when he first attempted to fill out the tuition reimbursement paperwork at work now felt like a hardened, un-movable wall. He enrolled in another extension course that spring.

Peter again did well in this beginners' class. Even though the material was still way below his competence, he talked a lot about it with his supervisor, parents, friends, and roommates, proudly demonstrating his grasp of the subjects, and expounding his own theories.

Peter was never one to brag, so his new boastfulness felt un-comfortable to him. Yet he couldn't seem to stop it. One day, af-ter he lectured at length to his boss on marine life, she impatiently stopped him midsentence. "Look, Peter, you're great. But you're telling me stuff I learned way back in college. I really wish you'd think more about attaining a degree and then putting some of these theories into action."

Her words were a blow to Peter. He could feel himself fall-ing from a high horse of his own foolish imagination. "Am I a slacker?" he asked himself. "Is this how things are always going to be?" He knew a lot of aging surfers in his town, how they bragged incessantly about their next "big idea" between hits of pot. Was he like them, braggadocios about being the head of a class filled with a bunch of high school students?

Peter felt a new urgency about college. Reaching the goal of being a marine biologist now represented more than a career for him; it was a status Peter desperately wanted, a way of distancing himself from the sad, self-deluding, aging surfers and catching up with his achieving friends.

Late that fall, Peter again focused on college applications, tar-geting ten schools.

But once he read the requirements for his major in many of the best universities on his list, Peter became dismayed by the basic level of the required courses. They were all so simple and rudimentary, less interesting than the extension course surveys, and almost like high school. They felt so distant from a future career. *I'm way ahead of this stuff already,* he thought. *I'm twenty-four years old, and I'm taking Intro to Marine Life? What do I tell people? What do I tell myself?* And then, as you might predict by now, *the blaming, demoralizing counterfactuals: If I had just done things earlier, I would be in a career right now. I should have taken all the effort I put in those stupid classes and just applied!*

Humiliation taking over, Peter hit that now familiar barrier blocking his motivation. Each box he completed in the application was another offensive reminder that he was so many years behind. Returning to college meant being equal to kids six years his junior. It was a painful image to reconcile with the vision he'd built of himself as someone *already* in the profession.

That feeling persisted as he tried to write his personal statement. He wrote about his year abroad, his time at the aquarium, the exciting classes he took. But on paper, these events looked so average—maybe even below average. *I look like a slacker,* thought Peter, *as if I can't get my act together.* After finishing a few paragraphs, he set the personal statement aside.

Now Peter waded into the general application. It came with a "Request for Transcripts." When he got to his high school transcript, he took a break. *Is this what I've achieved?* he thought. *Sure, I did well in the extension courses, but the bulk of my education was in high school. I come off like a kid.* Peter decided to get some lunch in town. When he returned, he couldn't get his concentration back. He put things aside for another day. He put it aside the next day too. And the next . . .

Peter missed the application deadline for three of the colleges. He called my office the next morning to make an appointment.

Peter and I meet a few days later. He engages seriously in our session, talking about "this weird feeling like I'm stuck in some mud" when he works on his college applications. He's just as earnest the next time we meet, telling me, "I have this embarrassed feeling like I'm a fraud," and complaining how this sense of embarrassment holds him back. On our third session, however, he seems a bit different, more relaxed than I've seen before, but also a bit distracted. Peter cancels our next meeting.

He never returns.

It's not a new experience for me to have people unexpectedly drop out of treatment after the first few sessions. I figure Peter is not ready to change. I hope he finds his way forward, but I have my doubts. Dropping out of therapy seems just another sign of his refusal to work on the forces holding him back from making the change he wants in his life. Sadly, I too can picture him becoming like those older surfers. There is something particularly frustrating in Peter's story. Here is a person with real promise—he has proven skills, acknowledged by people he respects (such as his supervisor), in a domain he truly values. He has identified a professional goal—marine biology—that fits with his values and aptitudes. All he has to do is start where everyone has to start—at square one. Yet for Peter, this starting place feels like a hurt to his self-image. He was the Boy Genius; now he is the Older Freshman. He balks at taking the necessary steps, and as a result never makes the big leap toward an ambitious and fulfilling career. And the longer Peter puts things off, the more humiliated he feels and the more stuck he becomes in this humiliation.

Peter's situation captures a central dilemma of change. Change demands that you look directly at where you are in life, despite the fact that it often feels lousy to do so.

Reason Not to Change #6:
Staying the same protects you from seeing where you are.

Personal change requires that you assess what you must change, taking measure of yourself in the moment, and thus have the uncomfortable realization that something about you remains incomplete.

If I decide to clean my office, I first need to admit that its messiness is a problem of my own making. To clean things up, in other words, I confront the mess I made. This dynamic in change is unavoidable.

When you move forward, you're acting on hope. When you muster enough hope to move forward, two things occur: 1) you appoint something as important, and 2) you see that you're lacking this important thing. If you don't want to feel the experience of something important lacking in your life (fitness, sobriety, love), you're going to have to stay the same. Conversely, you can only change if you are willing to look at something important that is lacking in your life. But what's lacking often makes you feel shame, since shame—this experience of being botched and tainted—exists always in comparison to some ideal of what is unbroken and clean, and you've set yourself up with that ideal by appointing importance to the goal at the end of the road you now travel.

Think about your own experiences of personal goals. Dieting, for example: When did you feel most fat? The day you noticed your pants didn't fit, or the day you started your diet? I'm guessing the latter. Sure, you were painfully stung when you noticed the change in your gut, but the sting only stayed with you if you moved toward dieting. If you didn't choose the diet route, it was likely because of excuses you made that lowered the pain of that original realization: *Too much salt at dinner last night*, *You bloat when you travel*, *My jeans shrank*. However, if you embarked on a diet, thus appointing losing weight as more important to you than it was before you started dieting, you became hyperaware of the thinness you lacked, you saw more clearly the distance between you now and your ideal weight, and you were unable to make excuses. Thus, the diet made the pain of facing something you didn't like about yourself worsen and last longer.

It's telling, and downright poetic, that the word "fathom" means both a penetrating come-to-Jesus moment of realizing something in its entirety, and is also a technical term for a measurement of depth. You're more likely to fathom your problems when you try to fix them because fixing them requires that you measure the distance between you and your goals. For this reason, the only way to reach your goals is to find a way to bear looking at where you are—blemishes and all—in relation to where you want to be. That's why most treatments for behavioral issues begin with the idea that a person must candidly evaluate her problem in order to overcome it. It's no coincidence, for example, that the first event at an Alcoholics Anonymous meeting involves people identifying themselves as alcoholics: "My name is Jane and I'm an alcoholic."

That kind of direct admission or confrontation with your problem, however, can also be demotivating. Like Peter, the would-be marine biologist, you stop any attempt at making the change you want if the necessary look in the mirror causes too much shame. That means that in order to free your energies to make change, you have to do something about the shame. And that involves finding a way to be more self-accepting.

THE CURIOUS PARADOX OF CHANGE

"The curious paradox," wrote Carl Rogers,[1] "is that when I accept myself just as I am, I can change." It's a "dialectic"—a tension between two seemingly opposite poles—that is at the core of all change, according to Marsha Linehan[2], the creator of a Buddhist-informed therapy called dialectical behavior therapy. Linehan, whose work is primarily focused on treatment for individuals diagnosed as suffering from what's called borderline personality disorder, believes that all kinds of suffering in our lives emerge from our inability to synthesize two or more seemingly conflicting thoughts. But she rightly marks the particular dialectic between self-acceptance and change as the core to every struggle to alter one's behavior.

Rogers, Linehan, and others come to very similar conclusions regarding the means to break free of the inherent tension between the need to accept yourself and the need to change: a nonjudgmental approach (that's why Rogers's humanistic approach is based on "unconditional positive regard," and why Linehan preaches the Buddhist ideal of "radical acceptance"). While my approach doesn't quite put judgment aside (I believe there are many behaviors we judge as "bad" that we can actually judge as altruistic but screwed up), and I've never in my own life been able to engage in the kind of pure Buddhist consciousness Linehan prescribes, I do believe that the concept of the force field of change involves reaching similar conclusions: You can be doing the best you can right now, while also striving to do better.

In the Lewinian "between space"[3] that spans where you are and where you want to be, the site of your current behavior exists exactly at the meeting point between driving forces toward change and restraining forces that push back against them. That means the balance between these countervailing forces largely determines your behavior. But just because you're doing the best you can at this very moment doesn't imply that nothing can change. Instead, it indicates that things need to shift in this field for you to want to move forward. That can mean that you find, or are shown, ways to build your own upward forces of hope and faith—through therapy, getting good at a hobby, spending more time with friends—or can decrease the power of restraining forces by succeeding more at other things in your life that will decrease your fear of hope—falling in love, getting on track with goals other than the one causing you so much consternation.

Decades ago, I witnessed a person conduct this kind of shifting of his field in a brilliantly intentional way, one that forced him to look directly in the mirror at his situation.

His name was Eric.

ERIC AND THE "IDIOT CARDS"

I knew Eric in the mid-1980s. During the day he worked as a master carpenter at a television studio in West Hollywood. He was a drummer in a punk band at night, roaming the clubs of Sunset Junction, Echo Park, and downtown L.A. Eric was a very cool guy. A leader, and someone people really respected in the underground music scene. He was a chain-smoker, and cigarettes burnished his image. Hanging precariously from Eric's lips, they were a permanent fixture, just enough spit between his cigs and his lip to keep them there. I remember him now, jumping out of his van for a gig, unloading equipment from the back, pushing everything up ramps and down hallways to the stage, a cigarette always there for the ride, bouncing lightly against his chin.

Eric was married, and his wife had recently given birth to their first child. His life was changing. It was time to grow up, and he desperately wanted to quit smoking. For the first time in his life he saw smoking as a serious problem rather than as a romantic prop, and wanted to find a way to recover from what he now saw as a dangerous addiction. He tried and failed at every intervention suggested by the experts (patches, gum, hypnosis, a smoking cessation group), inevitably finding himself back to the habit, feeling lousy and shameful about his inability to stop. That shame only grew when his wife regularly detected the smell of tobacco on his clothes, or caught him in their small backyard sneaking a smoke. She adored Eric, and was nothing but kind when she discovered his failings, but her gentleness only made him feel worse.

Finally, Eric came up with an ingenious idea. One day, he asked a bandmate to take a picture of him smoking. For the photo,

Eric did everything possible to look uncool, bending his head in a way to show off his slight double chin, sticking his stomach out, looking anxious and upset, his typically flawless pompadour ruffled into an ugly nest. Eric picked the worst of these pictures, wrote "Idiot" in giant red Sharpie letters across it, then took it to Kinko's and made a hundred copies, some small enough to fit in a pocket, others enlarged to portrait-size 8 x 10s. He taped the larger photos on the inside of the front and back doors of his house, on the dashboard of his van, even—with permission from the owner—on the exit doors and above the urinals of his favorite local bar.

Eric handed the smaller photos to everyone he knew, telling them to hold up the "idiot cards" whenever someone saw him smoking, making moves in preparation for the deed, or following suspicious activity, such as when the smell of tobacco emanated from his clothes. He warned people that he would likely become irritated with them when they held up the cards, and asked that they ignore his attitude.

Eric's friends, workmates, and acquaintances had a lot of fun with Eric's smoking-cessation plan. It became a sort of performance. Even though the photo of Eric portrayed him as an "idiot," he only gained the respect of those around him. Eric was acting boldly and doing something both creative and courageous by generating an audience for his own failings. It was also rather lovable, this willingness to expose the part of himself that acted like an "idiot."

The plan worked, and rather quickly—just a couple of weeks and he had quit smoking. Another month, and the idiot cards and posters were a thing of the past.

In Eric's previous attempts to quit, his attitude toward smoking was like a dentist's toward a rotten tooth: a direct intervention on the problem. In the new method, Eric was more like a farmer improving the nutrients in the Lewinian field around him. He did so in at least four ways:

1. *Eric changed how he dealt with the inevitable problem of facing his current position in relation to his goal.* By creating "idiot cards" he shifted from the dry and hardened position of a spirit of seriousness, in which his problem was out of his hands as "an addiction to cigarettes," thus requiring medical and medical-like interventions, to a spirit of playfulness in which the clay of change was in his hands, damply ready to mold. As a result, his smoking habit was less the source of constant shame than it was something pliable and manageable. By approaching the problem playfully Eric was also able to significantly increase the number of times he was willing to look himself in the mirror. That led to the second way Eric changed the field around him.

2. *Eric created multiple points of reflection on his problem that were more palatable than his self-image during prior attempts to stop smoking.* Everywhere Eric went he confronted a self-generated reminder that he was an idiot for smoking. He could bear this reminder because it was done in a playful way, by himself, to himself, for himself. Shame thrives in hiding. Eric's tactic weakened the restraining force of shame by bringing his behavior into the light of day, but in a less defamatory way than when reflections on his behavior occurred only because he either engaged in a new attempt, failed to quit, or was caught smoking. That fact leads to the third way Eric changed the field around him.

3. *Eric changed his habit by changing the way people observed his behavior.* He rewrote the script of "Eric Quitting Smoking,"

in other words. Prior to his invention of idiot cards, Eric mostly saw his failures to resist his habit as signs of weakness, and so he usually hid the fact that he was trying to quit. Inevitably, he would get caught by his wife and friends who knew about his new goal, and this would make him feel lousy and shameful. But now, with idiot cards as props in an improv he produced, Eric put on a new performance of himself—one less puppetlike, less a grim tug-of-war between nicotine and willpower, but instead one in which he was doing something heroic and endearingly vulnerable. Everybody was championing his effort, and this effort mostly generated in his audience a real admiration for him, while still reminding Eric that he was basically an idiot for smoking.

By creating his own form of street theater and seeing people take part in the thing he created, Eric made a different kind of mirror that combatted his own more shameful reflections. In this mirror, he was an effective individual making something happen in the interactions around him. That leads to the fourth way Eric changed what happened in his field

---

4. *Eric increased his experience of self-effectiveness (and thus his faith in himself) by taking charge of his problem and inventing his own solution for it.* Bandura, with his interest in self-efficacy, points out that being effective in one area can raise your overall sense of self-efficacy in others.[4] By taking his process for change into his own hands and seeing that the people around him were eager to engage in this process, Eric created secondary successes that boosted his confidence about conquering smoking. He gained greater faith in himself, in other words. The first time Eric resisted his urge to sneak

out of band practice for a smoke fueled his faith in his ability
to effectively manage his life. So did the second, third, and
fourth times he resisted smoking. If he had worn a nicotine
patch as his only means to quit, he might have felt some
sense of pride and some experience of greater effectiveness at
these moments, but nothing of the magnitude he felt when
he changed by following his own directions.

By making his own failures the source of play, and by gaining
the affection of those around him through his performance, Eric
found a key to unlock the dialectic of change: he discovered a
means to accept who he was in the moment in order to change
who he wanted to be. Those idiot cards served as both a sign that
he had to change, and also a symbol of his courage. He invented
a way to take a measure of himself and to measure his distance
from his goal, while simultaneously accepting that he had not yet
reached that goal.

It's been forty years since Eric's successful DIY intervention
on his smoking. Eric's story sticks with me because of its whimsical heroism and the true effectiveness of invention in personal
change. Like the child of Atlas and Amy Poehler, Eric stretched
his arms around his entire problem field, and moved it—one idiot
card at a time. I also think it imprinted on my memory back then
because it represented a positive opposite to how I was behaving.
At the time of Eric's idiot cards, I was performing in a dramaturgy much more complex than his, in which I too was managing
the mirrors around me. But the aim and result of my performance
were quite different.

Unlike Eric, who implemented his own plan targeting how
he dealt with moments of shame, making each of these moments
the subject of humor and kindness, I took a route most of us
take—sometimes grandly, sometimes in small spurts—in which

I avoided shame by performing as if I had already arrived at my goal.

PANTS PAINTERS, POSING, AND THE NARCISSISTIC DEFENSE

I lived in downtown L.A. with a couple of friends during the epoch of the idiot cards. We were very minor players in the burgeoning art scene there. My loftmates and I would often hang out at Gorky's, an all-night Russian café filled with artists and performers, and people watch. We became skilled at distinguishing posers from the true artists.

The latter group had a subtle style, a sense of color and pattern in their dress that appeared effortless. The former group often shared one particular "tell": paint splatters on their pants or shoes. "Just popping in for some kasha, then back to my work!" their Blockx—stained Levi's proclaimed. We called them the "pants painters."

Of course, my small group of twentysomethings, hunched together at our little table—Jeff, later a librarian; Mike, now a lawyer; and me, the sociology PhD—were also putting on our own performances for one another. Playing grown-up, we shared the unearned identities of snarky veterans of the art world, looking down our noses at the fakes. It was a brilliant pose we achieved, actually: wannabes assuming the role of insiders looking down at the posers.

My guess is that most of the pants painters went the way of my friends and me, while the more subtly dressed artists likely stayed with their careers.

Speaking from my own experience, I know my posing was a way to quickly escape feelings of shame that I was going nowhere (just a new version of me and my fellow stoners in junior high). Returning to our loft, the modest practice of my craft felt like an insult to my grandiose sense of myself as an already established creative person at the café, sipping tea, slurping borscht, and insulting the pants painters. The problem wasn't the natural tension between where I was and where I wanted to be that Lewin points out is so important to motivate us; it was between where I was and *the destination I pretended I'd already reached.*

I badly needed the sense that I was already making it to cover the always threatening shame that I wasn't.

Here's the problem with those thoughts: The threat of losing my experience of myself as an established artist made it impossible to engage in the actual work I needed to do to reach my goal. It felt too shameful to practice my craft, to learn the rudiments, to go to square one, since it didn't match the person in my self-scripted performance.

I faced two alternative ways of being, both fragile, but untenable: the shame that I was far from my ideal or the grandiose pose that I already reached it. Psychoanalysts have a term for the big-headed side of my vacillation between shame and pretense: narcissistic defense.

You don't have to be a full-blown narcissist to deploy this defense, and most of us use it at some time. When you engage in a narcissistic defense you are protecting your pride from shame by viewing yourself as exceptional. It's a brittle kind of defense, since it's often based on assumptions about yourself that don't hold up. When they don't hold up, they tend to exacerbate your shame.

Recall Peter, the would-be marine biologist. He experienced that kind of cycle between the heights of unearned pride and the depths of shame. Peter wished to feel as proud of himself as he did when he once held the crown of Boy Genius of the aquarium, and he wanted to feel that pride constantly. So by comparing himself to others in his extension course, he envisioned himself as having already reached the status of marine biologist. But Peter's pride was hurt when his supervisor suggested he work on getting into college, and when he actually sat down and attempted to fill out the college applications. Peter, in other words, used the fantasy of having already arrived at his goal as a kind of narcotic for the pain of being far from it. But when the narcotic inevitably wore off, he felt worse about his situation than if he had never taken it.

"I have this embarrassed feeling like I'm a fraud." Peter's comment to me captures the relationship between shame and our fall from pride unearned by actual achievement. We have a word for this brittle kind of pride: *hubris*.

In regard to personal change, hubris is the prideful belief you can skip the line of humbling effort—the anonymous progression from neophyte to master—but instead reach your destination immediately. Peter tried to skip that line. He engaged in a hubristic sense of himself by seeing his achievements in extension courses that taught information he already knew as a sign he had already arrived at his goal of full-fledged scientist. That's what I was trying to do by posing as the bureau chief of pants painting: creating a fantasy in which I had already achieved what I wanted to achieve without putting in the necessary and at times humbling effort. When Peter and I discovered we couldn't reach our goals by fantasizing or pretending that we had reached them, we felt a pang of demotivating disappointment and a resulting shame. That's the rapid dance of the narcissistic defense, a back-and-forth between shame and hubris, and hubris and shame. It's spurred when you measure the distance between your present actual self and your future ideal self.

You can get out of this frustrating, anxiety-filled dance by denying who you are, where you are. The denial will feel good. It will also prevent you from changing. So, as the proponents of self-acceptance tell us, you need to find a way to keep looking at yourself without taking flights into grandiose fantasies or falling into the depths of shame.

Change entails a particularly human strength, one unevenly distributed among us and often difficult to tap: enduring humility.

That's what garnered so much respect from Eric's audience, and helped Eric stay focused on his goal of quitting smoking.

THE MEDIATING STRENGTH OF HUMILITY

Humility is hubris's opposite and an antidote to shame. The absence of humility leads to narcissistic behavior.

If hubris is about grandiose flights of fancy, humility is about groundedness; its Latin root, *humilitas*, means "from the ground." Humility keeps you from getting too big for your britches, and prevents your head from swelling. But that doesn't mean this emotion keeps you small in your aspirations or stooped in self-abasement. When you truly have humility, you can marvel at yourself, love yourself, and find joy in your talents. Like Eric and his idiot cards, you can admit to your weaknesses but also be ambitious about the goals you want to achieve. In fact, you can be ambitious because you can admit to your limits. Here, humility acts as ballast to your off-the-charts ideas about yourself, weighing you to the ground, connecting you to other humans, preventing you from drifting into your self-fantasies. It also protects you from too much shame, keeping your face out of the mud and your eyes on what you want.

It would have been impossible for Eric to create the idiot card performance if he were overcome with shame. He might, of course, have simply fantasized about all that sweet applause and reverence the stunt would have earned him; but he never would have pulled it off if focused only on this secondary gain. No, humility holds you down *and* lifts you up. It's the general acceptance of your faults that flows from humility that makes it not only a counterweight to exaggerated and unrealistic images of yourself, but also the gentle gust of self-acceptance. Perhaps that's the point: humility is not humiliation; it is genuine self-acceptance. Accepting who you are, where you are.

Mariners at sea, with no visible landmarks, must somehow navigate their way to their destinations. They can only do so by first locating exactly where they are at any given point. Humility provides that ability to self-orient. If you accept where you are, you have a point of reference to where you want to go. I call this orienting space the humility zone.

The Humility Zone

The Greek myth of Icarus is a remarkable parable about humility. Icarus's father, Daedalus, was a great craftsman. He knew the importance of precision and patience in producing something beautiful. He famously made wings for himself and for his son. But these wings were delicate. The wax holding them together would melt if the wings got near the sun, and the feathers would be ruined if moistened by the sea. So his fatherly warning to his son was to fly neither too high nor too low; to chart his course between the hubris of flying close to the sun and the shame of staying so close to earth that ocean spray would soak the beautifully crafted wings. Imploring Icarus to remain between sun and sea, he was asking his child to fly in the moderate space between pride and shame: the humility zone.

When you're able to reach the humility zone, you feel enough pride to keep going but not so much that you lose track of where you are in that tension between what you want and getting it; you feel modesty, but don't get discouraged by the image you see in the mirror. When you operate in this zone, you keep going forward because you're able to withstand the notion that you are incomplete, without depending on the narcissistic defense, with its inevitable seesaw between hubris and shame.

It's especially difficult to reach the humility zone when your faith in yourself is injured by disappointment. Peter is a perfect case in point. As he felt increasingly helpless about traveling the distance from where he was to where he wanted to be, he found it more and more difficult to stay in the humility zone, instead rapidly flying between the hubris of feeling like he'd already arrived at his goal and the crushing shame of knowing he was far from that goal. Already feeling incomplete as a person, the experience of his incompleteness poked at his shame every time he sat down to fill out that college application. And here's where Peter's inability to access humility led to pretzeled behaviors: because he was unable to accept himself as he was, he didn't complete what he needed to complete because he didn't want to feel incomplete. And to avoid the shame that he actually wasn't completing anything, Peter created scenarios in which he could superficially feel some sense of completeness (ones that would inevitably make him feel *incomplete* once the narcissistic bubble of premature self-completion was popped). Twisted like a salted Bavarian snack, right? But hardly abnormal.

Like me in the 1980s, Peter was engaged in a perpetual narcissistic loop that killed his motivation to reach important life goals. But it would be wrong to say that either of us lacked motivation. In fact, we both exhibited a lot of motivation, putting in extra effort to reach our goal of seeming like we'd already arrived. We were motivated. It's just that our goal was different than what it might have seemed. Our goal was to find a salve for our shame in the reflection in the eyes of that audience of which we were members.

Social psychologists call our orientation toward external validation extrinsic motivation, and the attainment of this validation an extrinsic goal. They contrast extrinsic goals and motivation with intrinsic ones: goals that bring their own satisfaction and meaning, independent of external rewards. Like Peter and me, when your wish to achieve extrinsic goals overpowers your wish to achieve intrinsic ones, you risk losing the motivation to reach the latter.

Intrinsic Versus Extrinsic Goals and the Drive for Self-Completion

An athlete who is driven to work harder at the gym because it makes her more proficient in a sport she loves is intrinsically motivated. She's not looking for accolades; she's looking to get better at something that brings her satisfaction. "Intrinsic goals," write Peter Schmuck, Tim Kasser, and Richard Ryan—leading thinkers on what's called self-determination theory—"are those which are inherently satisfying to pursue because they are likely to satisfy . . . psychological needs for autonomy, relatedness, competence and growth."[5] Intrinsic goals, in other words, are good-faith goals. They are about you, improving on you, because you are in charge of you. Intrinsic goals are the ones you aim for when you're flying in the humility zone.

Extrinsic goals typically emerge from a wish to solve the anguish of helpless insecurity through external rewards. These sorts of goals, write the self-determination theorists, "generally reflect an insecurity about oneself." They tend to be bad-faith goals that see the outside world as the primary place of confirmation. An athlete working extra hard in the gym because she wants to win a trophy is doing so because of extrinsic motivation. Extrinsic motivation, however, is not always as simple as a contractual exchange between some expected behavior and a reward. Often we are extrinsically motivated because we want to be seen in a more positive light by others. For the athlete, it's not only the trophy she wants, but the applause. It might also be her new status as a winner, someone at the top of her game. And here's the problem: *The other-orientation of an extrinsic goal can mess with your motivation toward intrinsic goals when you seek to change something about yourself.* This is especially true when the thing you want has to do with your identity.

THE SUBTLE MAGIC OF IDENTITY GOALS

Social psychologist Peter Gollwitzer and his colleagues at New York University call extrinsic goals that place a person in a new exalted status identity goals—in other words, goals that express how you identify yourself to others.[6] Clearly, career goals are identity goals ("I'm a doctor"), as can be the goal to master a hobby ("I'm a fly fisherman"). But changing a habit can also be an identity goal ("I'm a thin person"). Gollwitzer and his group studies the relationship between identity goals and motivation.

This group has a theory regarding the relationship between identity goals and their too-early completion, called self-completion theory. They believe that when a person jumps too quickly into an identity for it to be earned, they ruin the propelling tension needed for sustained motivation toward the achievement that will earn them this identity. *That means that if you have a subjective sense that you've already reached your goal before you truly have, you'll suffer a loss of motivation.* To put it in the language I've been using, Gollwitzer's group says that when you hubristically take on a status you haven't really achieved, you kill your ability to reach that status.

The self-completion theorists are Lewinian, and you can see the imprint of Lewin's thought in their ideas. Think about that just-right tension of pursuing a goal you hope to achieve. Your mind, bent on completion, sees the goal, thus sees something incomplete, and motivates you to get there. But if you tell yourself you've already arrived, that tension becomes slack, since you've talked yourself into believing things are complete as they are.

That's what was happening for Peter. He thought of himself as already arriving at the goal of marine biologist, an imagined identity as a person at the top of his profession. By hubristically placing himself on the other side of the finish line, he lost that Lewinian tension between where he actually was and where he wanted to go. His extrinsic goal was satisfied, in other words, and that satisfaction made him feel less motivated to reach his intrinsic one.

A lot of self-completion behavior has to do with what these thinkers call symbolic self-completion. Symbolic self-completion involves those little things you do or say to others that associate your behavior with a particular identity goal. When other people recognize these behaviors, they become like mirrors to you, reflecting that you're closer to the identity you want. That's why a newly minted PhD is more likely to display her diploma in a prominent place in her home or office, while the famous professor may not display it at all. She's putting on a play for that audience in which she is a member, looking for confirmation that she has indeed achieved this status. Her older colleague doesn't need that confirmation.

Peter's experience in his extension courses is an example of premature symbolic self-completion. For a moment in those classes, when the teacher treated him like a peer, he was able to perform for others in a way that made it seem as if he'd reached the status of marine biologist, had graduated college, and was a master in his field. These moments of symbolic self-completion were fleeting for Peter, however, only achievable in that class once a week. In other situations, like talking to his supervisor or filling out college applications, he couldn't find a willing audience for his performance. As a result, he suffered a major disappointment in failing to reach his extrinsic goal.

My performance at Peter's age—as the Critic of Pants Painters—was much more enduring and complete than his. I entered into the hubris zone and settled in. Sticking with my gang of critics, never getting too close to any real artist for fear I would be revealed, never really working on my art, I took on the full character of the person I wanted to be without doing the work associated with the person I was pretending to be.

My intrinsic goals had lost the battle with the extrinsic, self-completion goals. Every day I put on the costume of someone too authentic ever to dress up, applied makeup to look authentic, and played a character so superior that he could spot an inauthentic poser at the other end of a café in seconds—all of this to avoid the shame of looking at myself in the mirror and seeing how far I was from my goal.

My posing was extreme, but there's a little poser in all of us wanting to reach a sense of closure and completeness without putting in the effort to get there. In subtle ways, that internal poser often decides the fate of our intrinsic goals. It's a sneaky little devil, often invading our interactions with others unnoticed.

In fact, just *telling* people about your identity goals can diminish your motivation. You'd think that the more people you tell about your goals, the more likely you'd be to stick to them, since telling people supposedly makes you more accountable. But Gollwitzer's group argues that the opposite is true: Their research shows that the more you tell people about your goals, the *lower* your motivation goes. Sounds counterintuitive, right? Here's how it works: When you tell someone your intention, and they validate that they understand you are on the course to change, your brain—hungry to complete all discrepancies—has a tendency to believe you've already reached the goal. "Hey everybody, I'm on a diet!" mistranslates to "Hey, I'm thin!"

In a sense, when you tell someone something about your identity goal, you approximate your extrinsic goal. Telling someone "I'm on a diet" places you on the road to losing weight as your identity ("I'm a dieter"). By placing yourself on that road in the eyes of someone else, your extrinsic goal of feeling better about yourself as a person losing weight is somewhat satisfied. That means that the chance for just a little hubris—that sense of pride unearned—is always just a quick, magical sentence away. When you do that—escape the pain of measuring the distance between where you are and where you want to be—you loosen the tension so important to motivating you to move forward.

When your identity goals become your main motivator for change, they trip you up in another way that can actually make this tension too strained to bear. This was Peter's situation. He wanted to feel like a full-fledged marine biologist, yet every time he sat down to work on his college applications it was a reminder that he was very far from the identity he wanted. Because moving toward a career in this field felt further from him when he tried to get on the road to that career, and because he badly wanted to feel close to that goal, he lost motivation.

Peter's extrinsic motivation to achieve the experience of identity completion overrode his intrinsic motivations to achieve something just for its intrinsic value. Because his wish for external validation muffled the intrinsic worth of doing the day-to-day work of actually reaching his goals, and because he didn't attain the intrinsic reward that only comes when a task is completed, he became discouraged. To put it another way, the reward Peter sought of validation that he was a marine biologist couldn't be attained in one giant leap, so he found his situation unrewarding. He generated the hope-crushing experience of disappointment by feeling like he had arrived, then, in another crushing blow, realized he hadn't.

Like Peter, when you find ways to feel as if you've reached some site of completion when you haven't, you either loosen too much or tighten too much the painful but motivation-enhancing discrepancy between where you are now and where you want to be. To put it another way, when you lack the mediating force of humility, everything is disregulated in your life, and you move back and forth between two turbulent forces.

Bouncing between hubris and shame, in a world always offering a quick fix, the easy-access route to premature self-completion can thus become a vicious cycle.

John's efforts to diet illustrate how a person can get trapped in such a cycle and end up abandoning the idea of changing as the only way out.

BACK TO THE FUTURE WITH JOHN

According to the chart his doctor hands him, John is officially obese. He's crestfallen as he leaves the office. He's been here before, and he worked so hard to lose weight previously. And now he's back. *I'm such a fool*, he thinks. *How the hell am I going to do this again? How long am I going to have to bear being fat before things change?*

John is in the zone of shame. He wants to flee from this feeling, and that focuses his mind on only one impossible thing: the urgent need to *immediately* get thin. He's not humbly looking at his location in relation to his goal, since a vision of the long road ahead only adds to his anguish. In his panic, he's about to destroy the very thing that will get him where he wants: the motivating tension that can only occur when he's able to take a clear-eyed look at his location compared to his goal.

What the doctor told me, that's a wake-up call, John thinks on his car ride home. *It's the news I needed to finally force me to diet.* That thought makes John feel a little better. He calls his girlfriend from the car, telling her the news, quickly describing how he's ready for a good plan to lose weight: "It's a wake-up call, I'm telling you!" he says. His girlfriend congratulates him and suggests a diet book she hears is effective.

John is now a "dieter," and with a little symbolic self-completion under his belt he stops off at the bookstore and buys the diet book.

Back at his apartment, John sits down on the couch and begins reading the first chapter. He then empties his refrigerator and cupboards of all tempting and fattening foods. He goes to the grocery store, book in hand, and stocks up on healthier ones. Returning home, he puts away his groceries, then makes himself a low-carb meal, following a recipe from the diet book. While eating his dinner, he reads online stories of people who successfully stuck to this diet. He then calls his girlfriend to tell her how excited he is to begin the trek toward losing weight.

From the outside, John appears as if he's taking all the right steps, preparing in so many ways to begin his diet, and learning as much as he can about it. But within his earnest and somewhat frantic pursuit of this diet is also his attempt to claim an identity. He's putting on a play titled *John the Dieter* in which he is, for now, the only member of the audience, and also the actor onstage playing "the Dieter." For confirmation that he is, indeed, now "the Dieter," he calls his girlfriend and offers a brief synopsis of the play. Caught up, she now joins John in the audience.

By the end of the evening, John is feeling remarkably energized and optimistic. In fact, he's happier and more excited than before he entered the doctor's office. *Deep down, I knew I needed to lose weight again. Now I'm losing it!* Getting the book, emptying the cupboards, buying the right food, reading the success stories—all these activities consume John's time that evening and give him the sense that he's not only dieting, he is now a dieter. Playing the Dieter becomes a salve for John's shameful sense that he's fat. And it works in the shame department at least: John savors a sense of himself as already successful and thinner.

John wakes the next morning, planning to focus on making it through the official Diet Day One. He feels proud of himself as he eats his second prescribed meal. At noon, he goes to lunch in the cafeteria with his workmates and gets a salad. When he sits down at the table, they immediately notice his choice. He proudly tells them, "I'm on a diet!" thus inviting them to his "play." They all congratulate him. The pride John felt earlier in the day has morphed into something much stronger—true excitement that he is seriously on the way to reaching his goal. As he sits down in his cubicle, he can almost feel the pounds melting from his body. He loves this feeling and wants more of it.

John calls his girlfriend about their date that night, proudly reminding her that they need to pick a place with "healthy options." He hangs up, reflects on how disciplined he's being, and again feels his pride tick up a notch. At dinner, just as at lunch, John discusses his diet with his girlfriend, how things went that first day, and his strong commitment to keep going "this time."

Walking home that evening, John feels as if he's entered a time machine, transported to that glorious moment in the future when his doctor reviews his weight again and happily reports a perfect BMI. It's marvelous: a moment of great satisfaction. Now, his thoughts red hot with optimism, he sees himself as on the verge of his goal rather than only at the beginning. The tension between where he is not and where he wants to be, in other words, is hazardously slack.

John's optimistic vision of his future doesn't match the fact that he's only three quarters of the way through the first full day of his diet. Overnight he's gone from the depths of shame to the heights of unearned pride. The mundane but motivating effect of putting his nose to the grindstone of a diet cast aside, he's rapidly sealing the gap between where he is now and where he wants to be. Lifted to the glare of pure fantasy, he's in danger of an increasingly precipitous fall back into shame.

When he gets home, John experiences a slight pang of hunger. He looks in the fridge, but nothing there looks satisfying. He searches the freezer for something healthy to eat, but his eyes land on an unfinished carton of ice cream hidden behind some frozen broccoli. *I'm doing so great on this diet already*, he thinks, *a spoonful or two of ice cream isn't going to kill me. Just a couple of bites to celebrate my accomplishments.* John finishes the carton.

The sweet and salty remains of the last spoonful of ice cream dripping over his tongue, John feels too burdened and heavy with shame to maintain those soaring experiences of pride that filled him only minutes ago. He has again enters the zone of shame, his image of himself as a diet hero smashed.

He calls his girlfriend and explains what happened.

"It's totally fine that you had a bit of ice cream tonight. Stop being so hard on yourself. This time's different, John, I can tell." He agrees that it's ridiculous for him to get so upset, but the sense of shame still lingers.

The next day, John does great on his diet, again checking in with his girlfriend about each success, and again receiving praise from his friends at work. That night, after a good day of dieting, and following a good conversation about his progress with his parents, John stops off at a market on the way home from his girlfriend's apartment. Picking out all the right stuff for his diet, the feeling of overwhelming pride comes back to him. *I made it through day two without a problem, and now I'm doing the good work of preparing for tomorrow,* he thinks. *The ice cream was just a blip. I'm really doing this!* Again, John is transported to the moment in the future when he's reached his weight goal. He's elated. Feeling an urge to celebrate his achievements, John adds a small bag of potato chips to his cart. He eats them as he walks the rest of the way home.

Entering his apartment, it's like he's back in the time machine, but it's moving in reverse to that moment in the doctor's office when he heard the bad news about his weight. He feels stuck again, seeing the goal of thinness as too distant to ever achieve. So he then counterfactualizes his problem: *For God's sake, POTATO CHIPS?! I just ate the worst thing in the world! What am I doing! Idiot, idiot, idiot! I could have added one day to my successful days! Why didn't I stop myself?*

John is deep in the cycle between hubris and shame. He protects himself from feeling that he lacks the power to get thin quickly by reaching too high into a sense of completion. Yet every time he reaches high, he's on his way back down to feeling low. From the hubris zone, the slow, pedestrian act of losing weight, one humble but motivating step at a time, feels shameful. It's a mismatch with John's sense that he's above it all. Yet every time his mood is propelled upward by the unmerited excitement of big success, the tension required to motivate him to diet is slackened.

Lying facedown in the pillow on his bed, John can't stand the feeling that overtakes him, a kind of shameful, almost bodily, agitation and impatience. He's disillusioned by foolish moments of delusional success, yet he doesn't want to feel like such a failure either.

John longs for that ancient golden time before the doctor told him about his weight. John, B.D.—Before Diet—that era when he wasn't pulled up and down between imagined heights of thinness and feelings of deep, ugly disappointment. He can't imagine staying on this diet without real proof that it's working. He starts weighing himself every morning, and every morning he feels more discouraged. *Nothing's changing! All that work, and I probably picked the wrong diet!*

By the end of the second week, John is back to his old eating habits. He is now embarrassed that he told people about the diet in the first place. *I should have kept my mouth shut*, he thinks. However, as the days go by, he returns to a calmer, more familiar existence, one with fewer emotional highs and lows, less shame, and no thoughts of grandeur.

Here's what happened to John: John set an intrinsic goal of losing weight, but that goal was secretly undermined by an extrinsic goal that was more powerful than his intrinsic one: to escape his shame by feeling self-completed now, through the confirmation of others. Feeling shameful about his weight, he sought out a balm, something that could soothe his sense that he was dreadfully far from his goal. By talking to people about his diet, and by obsessively attending to the diet, he created a fantasy life in his head in which his identity goal was more completed than it was in reality. John's subjective experience of already arriving at his extrinsic goal extinguished the all-important tension behind the motivation to reach his intrinsic one of losing weight. John's mind didn't only skip back and forth between shame and hubris; it also rapidly ping-ponged between the present and the past, rarely settling long on the present. John thought a lot about the Past John, who made all the mistakes that got him fat again. He also thought a lot about a Future John, thin and proud. But considering the humility required to face where he was on the road between what he wanted and getting it, he couldn't keep his mind focused on the John *right now* of his dieting.

Do you recognize John's experience as he attempts to make changes? I do. When I want to change something in my life, and I survey the long trek forward, I often stop at the point when I have to measure how far I am from the summit. But I also don't want feel like I've given up. I'm stuck then, stopped on the slope between looking at where I am and feeling the shame of turning around and heading back down.

It's at that should-I-stay-or-should-I-go point when hubris offers a seeming solution: *Don't give up! Come with me, I'll make it easy for you. I'll carry you to the goal right now.* But then, as I try to attend to the actual daily work of making the change, I discover that my hubris has actually tricked me, and I'm foolishly right back where I began. Ashamed, I then seek an escape from this feeling.

I bet you can guess what answers this call.

All along in the seesaw between shame and hubris, my humility is as overlooked as a middle child.

Premature experiences of self-completion, and especially symbolic ones, are candy to the hubristic, narcissistic part of you—sweet, empty-calorie ways to avoid the shame of looking at your location and its relationship to where you want to go, by pretending you've already arrived. But precisely because they keep you from seeing where you actually are, they also stop you from moving forward. This all gets us back to the importance of contemplation in regard to change. Self-acceptance is a prerequisite for change, largely because it is the prerequisite for contemplation. You can't contemplate your situation, weighing the pros and cons of a particular change, unless you stop, face the mirror, and take a long hard look at yourself.

Contemplation, the Stages of Change, and the Prerequisite of Seeing Your Location

In the therapy professions, and especially in the area of addiction treatment, we think a lot about the "stages of change." The idea comes from what's called the Transtheoretical Model of Change (TTM), developed in the late 1970s by James Prochaska and Carlo DiClemente.[7] When I assert in this book that the science behind contemplation is the key to change, I'm mostly referring to this work.

TTM proposes that you move through five stages of change: 1) *precontemplation*, in which you have no intention of taking care of a problem; 2) *contemplation*, in which you start considering that you must take action; 3) *preparation*, when you take the first small steps toward your goal; 4) *action*, when you actually start moving forward; and 5) *maintenance*, when you continue implementing whatever change you've made.

When we head toward change, most of us don't move neatly

from one stage to another and then take action; most of us switch back and forth between stages. We think, *Yeah, this is a problem, and I'm going to do something about it.* Next day: *Eh, it's really no big deal.*

John is a perfect example of these back-and-forth switches, and how this somewhat simple stage-based model helps us understand the complex workings of making a change.

From the outside, John appeared stuck in a back-and-forth between contemplation and action. He saw there was a problem—exhibited in how much he talked about it and how much he prepared to diet—and yet he had trouble taking what he was contemplating and making it actionable. However, in reality he wasn't contemplating at all. Here's the twist: John kept himself from looking in the mirror by doing stuff that made him seem as if he were a person fully aware of his place on the continuum between where he was and where he wanted to be. His performance as the Dieter, in other words, kept him in a precontemplative place.

The core of John's problem was his lack of humble self-acceptance. Without the ability to see himself exactly where he was in relationship to where he wanted to be, he kept jumping backward and forward between the stages of change.

John needed to do some good, hard work on himself before he started dieting, whether through therapy, yoga, or perhaps a meditative practice. He needed a method for reaching a higher state of self-understanding, a place in which he could confront life with less fear and more grit and resilience.

Well, sort of. And maybe.

Facing yourself in the mirror means facing your accountability and aloneness. Doing something with what you see in the mirror takes the ability to withstand the risk of profound experiences of helplessness. It also requires that you transcend your fear of hope and act on faith. But that's not all: to be able to look yourself in the mirror and contemplate your situation requires that you transcend a host of other things that are happening to you at the moment. In other words, if you believe self-acceptance is some sort of constant state you can reach by therapeutically working on yourself, I have some real estate in the Everglades to sell you.

The Independent Shifting of Arrows and the Unpredictability of Change

Unless you are the Dalai Lama or Yoda (or, who knows, Rogers or Linehan?), the ability to look at yourself in the mirror, warts and all, isn't something you always have. We live in complex fields of driving and restraining forces. When you set out toward personal change, you can do so with real confidence that one important driving force (hope) and one restraining force (existential anxiety) will always be there. But other than that, the arrows in your field are unique to your own situation. Many of these arrows—from your situation in society to the simple experience of a good or bad week at work—are outside your control.

Picture yourself speeding along in a subway car. You're looking at your reflection in the window across from you. First you're in a dark tunnel, so your reflection in the light of the car is almost a perfect mirror. Then the light outside the car rapidly shifts between bright and dark, and so, too, does your reflection. You arrive at a station and the image disappears. Passengers get on, the doors close, and you enter another tunnel. There you are again, bright as day. When the subway lifts to an aboveground track, you are gone from the window for a long time, until the train plummets back down under the earth, where you pop up again, sitting there, staring back at yourself in the reflection in the glass.

That flickering image in the subway window is how most of us tend to experience self-acceptance and thus our ability to see ourselves: it comes and goes—sometimes here for long stretches, sometimes oddly absent, and it comes and goes because of a combination of our own strengths and abilities and what's happening around us as we hurtle through space in the subway car that is our life.

The fact that self-acceptance is somewhat elusive and unpredictable, and relies on factors often outside your control, makes change mysterious.

Have you ever set a long-term goal, and after giving up repeatedly on the first step, finally, inexplicably, started to move forward? I have, often. For me, this sudden, belated vigor comes as a complete surprise. I look around and can't figure out why today.

My guess is that a change in motivation occurs because, between my last failed attempt and my current successful one, something shifts in my field that lifts my sense of self-efficacy and self-esteem, giving me enough security to look directly at where I am in my field—my location between me now and where I want to be. It doesn't have to be much: I have a nice day with my wife, and a sense of encompassing hope in all manner of aspirations envelops me; I enjoy a warm exchange with a client, and my general faith in many things rises a bit; I take care of a bunch of tasks that I was putting off, and suddenly feel that I can be effective in other parts of my life. These seemingly minor occurrences bring a little illumination and order into my existence. Something I often can't detect has made me more hopeful; a little more sunlight in my life strengthens my ability to move upward toward my goal, gives just enough extra *oomph* to my upward arrows to make things happen.

Peter, the would-be marine biology major, is an example of how our upward arrows aren't always within our control.

SURF'S UP, COUNSELOR DUDE

A year and a half after Peter dropped out of treatment, I'm standing in line at a Mexican takeout when I notice someone from the corner of my eye coming my way. It's Peter, sauntering over from a picnic bench, a young woman sitting there watching him and then us.

"Hey, man, I'm so sorry I just dropped out," he says. "That wasn't cool."

"It happens," I say. "Is it okay if I ask what you've been up to?"

"Totally! Basically, I stopped off at a bar after our second session and met this really awesome girl." He points to the young woman on the bench, who smiles and waves. "That's Samantha. We fell for each other big-time. She inspired me to get my act together, get those applications in, and go to school."

Peter, it turns out, is on break from a prestigious university where he's enrolled in every prebiology course. He lives with Samantha now. She's premed.

"I love it, man," he tells me, then introduces me to his girlfriend, who is sidling up. "Samantha, this is a counselor dude I saw a couple of times."

When I last saw Peter in therapy, he was heading into his sixth year of struggling over making important changes, each year placing him further behind his friends in the pursuit of adult goals. When he dropped out of therapy without notice, I assumed he wasn't ready for change, and I pictured him struggling to finally apply to colleges in the years ahead. But here he was, basking in a real sense of self-completion, excited, energized, bright-eyed—all systems go.

Peter needed greater self-acceptance to move forward. Yet he was dependent on unforeseen and unpredictable events to attain it: a chance meeting with the right woman and a new life together. These events changed the field around him, enhancing his driving forces and weakening his restraining ones. Peter might have found a way to move on to graduate school at some point even if Samantha hadn't entered the picture. But falling in love with her rapidly quickened the pace toward this goal and considerably raised the odds that he would reach it.

One shift that likely happened for Peter had to do with his attitude toward staying the same. Falling in love with Samantha lowered Peter's need to achieve external validation by going to graduate school. By lowering the noise of such extrinsic goals as reaching the same status as his friends, the intrinsic goal of becoming a marine biologist became clearer, less confused. It won out in the battle with his extrinsic needs. Once the intrinsic goal was Peter's main aim, he could approach his situation more dispassionately. He wasn't running frantically to feel complete; rather, he was heading toward a field of study he loved. That freed him from feelings of shame that caused him to resist moving forward.

Samantha, in other words, was much better for Peter than therapy.

Finding Beauty in the Capriciousness of Change

There's something so muscularly eloquent about the idea of being self-made—the master of your destiny, captain of industry, Atlas with the world in your hands. But that libertarian ideal is a trick, a tempting pool of grandiosity for the insatiable Narcissus in you, a permit for your Icarus to fly outside the orbit of the earth. When you get seduced into that ideal, its opposite—the Daedalusness of humbly approaching change as both a product of your actions and abilities and the messy interlocking fields of interactions, power relationships, and different levels of resources that surround you—can seem ungainly and ugly.

Personally, I find the fact that we live in fields beautiful.

I even find it beautiful that this fact means I can never quite celebrate my success in the amazing changes my clients make. I don't know what causes these changes. The people I see have whole lives, lived in whole fields that I don't control or ever even see.

Uncertainty about what shifts in their fields to add just enough self-acceptance and humility to move forward is a mystery.

As a veteran of the isolated attempt at self-completion, I wouldn't have it any other way.

I'm humbled by time.

CHAPTER 9

ARE WE THERE YET?

The heights charm us, but the steps do not; with the mountain
in our view we love to walk the plains.

—Johann Wolfgang von Goethe

- #7: Staying the same protects you from the insult of
  small steps.

Finally! After the long hard trek, you've made it up the mountain and you are now face-to-face with the Guru of Weight Loss. You've come so far, but he allows only one question. You think hard before asking it, then it comes to you—a mystery that has plagued dieters for decades:

"How often should I weigh myself?"

The guru contemplates your question then looks off into the valley behind you, a calm, mystical expression on his face, and says:

"The scale is your neighbor. Ask of it sparingly. Do not knock on its door more than once a week."

How wise, you think.

But wait! He has more:

"Research from Harvard University points out that 'Too much attention to the scale can be misleading and ultimately lead to frustration and discouragement.'" [1]

His answer is clear, and even backed by Ivy-League research: *Weigh yourself once a week.*

You thank the guru and turn to leave, taking your first steps down the mountain. But then you hear:

"Stop!"

You turn to look up at the guru, sitting on his summit perch.

"Maybe you *should* weigh yourself every day. It will drive you crazy to wait so long. Doctors at Cornell University offer this sublime proverb: 'Stepping on the scale should be like brushing your teeth.'[2] Yes, child, that is your answer: Weigh yourself every day."

He again looks off into the valley, then proclaims:

"The scale is a new lover; daily rejoice in its embrace."

A little confused, you stop to register this new and conflicting information, then settle in on the answer. "I understand. The answer is once a day," you say, gingerly stepping backward down the rocky path.

Just as you turn to start the long climb down, you hear it again: "Stop!"

For the third time that day, you are looking up at the guru on his perch. Now he's holding a book.

"I just remembered, my child, that this tome arrived by UPS," he says. He searches through the pages of *Eating Mindfully* while you stand and wait. "Here it is, yes: 'Put the scale away. Hide it, trash it, give it away, or tape over the numbers.'[3] Yes, this is the answer." His eyes a bit glazed, the guru looks out to the valley and makes this declaration:

"The problem is not how many times you step on the scale; it is the scale itself."

You head back down the mountain, more confused than when you reached the summit.

Scales preoccupy you when you diet: You check them, decide not to check them, weigh yourself at certain times, change those times, throw the scale out, then secretly weigh yourself at the gym, only to question whether the scales there are calibrated right. You get fed up with all this confusion about the scale and make that grave mistake of seeking health information on the internet, only to read conflicting advice, much of it useless.

What makes you so vulnerable to the power of these flat bathroom appliances? Scales measure your progress in, well, *scales*. They demand that you suspend your hubristic wish to feel you've arrived, in service of small moves toward that goal. That's often hard to stomach.

Reason Not to Change #7:
Staying the same protects you from the insult of small steps.

To change, you must take incremental steps toward a goal, each step an insulting reminder of where you are and how far you have to go to reach your goals. To stay on the track of incremental change requires the ability to envision the goal you want to achieve, while being able to act in a truly measured way, seeing things as they are, inch by inch.

The premise of chapter 7 was that changing requires a willingness to live in the both-and of wanting to change—which means both looking at something about yourself that dissatisfies you and accepting that you're doing the best you can. It's difficult to hold on to the second part of this formula, since change also requires the first part: a long, hard measurement of yourself in the very places you don't want to look. If change required this kind of measuring just once—so you could achieve change in a single bound, instead of having to take human-size steps to get there—a little self-acceptance would be quite manageable. But change typically demands that you continually look at where you are in relation to your goal, and the efforts you need to make and obstacles you need to overcome as you incrementally move toward it.

Reason Not to Change #7 is about the struggle over these small steps.

You may have grand plans for yourself, big dreams of a better you. But when you head toward change, it all comes down to baby steps.

Baby Steps Aren't for Babies

Change "means setting small, reasonable goals for yourself, one step at a time, one day at a time," writes Dr. Leo M. Marvin in his book *Baby Steps: A Guide to Living Life One Step at a Time*.[4] If you're a Bill Murray fan, you may recognize the doctor's name and the book title. Marvin is the fictional and ultimately villainous psychiatrist, played by Richard Dreyfuss, in the comedy film *What about Bob?*[5] Dr. Marvin's advice is actually spot on, as I will explain. Yet it's telling that Marvin, an uncaring, patronizing doctor, gives it. There's something inherently insulting about small steps. Having to make them can feel insulting, as if they were serial jabs about our ineptitude.

My friend Ann, the one learning Spanish, provides a great example of the way in which your motivation can die a thousand sword deaths when you face the necessity of incremental change rather than a single leap to success. One day over coffee again, she tells me about her most recent attempt.

"I feel like I can read a bit and say words," she says. "But when I hear the language spoken, I have no idea what is being said. I feel like that's my own stupidity."

"And what do you think when you can't understand what is being said?" I ask her.

"Basically: QUIT!" she says. "I think I'm never going to get this. I think, Maybe I'm just stupid in this area, or it's not my thing. So why should I bother? I mean, if I keep going, it's just going to mean more reminders of how stupid I am."

"Wow. Harsh."

"I know! And it's just so frustrating. I really don't feel like using Google Translate the whole time I'm in Mexico. It would feel so good to be able to talk to people, and know they see me as not some outsider. I would be less touristy than other people visiting. I really loved that idea when I first started thinking about learning Spanish: me at a small market stall, chatting it up with the owner. But now that I'm actually trying, it all seems totally impossible."

"I get that. So what have you done so far to learn?"

Ann thinks for a second. Then, as she tends to do, she begins to laugh at herself. "I've only been in one conversational Spanish class, and I've been using this app that teaches Spanish," she says.

I too begin to laugh. "How long have you been using the app?"

Ann doubles over a bit. "For about three days. I didn't even buy it! So far, I'm just using the sample version! And I use it a bit before going to bed, usually between playing *Candy Crush* on my phone. In total, I've maybe spent twenty minutes on it."

As we laugh together, she says sarcastically, "I thought I would be fluent by now! Like, I could go to Mexico tomorrow, talk Spanish to anyone on the street, and they would marvel: 'Do I hear just a hint of an American accent?'"

"So what are you going to do now?" I ask.

Ann stops laughing. She looks a little sad. "I don't know. It's not that big a deal to learn Spanish right now. And to tell you the truth, I feel like I fooled myself."

"Fooled yourself?"

"Yeah, between you and me, I feel like I've embarrassed myself in front of myself, if that makes sense: Like I had all these great images about me speaking Spanish fluently, but it was just a silly fantasy, since I didn't really do anything to get there. I feel like that person at a party who thinks she's a really great dancer, but she's not, and everybody is sort of laughing at her."

We both chuckle a little, but uncomfortably. We change the subject to other things.

Ann is in that loop I described in chapter 7, in which looking at the distance between her current state and her end goal hurts her motivation. But to get fluent in Spanish, Ann's going to have to measure that distance over and over again.

It's not as if Ann is completely stuck; she's taken some steps toward her goal, like getting that app and attending the class. But these first steps confront her with the distance she still needs to travel, and this reduces her motivation instead of inspiring her to take another step.

Here's what I think is happening for Ann: Before trying to learn Spanish, when she thought about speaking the language fluently, the idea was a satisfying fantasy; a lovely, self-completing thought bubble unpopped by the actual work of getting there. However, now that Ann has started studying Spanish, she is better able to accurately estimate the distance between her and her goal. The more realistic assessment invites disappointment.

Ann set herself up for a fall. She had unrealistic optimism about the process of learning a new language. Her end-goal images of chatting up local storekeepers eclipsed the less-romantic reality of learning a vast new vocabulary and a complex grammar, and the hours of effort needed to do so. Now, the gulf between mastering *uno, dos, tres* and fluently conversing with a native speaker has confronted Ann with her need to take humbling baby steps. She might feel less disappointed if she had never even entertained the notion of learning Spanish.

Stuck in this paradox, she feels a longing to fall back into her old state, where she could casually contemplate learning Spanish as a vague future goal, because it felt comfortable, safe from the series of insults that would surely come her way if she actually worked to learn the language. So, as she says, "Why bother?"

Before Ann are two choices: live happily in the thought bubble of "someday I'll learn Spanish" or deal with the painful experience of feeling incompetent by actually trying to take the steps to reach her goal, thus seeing how far she is from what she wants and getting disappointed. Facing these two choices, the protective part of her wins out. It's paradoxical: Ann feels happier about her goal when she's not actually pursuing it. But she feels hurt by every step she takes to pursue the goal.

Each hope contains the risk of disappointment, and the higher you hope for a better future the greater your possible fall into disappointment. Small steps not only raise your anxiety about future disappointments; they are a kind of minidisappointment in the present. Like a tired child strapped in the back seat, you repeatedly ask, "Are we there yet?" and inevitably you hear the disappointing, "No!"

Because small steps remind us of the distance to our goals and the disparity between what we want to be and what we currently are, they can be demoralizing and tempt us to return to sameness. The demoralizing property of small steps increases when returning to a previously attempted, but unattained, goal. The last time, you tried that Keto diet, planned to run a 10K, decided to learn how to cook French food—*and failed*. Now the slow, humbling path is littered with reminders of where and how you were previously disappointed.

Let's go back to my messy office. If I start to organize it, I'll be reminded immediately of all the little failures that came to light after I cleaned it last time.

1. Found my favorite pen, gifted to me in 2006 then promptly lost.

---

2. Discovered that extra car key I'd been searching for for years.

---

3. Located that USB cable I couldn't find, and so had to needlessly replace.

---

4. And so on.

As I survey this landscape of daily neglect, Ann's question of "Why bother?" makes sense to me. Tired of sorting through the artifacts of my own uncompleted tasks, and losing will to pursue or cut bait with them, it seems rather logical to stop all this effort and just sit down in my war zone of an office and write. Sure, I'll get frustrated when I can't find the printer ink, or when I knock over a coffee mug, the cold, stale residue spilling on my desk. But these little moments are easier to handle in the midst of the self-esteem-generating process of my writing, than is the insulting and painful work of cleaning my office and having to confront the chaos I've made, with nothing to soften the psychic blow.

I could try to motivate myself to clean the office by breaking the project down to baby steps, recognizing my success in each unit of change. But the ability to keep celebrating small steps gets worn down each time I discover yet another sign of my negligence, additional evidence that my faith in my ability to maintain a neat office is misguided.

Another word we use for insult is "put-down," vividly meaning the act of deflating another's self-esteem, ego, or status. When you insult someone, you are pointing to the gap between how they present themselves or think about themselves, and some lowlier version of them. Small steps have the stinging ability to point out this kind of gap. And you have to be able to live humbly within that gap over and over again to reach your goal.

Mind the gap! Mind the gap! These words, statically barked from the loudspeaker when you step off the subway and over the small but dangerous space to the platform in a London tube station, are the shortest proverb on change. Minding the gap between subway platform and train is easy: You simply mind it. But your stance toward the discrepancy between you now and how far you want to step toward a different kind of you can be difficult. To handle change, you need to be able to mind, but also withstand, this gap. You have to look at it, accept it, and, most importantly, be able to live in it—that in-between space between action and completion.

You are motivated toward change when you keep your eyes on the gap between where you are and where you want to be, and withstand all the reminders that you lack what you want. And as I reviewed in the previous chapter, you deflate this motivation when you talk yourself into thinking you've closed the gap and achieved your goal, before actually having done so. The job of making incremental change, then, depends on your ability to accept where you are; to fly as evenly as possible in the humility zone. Big changes require incremental steps, and these in turn require two kinds of toughness—one is to persevere through the simple hard work that these steps demand; the other is to accept the humility that small steps demand.

Incremental change is all about how long you can bear feeling you lack something. It's a challenge to the you-here-now/you-where-you-want-to-be tension in all change: a battle between repeated reminders that you haven't finished acquiring something missing in your life versus your need to keep your head up, remaining hopeful and full of faith for a series of steps. And that's just the point. Personal change is not about having one lovely nirvana-like moment of self-acceptance. It's about accepting yourself where you are—and accepting the fact that, right where you are, you lack something you believe will improve you—over and over and over again. In other words, it's about staying in the humility zone over the long haul.

To take small steps you need humility in regular doses, since having to take small steps is rarely gratifying if you're seeking extrinsic rewards about how great you are. The more your humility outbalances your pride, the less small steps hurt. That ratio prevents you from engaging in Ann's folly in learning Spanish: a dream solidified into a fragile thought bubble and pride unearned by actual effort that is threatened every time you try to move forward in a concrete way.

It's no coincidence that Daedalus, the builder of wings, was a craftsman. It might not be a coincidence that Eric, the abstaining smoker with idiot cards, was a craftsman too, a master carpenter and musician. In real life, one *works* on his or her craft, they *hone* it. No matter the beauty of their last piece, they keep working at their craft. They are as focused on the inner satisfaction—the intrinsic experience—of practicing, as on the beauty of the final product. Successful craftspeople and artists, in other words, are individuals who have learned how to aim for the humility zone, for those moments of honing. These people have a lot to teach us.

THE CRAFT OF PERSONAL CHANGE

John Coltrane, the great jazz saxophonist and the composer of the groundbreaking *Giant Steps*, knew the intrinsic importance of the small, precise, well-scaled walk toward a goal. There are various accounts of how much he practiced each day, but everyone agrees that he was obsessive about it. Some accounts say up to twelve hours a day. It's reported that Coltrane sometimes spent more than ten hours working on a single note. He was rarely seen around the house without his sax hanging around his neck by its strap. One day, his wife, noticing that his practicing stopped rather abruptly, went searching for him. Coltrane was asleep on the couch with the instrument still in his mouth.

Jazz musicians have a perfect term for practicing their craft: "Woodshedding" refers to honing their skills alone and away from others, in the shack outside the main house. They "practice their chops" out there. A lovely poetic yet coincidental term for the usual activity in a woodshed, "chops" refers to the jaw, mouth, and lips of a trumpeter, and the need to keep this embouchure physically fit. Woodshedding is mundane and repetitive work. It requires patience and the need to focus on weaknesses, kneading kinks and knots into working muscle. "When you practice," said the great jazz trumpeter Wynton Marsalis, "it means you are willing to sacrifice to sound good. . . . I like to say that the time spent practicing is the true sign of virtue in a musician."[6] "Sacrifice" and "virtue": Marsalis's language describing something as seemingly mundane as practicing musical scales borders on the spiritual.

Artists and musicians as humble servants to their crafts, monklike in their humility and patience. Is something missing here? We often describe artists as "arrogant" or "egotistical." And so some of them might be in their social behavior. But this is not their attitude toward their craft. No one has more respect for the blank page than the master novelist; no one more regard for chord changes than the virtuoso musician. The artists who truly bring something new into the world are the ones who are so ambitious that they're able to put aside their (often considerable) ego needs in order to woodshed. Humility, for them, is intrinsic to success. In fact, it's often their significant confidence in themselves that allows them to repeat those humble steps every single day of their lives.

My father was a successful jazz clarinetist and saxophonist before he changed careers and became an organizational psychologist. He played jazz until the day he died. I have recordings of him playing with his combo and of his session work on soundtracks in the 1950s and '60s. Tragically, I have no recordings of him practicing. And that's how I remember him, much more so than in any performance: doing his scales, over and over again, our home filled with rapid, repeated arpeggios, his woodshedding the soundtrack of my childhood. This was Dad at his core, and it was Dad at his most heroic: honing, honing, and honing.

I wouldn't say he was a person who shied from accolades or dodged attention. Far from it. But when he practiced, he was selfless.

My own Daedalus, right there in the den—yet it took me decades of getting scorched for posing as an artist for me to appreciate what he taught by the example of daily practice.

Most of us lack the ambition of the artist, as well as the quantum of talent that can justify even to ourselves sustained practice, and the ego one needs to be humble enough to take small steps. So in our lives, we meet these baby steps with a lot of trepidation and a related wish to reach our target as soon as possible. This is especially true if we are injured in some way by disappointment. As granular messages that you haven't attained your appointed dream for yourself, small steps are salt on the wound of disappointment. If you are mainly worried about disappointment, they are bitter to taste. Small steps also require that you delay the gratification of feeling you've arrived at your goal, and that you bear the insults of small steps without getting humiliated by the fact that you aren't where you want to be. They are a test to your wish for self-completion.

Here's the problem, one I've raised a few times in this book already: within small steps are also granular messages that can inspire you. Taking them is a means to building your fortitude to take more small steps. So if you find small steps difficult because of your fear of hope—each step both a reminder of how far you have to go, and step higher from which you can more deeply fail—you miss out on the very important motivating qualities of small steps.

The Bitter but Necessary Little Pill of the Small Step

When you're able to mind the gap between where you are now and where you want to be, *you are able to see successful small steps as signs of progress and achievements to celebrate*, each step its own minitension between aspiration and goal, and each step coaxing and nurturing your driving forces.

In fact, sustaining yourself within the gap between where you are and where you want to be is the only route toward positive change. As we learned from Lewin[7] regarding hope, and from Bandura[8] regarding self-efficacy, if you can remain within this gap you actually take a 180-degree turn in regard to your experience of small steps. They raise your hope and they increase your self-efficacy. When you stick with small steps, they add up to larger gains, which themselves motivate you to continue onward.

Achieving small steps not only gets you incrementally to your goal but also provides the motivation you need to get there, which is why you become intensely engaged in a routine when you exercise and why musicians obsessively practice every day. If you were to skip a day of your routine, that one lost day wouldn't really change much in regard to reaching your fitness goals. But you'll feel as if you're taking a big risk if you do skip it. That risk is real, but it's not about a little less muscle or a pause in your improving heart rate. Instead, it's about the risk of losing motivation.

You're worried that if you break the routine, you'll break it again and again and again. By skipping one day, you also skip the motivating energy of one small step. So the next day, when you try to go back to your routine, you won't be able to rely on that aspirational energy. If you then miss another day, whatever residual inspiration is left from your last achievement is now gone.

Think of it this way: The way you approach small steps is like a micro–force field within the larger force field of incremental personal change. If you approach small steps as insulting, you empower the restraining force in this field, which holds you back from taking more steps. If you mind the gap, on the other hand, and keep your eyes on each step as an achievement, you strengthen the driving forces that give you the fuel to take more steps.

Your approach to small steps either makes or breaks your motivation. That's a cardinal rule of incremental change. Each time you face a small step, this rule comes into play. Will you see it as an insult or as a modest challenge worth achieving? How you answer that question decides the fate of your larger goal.

The inability to humbly look at the small steps immediately in front of you has profoundly negative implications regarding your ability to move forward. When you leave the humility zone—as Ann did in regard to Spanish and as did John, the would-be dieter—you lose the opportunity to let incremental change incrementally raise your aspirations, earned pride fueling your motivation.

Facing small steps, you can either experience them as insulting or as small, precious achievements. You can't move forward if you can't find the humility to experience them in the latter way, and you'll also stay the same if you experience them as shameful reminders of your failure. That fact reflects a paradox: Small steps are the only way to move forward on your path to change, but the meaning you may invest in them—as too modest for your self-image, or as a shame-inducing indictment of your felt inadequacy, can also deflect you from change.

It's a real dilemma. Alcoholics Anonymous has developed some interesting ways to deal with this dilemma. In fact, a lot of what they do is aimed at keeping people focused on small steps while containing them in the humility zone.

Putting a Box Around Humility: Rightsizing

Alcoholics Anonymous is a bit of a mystery for many of us in the behavioral sciences and helping professions. Research doesn't really support its reputation as the prime means to recover from problematic substance use. In fact, some very good research shows that AA, and twelve-step programs in general, have a questionable effect on long-term sobriety.[9] Yet many trustworthy, smart, and self-aware people describe it as lifesaving and the central conduit to their recovery.

My friend Jack, the stand-up comedian and substance abuse counselor, is one of them, and I trust his opinion. Remarkably, Jack describes the problem of maintaining sobriety in a way that matches what I've called the narcissistic defense—that bouncing back and forth between hubris and shame: "Addicts feel either better than or less than. We're egomaniacs with an inferiority complex. It's all about insecurity." Jack explains that this back-and-forth between feeling "better than" and "less than" led him to drink. "When I felt like a piece of shit that's when I wanted to do something wrong," Jack explains. "But when I felt really good, that's also when I was likely to drink."

"So what's the way off this seesaw of feeling too low or too good?" I ask.

"To get sober you need to understand how to rightsize things. 'Rightsize' is an AA thing we say. Rightsizing myself was about getting myself into a stable place where I was comfortable in my own skin. Comfortable but not cocky and thinking I had the answer to everything. I'm not a dormouse, but I'm also not some arrogant big shot."

Comfortable but not cocky: As I listen to Jack, I begin to understand rightsizing as a sort of Goldilocks alchemy of "just-right" modesty combined with the "just-right" pride of accomplishing small steps. I start to see the process of AA as really an attempt to get its members into the humility zone in order for them to take the humbling small steps of sobriety. I imagine a kind of therapeutic box, one that holds humility, protects against hubris and shame, and assures that small steps are noticed and even celebrated, but always held within the box. AA's most famous part of this box is the concept of one day at a time.

ONE STEP, ONE DAY AT A TIME

"One day at a time" is AA's way of breaking things down into twenty-four-hour units. Once you complete one unit, you move on to the next. "I think 'one day at a time' is *really* helpful in early recovery because the idea of avoiding, *forever*, a substance I've been dependent on is daunting," says Jack. "In the beginning, I could never imagine permanently being without alcohol or drugs. I felt mostly like a fuckup. Keeping things 'just for today' was more manageable. On extremely tough days, when cravings were strong, I learned to break it down to hours at a time. 'Stay sober until after lunch . . . after dinner . . . until bedtime.' Eventually it got easier."

Jack finely diced his recovery into small increments when he first started out, focusing only on what he could achieve that day, that hour, that minute. By giving him a sense of his success in this way, one day at a time was a way to circumvent the shame of being a "fuckup" or a novice on what felt to him an impossibly long road. It also increased his driving forces toward change, as each incremental step raised his sense of hope and self-efficacy.

AA offers a ritualized way of noting a person's sobriety. They hand out "chips," coinlike mementos, each a different color, marking the amount of time a person has been sober. The chips ritual fortifies the internal, intrinsic rewards of daily success with an extrinsic social reward. It makes meetings a place where people not only surrender hubris by acknowledging their substance dependency, but also where they have an appreciative audience that validates their incremental successes. Simple but meaningful, they are a *humble* celebratory token.

I see the sobriety chips as the way things are celebrated in the humility zone. They recognize a person's capacity to make change and the fact that the goal hasn't been reached. This is precisely the kind of celebration we all need when we're taking small steps: markers for change that are contained so they don't lead to the hubristic belief that we have arrived, and have thus completed our journey toward change.

For Jack, such things as the tokens and other small gifts he gave himself—a new music CD, a nice dinner—were ways to support himself without indulging himself. "Replacing how I celebrated was a big shift for me," he says: "Getting sober takes a long time. I needed to be kind to myself, but in the right way."

However, there's risk in being *too* kind to yourself, even if success is marked in twenty-four-hour increments. As Jack likes to tell the people he now helps: "Don't celebrate your sobriety with a rum cake." Just as with John and his diet, if one day's success causes you to unrealistically inflate your progress, you're in trouble: *I did so great yesterday, I'm in such better control than I was before, what's wrong with a little sip of Crown Royal today?* AA has developed a smart way to control for this risk of resurgent hubris through its explicit orientation toward humility.

GETTING TO THE HUMILITY ZONE BY RIGHTSIZING

Humility is an essential part of AA, clearly expressed in the myriad slogans taped to the walls of church basements and community centers around the planet: EASY DOES IT, FIRST THINGS FIRST, DON'T TAKE YOURSELF TOO SERIOUSLY, SOBRIETY IS A JOURNEY . . . NOT A DESTINATION, THIS TOO SHALL PASS, LIVE AND LET LIVE, "The serenity to accept the things I cannot change. . . ." These slogans help contain the sense of invincibility that often accompanies dangerous habits and the potential hubris that comes when we succeed a little at breaking them. So, too, does the ritual of introducing oneself by name followed by the open declaration of being an alcoholic. The point is not to humiliate, but to root members in the reality of where they are, so that they take the small steps needed to get to where they want to be.

AA thus prepares members for the long, incremental road of sobriety by keeping them focused on the humility zone, their eyes on the intrinsic goal of staying sober as a process, not only on the long-term wish to reach some imagined destination of complete and permanent sobriety.

Combining a focus on incremental achievements with an ethos of humility, the AA philosophy aims to help its members mind the gap between where they are and where they want to be. That philosophy is not just a great antidote for addiction; it's helpful for all of us. As you move toward changing, balancing the small steps while keeping your eye on staying humble is the central means to staying motivated over the long haul.

Think about dieting. Let's say you've been faithfully following your diet for three weeks and someone offers you a cookie. One cookie is not going to undo three weeks of dieting; it will not instantly add all the weight you lost. But you refuse. You refuse the cookie because you've built a routine in which daily success raises your aspirations and motivation. You don't want to give up this aspirational quality of small steps. So it's not really about the cookie and those few added calories. Instead, you refuse the cookie because you don't want to lose even a day of small steps and the way they keep you motivated.

INCOMPLETE COMPLETENESS AND THE NOTION OF A CHRONIC DISEASE

"Once an alcoholic, always an alcoholic." AA regards substance abuse as a chronic disease, and approaches sobriety as a lifelong process. It thus offers a kind of self-completion: a full identity, but one based on the idea that the road to sobriety is never-ending. It's thus an incomplete kind of completion. Paradoxical but true, it's a way of feeling less lacking in your life by accepting your lack of something as part of a complete self.

The focus on addiction as a lifetime disease has its problems: It has spawned treatments that target full sobriety as the only good outcome, a diminishing of a person to an identity based on deficits, and cultlike pressure to regularly "admit" that you suffer from something a little like original sin. However, this focus also has an important purpose. It reminds members that the place between wanting to achieve something and achieving it isn't just some empty but necessary causeway connecting two important terrains; it's a vital terrain itself. The journey, in other words, is as important as the destination, with its own specific experiences. The most important of these experiences is that something is lacking in the life of the person on this journey. That means that the painful recognition that you are not where you hope to be isn't some sign that you are doing something wrong, but the legitimate experience of someone on a trek in the land of betwixt and between.

What happens, however, when you face the path leading to

your destination, but you don't have the hope and faith to start on it? As much as telling yourself you have a disease might make that road more palatable, you still need to be willing to take those aspiring steps. Without doing so, you can't generate enough hope and faith to keep going. So you need some way to keep going on the path, even though you lack confidence in your ability to reach your goal. You need, in other words, to "fake it 'til you make it."

FAKE IT 'TIL YOU MAKE IT

I describe this idea in chapter 7. It captures the idea from behavioral psychology that "action precedes motivation." It's a way to prime the pump for movement toward your goal.

When you fake it 'til you make it, you take a leap of faith, perhaps supported by the advice and assurances of others, even if you lack faith in yourself. It's a sort of external command that you simply follow when you can't muster your own internal driving forces to propel you forward. This faith is most needed when you are severely insecure, because it gets you on the path toward change and thus provides access to the hope- and faith-generating experiences of achievements, one day at a time.

When you are functioning in the hubris zone, you see yourself as way too omnipotent to ever need to break things down into one day at a time; you view rightsizing as too constraining for your marvelous abilities, and the label of alcoholic too limiting considering your amazing and complex personality. In the same way, if you're flying in the zone of shame, "one day at a time" pokes at your shame, reminding you of the distance between where you are and where you want to be; and rightsizing feels like another jab, another reminder of your distance to some ideal; and calling yourself an alcoholic is like a stab in your heart, a deep offense to an already vulnerable self-esteem. So you need this final wall of fake it 'til you make it—this use of bad faith in order to reach a place in which you can act on good faith—to use the other processes that box in humility, protecting it from the temptation of hubris and the dangers of shame.

When you set out to change something in your life, AA's way of containing the humility zone can help you. Imagine John and his diet once again. He was painfully flailing between feelings of shame and hubris, and unable to comfortably settle in the humility zone. Now think about what would have happened if, knowing the dangers of hubris, he took a more incremental approach to his efforts. If John forced himself to humbly focus on one day at a time instead of on the frustrating experience of only looking at the long haul, his chances of losing weight would rise. If he spent less time trying to feel more complete by talking to others about his diet, and kept his eyes on the intrinsic satisfaction of achieving small steps each day, these chances would increase further. If he recognized that his despair over not losing weight immediately just came with the territory of change, his odds would improve again. If he kept to the plan described in the diet book, even when he had little faith in its ability to help him, he would be one step closer to success.

In many ways, John's inability to stick to his diet had to do with how consumed he was with dieting. In fact, the problem for John was never really about dieting, per se. Instead, it was always about how he managed feeling overweight while wanting to feel thin. His chance of getting thinner depended on whether he could focus on ways to nurture his humility on the road between where he was and where he wanted to be, instead of hurtling overnight into a new identity as a thin person.

The way Jack describes AA, it sounds to me like a kind of needed prosthetic for people who have lost a lot of faith: a humility box holding them until their steps become little drops of self-propelling fuel.

Sometimes we need that level of help. Often we don't. Like Peter and how love propelled him forward toward his marine biology degree, our capacity to handle small steps can come from unforeseen upward arrows. For Peter, the arrow that moved him forward was his new relationship with Samantha, something that came partly from a world outside him (*partly*, because without Peter's "inner" ability to love and be, his chance meeting with Samantha at the bar that night would have gone nowhere). Sometimes the upward arrow comes more from accessing untapped strengths in ourselves. Ann, the learner of Spanish, is a fine example of that.

JUST A BRAT

Another month goes by, another date for coffee with Ann. I ask her about her progress in learning Spanish.

"*Muy bueno*, actually," she replies.

"Really?"

"*Es verdad!*"

"I have to tell you, I'm surprised."

"*¿Por qué?*"

"Okay, I get it! But you seemed ready to quit last time we talked. How did you keep working at it?"

"Well, actually, it was our conversation that got me motivated again."

"Really? Why? What did I say that helped?"

"Don't get a big head. It wasn't you, it was me."

"What do you mean?"

"When I started laughing at myself, I saw this pattern I always get into. I'm like this little kid who wants it *now*. I get discouraged before I even give things a chance. And something about that just cracks me up. I love it, I think it's funny. I was with a bunch of friends the other night and I told them about all this, and they totally got it. They called my brattiness 'adorable.' I kinda agree, if I can say so myself."

"Adorable?"

"Yeah, it's like this funny cartoon character inside me. Once I saw her this way, I relaxed. The whole process got more fun and interesting. She wasn't some horrible, incompetent failure. Just a brat. She wanted to *speak Spanish now*! I get that. I see why she would want that. I'm like that with all kinds of things."

"You sure are!"

"I know! Like I don't really enjoy going to museums because I can't leave with the paintings under my arms," she says, laughing. "But you know what?" she adds. "That's not totally a bad thing. It means I feel like I deserve things. And I do. Why shouldn't I have my own Monet? I like that about myself."

"It's funny. The more I think about what you're saying, the more I see that brat as one of the things I like most about you too."

"Thanks! Exactly! And, here's the thing: that brat's also the part of me that wanted me to learn Spanish in the first place. She didn't just want to go to Mexico and take a bunch of pictures; she wanted more out of the experience. Something deeper. I know that's kind of silly, like speaking Spanish isn't going to change everything. But still, she wanted to go home with the Monet, and that made her try to achieve something."

"The brat wants to eat up the world."

"*Sí.*"

Ann recognizes that her wish to "do it now!" is the root of her problem learning Spanish. But she also sees this quality as an "adorable," likable part of herself—in fact, it's a part she cherishes. In this way, Ann extinguishes the potential shame of her inability to stick with her lessons. She sees the reason she isn't changing, accepts it as understandable and emerging from good intentions, and is thus able to move into the humility zone instead of skipping this zone and reaching for the high of feeling like she's already achieved it.

By seeing the reason she was holding back from learning Spanish as something that mostly helps her in life—that brat who wants to go home with the Monet—she also tapped into an upward arrow that was frozen by shame. Brattiness was mostly a good thing. It got her in trouble because it always wanted things NOW! but it was also the part of her that felt entitled to deep experiences.

That's a central lesson as we look at all Ten Reasons Not to Change. From a place of insecurity, you see staying the same as a sort of enemy across the lines that you must battle, step by step, to win the war. In one fist you raise a swift sword, violently hacking at those wicked obstructions to change. In the other fist you carry a shield of grandiosity to defend yourself from feelings of inferiority.

But from a state of self-love, your approach to sameness is very different. Stable in your hope and faith, ready and eager to be accountable for yourself in the long journey ahead, you lay down your sword and shield. Standing straight and vulnerable, you act generously, kindly, to sameness. You regard it in peace. The war ends, and you are able to make progress, arm in arm with the forces of sameness, often finding hidden resources in them.

The capacity to make peace with sameness is instrumental to taking the small steps of incremental change. It might come first from an intentional attempt to fake it 'til you make it, repeated in slogans and reminders at AA in a church basement; it might arrive through an unexpected and transformative event at a bar one night or in a delightful moment of laughter in a Manhattan coffee shop. Wherever you get it, you know when you have it, since change becomes easier. You neither focus on sameness like a painful wound, nor do you try to escape the pain of your shame by seeking a sense of unearned success. You exist in the humility zone, rightsized for the task ahead. Your wings gently moving, feathers warm and dry, you migrate at a well-measured pace toward your distant goal.

Scaling the Long Trek of Change

Finally! After the long, hard trek, you've made it up the mountain, and you're now face-to-face with the Guru of Weight Loss. He sits cross-legged above you on his perch, a mysterious black orb resting at his feet.

"How often should I weigh myself on the scale?" you ask.

"That is not a good question," says the Guru.

"What? But I came so far! I need an answer!"

He picks up his mystic orb, shakes it a bit, then looks deeply into a small triangular window cut into its surface: "Magic Eight-Ball says DON'T COUNT ON IT."

"What? Why? I need an answer!"

He looks intently into the object again. "OUTLOOK NOT SO GOOD."

"Come on! I have a right to know!"

"Do you? "

"Yes! I just made this lousy trek to see you."

"Well, that is true. But, look at your FitBit. Did you not complete many steps today? Congratulations!"

"Please! Just tell me what I should do with the scale. It's the answer to my shedding all those pounds."

He shakes the black orb again and again looks into the oracle's tiny window: "I'm sorry, my child, but once more the answer is DON'T COUNT ON IT."

"Come on! Can you help me or not?"

"REPLY HAZY, TRY AGAIN."

"Oh . . . my . . . God! The work it took to get here, finding the right outfit, the packing, the long flight in the middle seat, and then the horrible hike to reach you!"

"Magic Eight-Ball says CONCENTRATE AND ASK AGAIN."

"This is ridiculous!"

He again shakes the orb. "ASK AGAIN."

"Just tell me—what's the best way for me to measure my success on my diet?"

"Ah . . . *That*, my child, is a good question," the Guru says, returning the orb to its place at his feet. "When you took the path to reach me, did you keep your eyes upward on the summit?"

"Yes, every once in a while."

"Why did you stop looking up?"

"Because I had to keep my eyes in front of me."

"Did you ever stumble, then look only at your feet?"

"Of course! Who doesn't?"

"And did you keep your eyes on your feet the rest of the trek?"

"Of course not!"

"Why?"

"Because, like I said, I had to keep my eyes in front of me."

"So you made it up here safely because of what?"

"Because I didn't look too high or too low."

"And?"

"And that's how I should be looking at losing weight?"

"Magic Eight-Ball says OUTLOOK GOOD."

CHAPTER 10

THE WEIGHT OF DESPAIR, THE LIGHTNESS OF HOPE

The heavier the burden, the closer our lives come to the earth, the more real and truthful they become. Conversely, the absolute absence of burden causes man to be lighter than air, to soar into heights, take leave of the earth and his earthly being, and become only half real, his movements as free as they are insignificant. What then shall we choose? Weight or lightness?

—Milan Kundera

- #8: Staying the same protects a memorial to your pain.
- #9: Staying the same protects you from changing your relationship with others.
- #10: Staying the same protects you from changing your relationship with yourself.

A colleague and I were giving a talk to a small audience of professionals in a conference room lent to tenants in the building where one of my programs is housed in New York City. The talk was about our research on fear of hope, the first one we'd given since reviewing the promising initial data from the FOH scale. We were excited to see how our ideas would be received, introducing them to this group of twelve or so. As my colleague was engaged in his PowerPoint presentation, a man in a business suit entered the conference room. Behind him a group of young professionals stood in the hall peering into the room, lunch boxes and take-out bags in their hands.

"What are you doing here?" the man asked. "We have this room reserved for this time." He was clearly angry.

"Sorry, but we reserved this for today at the front desk," I replied.

"No, you didn't. It's ours."

"Um, no, sorry, please check the reservations schedule and you'll see us on there."

"Nope, it's ours," he said as he angrily stepped farther into the room, holding the door open for his staff in the hall to enter. The lecture stopped as the audience watched this drama unfold.

I asked him to step outside into the hall with me to figure things out. Once there, his employees surrounding us, the businessman continued to angrily ask me to exit the conference room.

"What do you want me to do?" I asked. "Make all those people leave?"

"Well, what do you want *me* to do? We have a staff meeting here every Friday and you've taken our space." He was in my face, chest puffed out. I was now worried that he wasn't going to back down and we would have to end our public event.

Finally, the building manager showed up and explained to the gentleman that the room had indeed been reserved for our presentation. The man left in a huff, his gaggle of young employees following him to the elevator.

I returned to the room, listened to the remainder of my colleague's presentation, then gave my own. Our talks were well received, and we left the meeting with a palpable sense that we were on to something in our research.

If I recollect all that happened during our presentation, I can clearly measure the event proportionally: those two hours of honeyed success, with a ten-minute belligerent fly in the ointment. But if you were to ask me, "How did the presentation go?" or even "Did anything important happen to you on that date?" I would tell you about that jerk in the hall. My feelings about the event, and about that entire day, are of the interloper and how he angrily invaded our presentation.

The bad, brief, and useless experience that day completely marred the good, long, and important one. This happens often for me; this tendency for negative experiences to strike more deeply into my consciousness than positive ones. I'll obsess over two negative scores among a hundred good ones in the evaluations of a seminar I ran; ruminate about the one employee who expresses dissatisfaction with her job when all the other employees report being happy; and compulsively review the ins and outs of an argument with my wife, much more so than the intricacies of all the joyful times we spend together.

I'm hardly alone.

Research offers plenty of evidence that negative experiences typically trump positive ones. "The greater power of bad events over good ones is found in everyday events, major life events (e.g., trauma), close relationship outcomes, social network patterns, interpersonal interactions, and learning processes," writes social psychologist Roy Baumeister, in the aptly titled paper he coauthored, "Bad Is Stronger Than Good":[1]

> *Bad emotions, bad parents, and bad feedback have more impact than good ones, and bad information is processed more thoroughly than good. The self is more motivated to avoid bad self-definitions*

than to pursue good ones. Bad impressions and bad stereotypes are quicker to form and more resistant to disconfirmation than good ones. . . . Hardly any exceptions (indicating greater power of good) can be found.

According to Baumeister and his colleagues, learning something bad about a person you meet for the first time carries more weight than learning something good; lottery winners don't report greater happiness than people who haven't won, and the only lasting effects they report are negative;[2] women who lose important, life-enhancing resources prior to giving birth to a child have a greater chance of a more complicated postpartum depression, yet there is no positive effect on such a depression for women who gain similar resources.[3] If you have a great day, there is little emotional effect on the next day. If, on the other hand, you have a bad day, the experience lasts until the next and the next.[4]

For married couples, the good, affectionate parts of their marriages have less effect on their sense of marital satisfaction than the impact of negative experiences with their partners.[5] In fact, couples rate adverse events in their marriages as influencing 65 percent of their marital satisfaction, even though they actually record three times as many positive events.[6] Bad sex has a stronger effect on your sexual functioning than good sex. One night of a negative sexual experience can affect you for years, but a positive night typically has little effect other than the pleasure of that one night.[7,8,9] Children more strongly rate the negative characteristics of their adversaries than they positively rate their friends.[10] Perhaps the most indicative fact about the power of bad experiences is the concept of trauma. When we speak of psychological trauma, we are addressing how one or more events can indelibly wound someone. We have no word or concept for something good happening to someone that has the same deep and lasting effect. ("Epiphany" and "salvation" come a little close, but they don't have the weight of "trauma.")

I could go on and on about the power of negative experiences. In fact, I want to. I'm drawn to the unpleasant fact that people are more interested in these experiences than good ones. My attention would be cut to a very tiny portion if the data proved the opposite was true.

In most languages, there are more words, and more nuanced words, for negative emotions than positive ones (and don't get me started on German—from *angst* to *weltschmerz*, it's a lexical catalogue of horribles). Psychologists' catalogues of basic emotions show the same dominance of the negative: happiness versus anger, sadness, anxiety, fear, and disgust. Your emotional responses to bad experiences are simply more palpable than good ones; they make themselves noticed, sinking to the pit of your stomach like fried dough and sitting there for days. Get angry, and you feel that anger agitating through your body like a jackhammer; become despairing, and you're hit by a ton of bricks; fail at something and you run smack into an emotional Jersey barrier. Good emotions, on the other hand, float like cotton candy, a pleasant meringue that quickly dissolves in your mouth. Be forgiving, and you might detect a little lightness in your chest; feel happy, and it's the slightly sunny scent of an orange being peeled; succeed at something and your pride is as fleeting as the first snow; have hope, well, you know how that goes.

This is not to discount the many ways that positive emotions and positive states are good and good for you. For example, forgiveness reduces depression and anxiety and even improves your health.[11] Happiness has similar benefits.[12] But although these states are good for you, we don't weigh them as heavily as we do negative states.

I touched upon this phenomenon of the bad walloping the good in chapter 6, when I discussed loss aversion theory, the idea—best evidenced in the data that winning a hundred dollars is half as appealing to a person as losing a hundred is unappealing—that we are more protective of losing things than we are attracted to gaining them. As with that theory, the fact that bad experiences or interactions are stronger than good ones is likely based on our evolution. A lion's chances for survival aren't significantly increased by the mouthwatering taste of baby wildebeest, but its survival does rely heavily on remembering the sharp horns of the wildebeest mother nearly gouging its belly.

Laughter or a scream—which one is going to jar you into the present, wake you to what's happening around you, and resonate in your skull for days or longer? The scream obviously (unless the laughter is menacing).

The bad generates stronger, longer-lasting experiences than the good. That fact makes you want to avoid bad experiences. It's their power and durability that is so aversive, but it also makes them alluring. Most literature, film, and theater is about some sort of tragedy; even when there's a happy ending, it comes after a long arc toward conflict and strife. Almost 70 percent of all articles in psychology journals are about negative psychological experiences.[13] Ninety percent of the news is negative.[14] That's what readers want. People are 30 percent more likely to click on negative headlines with negative superlatives like "never," "bad," or "worse," than positive ones like "always" or "best."[15] In fact, when a Russian news site—City Reporter—changed the approach of their stories to be less negative and increased the quantity of uplifting stories, their readership dropped by two thirds.[16]

I think bad experiences are attractive for the same reason they are aversive: they force you to feel, and to feel strongly. They dictate your feelings, while good experiences are a little more governed and elective. If you don't want to feel alone, or want to feel like things are certain, or even long for a potent reminder that you exist here on earth, you're more likely to reach these destinations on the thousand-ton locomotive of bad experiences.

When things are bad, you're going to feel more depressingly grounded, feel more feelings, and feel them more deeply than when things are good. You might not enjoy feeling bad, but there is gravity and a solidity to negative feelings, and perhaps a security in their weighty reality. So as you try to make positive change in your life, you need to understand that you're cutting the chain to a really heavy and reliable anchor—the power of the negative. The final three reasons not to change concern the struggle to relinquish the bedrock of negative feelings when attempting to do something positive for yourself.

Reason Not to Change #8:
Staying the same protects a memorial to your pain.

Staying the same is often the only means of protecting an enduring memory of past events that were painful or traumatic. Changing is thus like demolishing a memorial. It's tantamount to forgetting.

In California, the coastal cypresses sit at cliff's edge. Without any protection from the wind that comes off the ocean and up the cliffs, they are often bent landward. Over the years, they develop a posture molded by the constant force of the wind. Even on a day with no wind, they look as if they strain against a forceful one. The bending of the cypress is a kind of memory. It's not "stored memory" like in a brain or computer, but it does the job of "re-membering," *bringing together* the past of the wind hitting the trees in the position of the trees now. On a calm day, as you look at the cypresses you know they survived significant forces over many years. You mentally evoke that wind when you look at those trees. No matter how calm, it's a picture of a windy day. Staying the same can be an act of this kind of memory by posture: a way to give testament to bad experiences through one's position toward personal progress. In this sense, staying the same is being like coastal cypresses; it's a kind of memorial.

From Hiroshima to the Holocaust, we erect all kinds of memorials for suffering and loss, stone markers that assure we never forget and that ensure we keep remembering together: the *com-* in "commemoration" for the damage of the past. However, we don't erect physical memorials to our more personal, private suffering and trauma, to the damages, injuries, and wrongs done to ourselves. Sometimes, a bent posture away from the winds of change is the only way to ensure that these events are memorialized. By staying the same we give testament to something that happened to us. The more traumatic the event, the more we may at some level feel compelled to memorialize it in the shape of our character and in our stance to the world.

Trauma Memorialized

Decades back, a client in a group I ran had a perfect way of describing this issue of consecrating one's past hardships by adopting a fixed posture toward life. Alison had spent years courageously getting psychological help for significant trauma caused by abuse by her father when she was a child. Through the years, she had done a remarkable job of developing a productive, meaningful, and socially connected life despite this trauma. She found work she loved, got married, and had a close network of friends. Alison attended the group in which we first came up with the Ten Reasons Not to Change. I think we had about seven reasons figured out when she suggested one more.

"Change means bad things were a little less bad than they seemed when you weren't changing," she said.

"What do you mean?"

"Well, like, if you can recover from the bad things, then the bad things didn't completely ruin you."

"I'm still not quite getting it."

"It's like destroying the negatives," Alison said.

This was a time before cell phones and other digital cameras were ubiquitous. In spy novels, TV shows, and films, when someone "destroyed the negatives," they destroyed the photographic evidence that an event occurred.

"You mean you can't really prove anything happened?" I asked.

"Yes, it's a little like that. Like that horrible thing people say: 'Get over it.' When you get better, you're getting over it. And if you get over it, you kinda destroy the negatives that it happened. If you don't get better, you keep the negatives in that little envelope they come in."

Another group member, Erica, spoke up. "I totally get that. It's like, if I recover, people aren't going to see what I went through anymore."

"Yeah," said Alison, "it's definitely partly that. It's also that *I'm* not going to be looking at my pain that much anymore either."

"So maybe it makes sense to find other ways to remember what happened," I suggested.

"I'm not sure you're getting this, Ross. Once you get better, the only way to remember the pain is to remember it. I'll always know the things that happened to me. I just don't need to protect the negatives anymore. I don't and I can't. Once you get better they are at least a little bit ruined, and sometimes destroyed."

"And what about what Erica said? That it means other people aren't going to see what you've been through."

"Yeah, that's the real hurdle. But there's really nothing you can do about it. Especially with new people you meet. I mean, for them, it's like 'here I am, a totally functioning adult.' The only way to get them to see my pain is to tell them about my past. For a lot of them, I'm not sure I want to do that. Plus, it's not going to work anyway. If I'm doing fine, my past is mostly just a story to them."

Like Alison and Erica, if a person who has been injured by something bad in their past does well, their progress threatens to indicate that the past events, while painful and even traumatic, were not so oppressive as to ruin their ability to survive. Thus, change in this situation is a form of weakening or even "destroying" the memorial to the event. Change, in this situation, has an almost sacrilegious element to it: the profane act of destroying a valuable edifice to past wrongs.

Part of change is chiropractic: You adjust a posture toward life, one that is bent in muscle memory from past events. As you adjust it, you no longer give testament to those events. You'll know they happened, and you'll see evidence they did, every inevitable time your posture poorly aligns and you feel the pain again. But others may never again see the damage done. That's a big sacrifice to make—to live a life in the eyes of others as if nothing happened, or that what happened wasn't powerful enough to destroy you. But it's often a necessary sacrifice you have to make in order to change. That's one reason why therapy is helpful in recovery from trauma: It offers a witness to the event, someone who will hold that memory even after you no longer see them for help.

It takes a lot of work to build a meaningful and engaged life following the kind of psychological trauma Alison experienced. The step toward moving on, despite the threat of dismantling a memorial to past events, best comes late in a person's recovery, as a natural part of their movement toward hope. It typically isn't a central part of trauma treatment, and perhaps it shouldn't be.

If the attempt to relinquish traumatic memory occurs too early in therapy, or becomes prescribed as a therapeutic step, then the need to honor one's past can impede recovery. It can feel like an assault on one's integrity, a moving on without some assurance of giving a memorable testament to what happened.

Current thinkers on psychological trauma now speak of trauma as the damaging aftereffect of voicelessness following a life-shattering event.[17] The devastating event leads to greater traumatic injury when there is no opportunity to testify to the event. Thus, it is not only the immediate harm and hurt created by the traumatic event, but also the silence around it, imposed by others or by oneself. But once the process of emotionally testifying has started, it may have to go on for years—the event so deep that it takes that long a retelling, and requires that much repetition to etch the event into another's consciousness. But the retelling—often in different forms than talking, such as dance, yoga, art, and writing—appears to be the key to recovery.[18,19,20,21,22] Staying the same, too, is a form of retelling—a portrayal of what happened through a fixed posture that implies "I am not okay enough to move on with my life." A person may need to tell that story, that way, for years before they are willing to risk destroying the negatives.

Alison's story is about the deepest of psychic injuries. Most of us are lucky not to have endured such trauma. However, for all of us, the temptation to hold on to the experience of the bad deeds of others is strong. We call this posture resentment.

THE RESENTMENT MEMORIAL

Sentir is from Old French, meaning to feel. *Re-* is the prefix we use for repeating something. Put the re- before the *sentir,* and you get *resentment,* the experience of feeling anger and disappointment over and over again. That makes resentment the grumpy cousin to "(re)member" and "(re)collect." When you resent someone, or some group, you hold on to them, keeping the past in the present. That's why we say, "Let go of resentment," when we refer to no longer resenting someone. That's also why we suggest that forgiveness—the freeing act of giving away a grudge—is the antidote to resentment. Resentment is thus an odd emotion; it binds you to someone you want nothing to do with, and keeps you connected to them through repeating the heavy emotion of anger toward them. In psychoanalytic terms, when you resent someone in a fixed and intense way, you are engaged in a *cathexis*, imbuing the other person with an emotional power that connects them tightly to you. In all of our lives, there are positive cathexes, like deep love, and negative ones, like resentment.

Staying the same is often a means of holding on to resentment in an externalized way, in other words, through your actions. My client Dave is a good example of this.

Dave came to me months after being fired from his job at an insurance company. He had an excellent work history and a specialized skill set valued in his field. But after being fired, he couldn't get himself to apply for jobs. His wife asked that he "see someone," since his growing lethargy was starting to be a problem.

Dave had been fired by Andy, a new boss at his company. As Dave tells it, despite the glowing reviews in his own employee file, Andy took an immediate dislike to him for some reason. Dave suspected that Andy was intimidated by him, the new boss having little understanding of day-to-day operations at the office. Whatever the reason, and for the first time in his career, Dave felt attacked by a superior. Andy's antagonism was expressed in passive-aggressive comments, the way he treated Dave differently from his peers, the scowl on his face, his tendency to be dismissive when Dave made comments at meetings, and in an occasionally critical group email. Dave hated going to work, and he felt uncomfortable talking to his colleagues about the situation, not wanting to seem overly sensitive or paranoid. As a result, he kept increasingly to himself.

Before his new boss assumed his position, Dave was often the person in the office who planned social events for the staff—a few drinks after work, joining a softball league, and more. Andy, however, now assertively took charge of these things. When Dave attended them, he continued to face Andy's constant but subtle aggression. Laughing over drinks, listening intently to the other employees, Andy would stare blankly at Dave when he tried to participate. Dave stopped going to the social outings he so enjoyed before.

Finally, Dave went to HR to discuss the situation. The woman in HR was very nice, and promised Dave that she would keep their conversation confidential. She recommended a few strategies for Dave to help him get along with Andy and offered to mediate a conversation between the two. Dave declined the latter offer, since he was sure his boss would deny any problem.

A few days after the meeting in HR Andy called him into his office.

"Look, Dave, I don't know what's going on, but I just got a call from corporate that you've filed a complaint against me."

"What?"

"You don't know about this?"

"No, I swear."

"Did you meet with HR last Thursday?"

"Well, yeah, I did. But I didn't file any complaint."

Andy appeared both skeptical and angry. Dave tried to explain the situation, describing his experiences of being shut out and criticized by Andy, as his boss looked on, that same blank expression on his face.

"I have no idea what you're talking about, Dave. All I know

is someone filed a report stating I create a hostile work environment. Does the environment here seem hostile to you?"

"Well, not exactly."

"'Not exactly'—what does that mean?"

The conversation continued in that manner for a few more minutes, Dave feeling increasingly helpless defending his position and increasingly concerned about his job. It ended with Andy telling Dave that he set up "mediation sessions" with HR.

"That's what we do here, Dave, when someone gets blamed for a 'hostile work environment,'" his boss told him, sarcastically using finger quotes.

No one in HR would give Dave a straight answer on how and why his supposedly confidential conversation about his boss ended up as a filed complaint; and the mediation sessions were disastrous, the person from HR appearing to take Andy's side, his boss putting on a show of sensitivity and concern for Dave, and Dave increasingly appearing brittle and paranoid. At the end of the final and third meeting, after they drew up an action plan for the two of them, the person from HR asked Dave, "Do you feel like we've solved this issue for now?"

Dave didn't know what else to say but yes.

"Good, and that issue of a hostile environment, do you still feel there is hostility?"

"Well, I never said I felt there was a hostile environment, I don't know where that came from."

"Well, good," said the HR person. "Then I'm sure you won't mind signing this form stating that you feel safe and supported here."

This felt like some sort of trap to Dave, and he began to wonder about the real intention of the meeting. But he signed the form.

Things went downhill rather quickly from there, Dave and Andy barely on speaking terms. His job ended on a Friday; first, a call from HR, then a quick dismissal with little explanation other than the repeated comments that he was "an employee by will." The company offered him a small severance for all his years of services. Signing off on the severance package, he agreed not to take any legal action against the company.

Dave was understandably furious with his boss and disappointed in a company that once offered him a real sense of belonging and purpose. The anger and disappointment consumed him. However, he had no one, other than his wife, to talk to about this injustice. He wasn't sure if anyone would believe him, and was concerned that if he talked to friends or family members about it, he would be doing himself more harm than good, since they would probably feel Dave had been and was still being oversensitive. In fact, even in his conversations with his wife, this concern sat there, especially as she grew more exasperated with him and his repeated retelling of the story.

On his third session with me, Dave came in with some good news: An old friend of his was starting his own insurance agency and had asked Dave to come on board in a management position. He would be making a better salary than at his previous job, and he would have some stake in the company, probably receiving a percentage of the profits each year. Dave knew this was an excellent offer and was prepared to take it. Yet all he felt about the development was sadness and a strange disappointment. As we talked further about this, the reason for the dark feelings came into focus.

"I feel like they're getting away with murder," Dave said to me, referring to his previous employer. "I can't stand it that they could do that and nothing's going to happen to them."

"I know, Dave, it really sounds like an injustice. But what does that have to do with this new offer?"

"I have no idea!" he replied, smiling a little and shaking his head. "But I do know that if I accept this new offer, it's like nothing happened. I mean, they do this really screwed-up thing and I end up better off. That just seems wrong."

"Okay, I think I get it. So what would have happened if you were never offered this new job and you ended up never finding a job again? Would that fix the problem?"

"Well, that's what's weird: Somehow it would! Like my unemployment says, 'Look what you did!'"

"Like there's more justice if you stay unemployed?"[23,24]

"Yeah, in a really weird way, there is. I've got this strange memory right now. Somehow it fits. One night when I was a little kid, my mom promised that we would have mac and cheese for dinner. Somehow she forgot, and instead served hot dogs, which were my sister's favorite. I was very upset about it. The only problem was I actually liked hot dogs a lot. They were my second favorite meal! But I pretended I didn't like them, acting like I was gagging on something horrible as I 'tried' to eat the hot dogs. Somehow this whole thing is like that."

"Like the new job is the hot dog?"

"Well, yeah, but it's actually the mac and cheese." Dave shook his head and laughed. "What am I doing here? This is like the greatest thing I could have hoped for, and I'm acting like a real downer!"

"Well, it really does sound like you were screwed at that last job, Dave."

"Yeah, I was. Definitely. But screw *them*. This new thing's great."

Dave's experience of being fired is not, in any measurable way, as injurious as Alison's experience of being abused as a child. But they have one thing in common: injustice. When we see an injustice, we see a discrepancy between how we believe the world should be, how we believe we should be treated, and an event that violates those beliefs. Remember that Lewinian idea that our minds tend to keep unfinished tasks alive in memory? Refusing to move on, to stay stuck on a past injustice may reflect that need to repair a past injustice, to reconcile a belief about how you should be treated with how you were treated.

Memorializing the injury by staying the same is often about the wish for justice; it's a self-defeating way to right a wrong. In this case, staying the same is a form of waiting, of holding on to the bad until good is restored. The problem is that this mode of seeking justice never really works, since the actual way to close the discrepancy is to recover what you can of the person who you were before the injurious event—and that means moving forward despite the event having occurred. Your choices are staying the same to spite the other or moving on despite their behavior. The former doesn't actually work. As the saying goes, "Resentment is like taking a poison pill and expecting the other person to die."

Results from the Fear of Hope Scale show that the more you fear hope, the greater you believe the world is controllable, but the less benevolent and the less generous you feel this world is. These relations are correlational, so we can't say whether FOH causes these beliefs or if the beliefs cause FOH. That said, Alison's and Dave's stories suggest a causal path: that when we believe in a world that is just and we experience an injustice, we fear hope. We do so because hoping, and allowing hope to move us in its forward-moving direction, means moving on without justice. In this situation we fear hope because hope threatens the memorial we've built to our pain by staying put, in a posture of dejection.

As Alison made clear, change toward recovery means changing the way you approach your past injuries and how *other* people change their approach to your injuries. That's actually true for all change, whether you've had something bad happen to you or not. When you change, you potentially change your relationship with others, and your relationship with yourself. Reasons Not to Change #9 and #10 deal with the threat of these relational changes.

Reason Not to Change #9:
Staying the same protects you from changing your relationship with others.

Positive personal change inevitably creates the real chance of uncertainty, and even conflict, in your relationships.

One of the things—perhaps the most important thing—that I love about my relationship with my wife is that she has significant affection for my foibles. Rebecca keeps a sort of running top ten list in her head of all the awkward, funny things I've done: the one, early in our marriage, when we had little money, and I tried to return a Mamasan chair we found in the trash to a local Pier One, only to be reprimanded by the teenager at the counter; me, backing toward the exit door, denying the charge of fraud, then running for the car; the one when I raised my hand to stop a waitress midsentence as she described what I thought was the beef list, saying, "You can hold it right there. We're vegetarians," when she was actually describing the *beer* list; the one when I loudly yelled "IT'S TOO VAGUE" to my wife across the airport security line, everyone turning their heads as I frantically held up my home-printed ticket just rejected from the scanner.

These are little, silly, cringeworthy things, but they betray the public persona I like to keep of someone serious and, maybe even that grandest of modern accolades, cool. They are about a sometimes awkward, sometimes confused, sometimes error-prone person. I love to tell Rebecca about such events. When she listens to my tales, or actually witnesses my misadventures, she often says,

"That's so great!" and I know what she's about to do: add the event to her top ten list. Sometimes we review the list, and it's like viewing an old Steve Martin film together; a couple, holding hands at a theater, sentimentally watching a schlemiel trip over a rake. Rebecca's the one person in the world who loves the messy broken parts of me as much as (and often even more than) she loves my successes. I cherish that. In fact, if I had to choose between her appreciation of my accomplishments and her affection for my foibles, the choice would be easy: the latter, no questions asked.

I'm convinced that forgiveness toward oneself is a prime virtue, an antidote to a lot of suffering, and a key to having fulfilling experiences. Having someone along the way in life who finds humor in your mistakes, bringing lightness to places in yourself you otherwise see as heavy and dark, fosters this virtue. So what good is cleaning my office, always knowing where my car keys are, following directions? If I aim toward perfection I lose something I find most nurturing for me in my marriage. I'm sure that somewhere in my subconscious this fact might even sometimes stymie my attempts at change. Every time I change, I risk changing a sustaining feature in my most important relationship.

The example of the dynamic between personal change and what I can lose in my relationship with my wife is quite specific. But there are vast numbers of things that can change a relationship—some nurturing, some neurotic—if someone makes positive changes in themselves. From making others feel unneeded and invisible, sparking envy in your best friends, losing the familiar rhythm of intimacy, or disassembling networks of social support, positive change can change your relationship in ways you don't like.

Strangely, this fact is often ignored in the therapy professions. Emily is a case in point.

EMILY IN (LIVE) ACTION

Emily was twenty-three years old when she came to our program. She had dropped out of college after one year, following a bad breakup with her girlfriend, her first real committed relationship, which had also prompted her to "come out" to her family and friends, who mostly welcomed this news. Emily was now living with her parents, spending her days online playing role-playing games, often joining a team with gamers from around the world. Through the games, Mary had built strong relationships with many of the members of her teams without ever meeting them in person. They would chat back and forth, both during the games and after them. Before meeting with us, Emily had attended three different therapeutic programs far from where she lived, for people suffering addiction. In her case, this was an addiction to online gaming. Each of her admissions to these programs followed a session with a professional interventionist her parents hired, someone trained in persuading people to seek treatment. The interventionist her parents hired specialized in twentysomethings who—in the professional parlance for adult children who won't leave the nest—had the problem of "failure to launch."

Emily absolutely hated the treatment programs. When she would return home from these programs she would find the Xbox locked up, and the family wi-fi passcode changed, as her parents had been instructed to do. She would become depressed, staying in her room all day, lying in bed. She grew sullen, and her otherwise close and affectionate relationship with her parents would sour. After a few weeks of this acrimony, her parents would let her unlock the Xbox and permit her back online, where she would start back up, gaming all day long.

Considering her situation, my program was a good match for Emily. It offers services for individuals typically described in the psychiatric nomenclature as "difficult to engage"—people who miss treatment appointments and typically drop out of treatment. We do all kinds of innovative things to help them reconnect in the world, often going with them to events and helping them keep up with work by meeting them during their lunch breaks. Our approach to Emily's problem was quite different from those of her past treaters.

I was assigned as the therapist on Emily's team, and I met with her at her home. Now, the last time I played any video game, it was likely *Donkey Kong*, so I had no clue when I met with Emily about the depth of her relationships with other gamers. As we continued to meet, however, I came to understand that while the relationships had their limits, they were deep and offered Emily an authentic sense of social support and social connection. In fact, as far as the quantity of her interactions, Emily's virtual social life significantly dwarfed mine in the non-virtual, but "real world" of actual eye contact, leaning in to listen, handshakes, backslaps, hugs, and a good night of food and drink.

The idea that Emily had a gaming addiction really missed the point. Her gaming behavior may have been rewarded by intermittent cyber wins, but the games were also offering something much more interpersonally and internally gratifying. She was feeling like she fit in, that she was needed, that she had a purpose and role in the lives of others. In a "real world" in which these crucial experiences were hard to obtain, she found them in the virtual world of online gaming.

Spending the day with a friend trying to cop a fix is also a sort of social experience; sitting at a bar definitely is, as is spending a night at a roulette wheel. Not always, but a lot of the time addictive behaviors happen in groups. It follows that when a person aims to recover from their particular problematic habit, they often have to give up their membership in these groups.

At work here is a compounding challenge to making personal change: A growing concept in addiction research is that problematic habits often co-occur, and are sustained by, an attempt to feel connected to others. The same chemicals released in your body when you are warmly attached to other people are generated by your body or activated when you engage in dangerously habitual behavior.[25] That's what makes addiction so tricky: It taps into the very part of your brain that nature and evolution use to keep you connected to others. To put it another way, addiction hooks into the part of you that makes you most human: your collaborative social part. Addictive behavior, whether a process addiction (like gambling, shopping, and sex) or problematic substance use creates a sense of human connection. When you quit an addictive behavior you often have to leave a group to which you belong, an identity that you comfortably present to others, a repertoire of social behaviors you have mastered, and a synthetically generated experience of belongingness.

Back to Emily: Once we understood the relationship-oriented value of her video gaming, we knew that the worst thing for her would be some office-based, or even worse, hospital-based or treatment-program-based therapy. Instead of providing only therapy outside the home, we took three steps with her. First, with her permission, we brought Emily to a video game convention in town. This strategy, of course, would seem absurd, if not downright dangerous, to someone who believed Emily's problem was purely a chemical hook to a behavior: like taking a drunk to a bar. But we believed there was a chance that she would experience some positive moments at the convention, ones that might pique her interest in heading outside the confines of her bedroom to make connections. The strategy worked, as Emily discovered that thousands of people shared her interests and spoke her language. She actually asked the clinician accompanying her to leave her on her own at the convention, and went out for a night of Dungeons and Dragons with a group she met there.

The second step was membership in the Greater Boston LARP Society.

LARP stands for live action role-playing. These are games people play, typically on playing fields, in which they dress up as characters—like costumed avatars—to do battle. They are taking the experience of a video game and performing it live. Emily was part of an LARP club in high school, but she stopped playing once she left for college. We had found one for adults, and the clinician in charge of Emily's overall treatment offered to participate in one of the games. They both dressed up in medieval costumes and went. That, too, was a success, and Emily kept attending any game she could find, doing so on her own. Through the LARP games and the festivities after the games, Emily began to develop real-world, face-to face, actual friendships. Through one of these friendships, she got a job at a local shop, selling used video games. With our help (the third step), she soon moved out of her parents' house and into an apartment with one of her workmates.

Emily was able to change her relationship with video games from one in which they preoccupied her day and kept her from being self-sufficient, to finding ways to stay connected to people with whom she could engage outside "the Matrix" of virtual relationships on which she had depended. She couldn't achieve this lifestyle change in programs focused on changing her behavior. Such programs required that she also change her social network, since avoiding gaming would end in her disconnecting from that network.

Prior to her reconnection with LARP, Emily was hooked on a habit that was problematic, keeping her indoors, unemployed, and disconnected from face-to-face interactions. I'm sure the virtual games she played pulled her in with the promise of an occasional win. But she was also hooked on something that is irresistible to most humans: playful, engaged, and collaborative contact with others. By sustaining these kinds of relationships, while simultaneously assisting Emily in leaving the confines of her house, we provided her a way to maintain valued social connections while diminishing the strength of the online games that had kept her disconnected from the wider world.[26,27]

Emily exhibited a significant amount of hope. Offered the opportunity to move back into the world outside her house, she grabbed it, heading toward the lightness of hoping and away from the solid rocks of inertia and despair. Emily was very ready to leave her problems behind (ironically, traditional treatment approaches were the only thing really holding her back). She just needed the right social-psychological resources—like social support, self-esteem, and self-efficacy—to move ahead. Once those were in place, she could change. For many other people, access to social connection is much more narrow, and maintaining a harmful addictive behavior is their main route to getting the benign fix of connecting to other human beings.

PROBLEMS AS KEYS

Here is a famous triangle representing a concept of three facets of an individual, with roots in ancient Egypt and showing up today at the top of the Y in YMCA.

Here is the Alcoholics Anonymous version of the triangle.

"Unity"—group connection and social support; "Service"—purpose, contribution, role; these lead to Recovery. AA's emphasis on fellowship is a fundamental aspect of its philosophy and approach; through fellowship, the organization offers an alternative to a barstool or shooting den. If you talk to most people in AA, they'll tell you that their recovery grew as much as or more from the interactions they had before meetings ("the meeting before the meeting," as some people call it); on car rides there with a group; mingling before and after dinner with a group at a local restaurant; a shared smoke before they hit the road; the drive back. All of these opportunities to interact, engage, and bond were more important to their recovery, they say, than actually going through the prescribed twelve steps.

AA provides an experience of group connection based on recovery as an alternative to group interactions based on use. By focusing on fellowship, it goes right to the place we're only now discovering is the site of problematic substance use: human connection and the lack thereof. In some ways, AA uses the spirit of a guild or religious group (all of them focused on service and unity) to help people recover from a problem of disconnection. The not-so-secret handshake, special knock or password at the door, however, is meaningful: You must admit that you have an incurable disease to enter.

Your illness, a blemish on your personhood, in other words, is your key to AA. If you come to the conclusion that you, like many people, have actually "kicked the habit" (a possibility increasingly supported by science[28]), leaving problematic substance use behind you in the rearview mirror, you lose the fellowship. You may even lose your friends in AA, your actions speaking to the blasphemy of "denial." If you decide you can still intentionally drink or take drugs, but in a safely moderate way (another behavior supported by a lot of science on habitual use), forget about it: you're out of AA.

All behavioral treatments have this potential problem of offering recipients the promise of social connections that can only be attained by an admission of self-deficiency. In fact, good psychotherapy offers this promise in a paradoxical way. Psychotherapy works when client and therapist build a collaborative bond that approximates and even reaches the experience of love. However, it's a loving relationship with the purpose of the client becoming more their own person. Therefore, the better the client gets, and the more the relationship is working for her, the closer she comes to a divorce from someone she feels very close to.

In a previous book,[29] I wrote about how this dynamic can be difficult to deal with for the individuals I work with, who have spent long periods of time in the mental health system. For many of them, their main source of social support and social contact comes from professionals or fellow clients. Their social world, the world where they are known, accepted, and which they know how to navigate, is the world of psychiatric treatment. So for these people, to get better means to lose a basic resource that all of us need to move forward in life. Thus, they unconsciously and understandably resist change, becoming professional patients, or "patient careerists," as I put it.

That book is specifically about individuals who engage in parasuicidal behavior, that is, repetitive suicidal gestures that typically do not place the client at physical risk (superficial cuts on the wrist, taking a few extra pills than prescribed, threats with no action), but inevitably result in increased professional attention and intervention. I argue that these parasuicidal behaviors increase the more a person has a "career crisis." The types of events that spur this crisis are opposite in nature to your typical crisis at work. At work, you feel worried about your career when things go wrong. A person engaged in a patient career, however, gets worried when things go right; they get a new job, receive a good grade in a class, even start doing better in treatment. These successes threaten the patient careerist, who becomes concerned about all they can lose if they get better. Parasuicidality, that dramatic act of potential self-harm, pulls them back into their limiting but comfortable patient career.

The story of patient careerism is one of extreme insecurity and a correspondingly extreme behavior to relieve existential anxiety regarding aloneness. But the paradox of losing a relationship due to your own increased self-sufficiency is not abnormal; it's a basic feature of parent-child relationships, and relationships we have throughout our lives.

ALONENESS IN THE PRESENCE OF OTHERS

If you are a parent, you will know this phenomenon: Your child is in another room playing by herself. You can hear her in there, alone, talking, singing, making noises. She seems so focused on play, so separate from your presence in the other room. Then the phone rings. You answer it. All of a sudden, she is by your side. You try to stay on the phone, to concentrate on what the other person is saying, but all you hear is, "Dad-Dad. Dad-Dad-Dad-Dad . . . " At this moment, you may realize that your child was never quite playing alone. All along, your presence facilitated her playing. She was able to be alone because she knew you were only a room away, hearing her, thinking about her. She was, as D. W. Winnicott succinctly put it, "alone in the presence of other."[30] Her ability to be alone, and to be able to play and imagine, was actually dependent on her sense that she was "held" somehow, in your mind. The phone call broke the spell of your presence, and thus damaged her ability to be "alone."

To approach life securely, adults also need this sense that someone is thinking about them; that they exist in the consciousness of someone else; that, while alone, they are vital to others. When you know you are held in the consciousness of another, you may be playing or working alone, and you may accept this aloneness and the resulting feelings of accountability it fosters, but your aloneness is less stark. Less *lonely*.[31,32]

You can be held in another's thoughts by succeeding at something, but success very likely won't hold their attention very long: because the bad outweighs the good, and you will likely only get a fleeting bang of attention for the buck of your success. If, on the other hand, you cause another to worry about you—because you are suffering, you failed, you're injured or in some way in jeopardy, the strength and duration of their attention is likely to be stronger, more constant, and more enduring.

Back to the parent, the child, and the phone call. Let's say you ignore the "Dad-dad-dad." What comes next? It's predictable: A crash, a cry, a gesture of risk. When a child can't get your attention, and they are threatened by feelings of aloneness outside the consideration of someone important to their security, they tend to choose the siren of the bad over the serenade of the good. By doing so, they tap directly into the primordial program—the call-and-response of danger and protection—in the parent-child relationship.

Young children are completely dependent on their parents. That dependency, for both nurturance and protection, defines the parent-child relationship. The emotion that ensures that parents do their best to care for their kids, and that kids bond with their parents in order to grow safely, is love. But here's the trick to all this: The parent's job is to help the child reach a point when the child becomes independent of the parent, no longer in need of behavior associated with parental love. The love exchanged in a parent-child relationship is always about need and satisfaction of this need, risk and protection from risk, growth and the supportive connection to keep growing, all with the goal of ending this back-and-forth. Some fortunate parents and kids more easily achieve the balance in this dynamic needed for the child to leave cleanly, and to more easily experience an adult relationship with the parents, at once independent and affectionate. Many of us don't. Many children rely on the strength of the bad (needs, fears, vulnerabilities, weaknesses) to occupy their parents' attention. This definitely was my experience when I was first attempting to become independent.

It took me a very long time to find a way to have a relationship with my parents that wasn't based on my needing something from them. It took them (both children of the Depression, and one of them Jewish, with all the historical baggage and trauma of living in a capricious world) a long time to build a relationship with me in which they weren't automatically either providing resources or finding ways to protect me. My early twenties, that period when I lived in downtown L.A., directionless, posing as an artist, and making very little of myself, were shaped partly from my conflation of love with need. During that period, my own problems and my own lack of progress were my means to remain connected to my parents. I didn't know if I could have a new, different kind of relationship with them, and I was scared of losing my reliable link of needing them.

I remember one night when I had just gotten into a car accident, and my parents made the hour-long trek into L.A. to take me out to dinner and comfort me. It felt so good to receive their help and care—like I was back where I should be, my sense of homeostasis, of "how-things-should-be," reestablished, my experience of psychological well-being greater than it had been in months. If I changed for the better, becoming more self-sufficient—maybe keeping my eyes more on the road, and using my car's turn indicators—I risked losing the all-comforting embrace of loving, caring parents.

My attraction to remaining the same, and continuing to make enough mistakes to keep my parents involved, was perverse, for sure. But this dynamic, in different degrees, sits within all of us. This feeling that falling down less—quieting the heavy thud that calls for care—means losing the comforting experience of being picked up. That wish for the comfort of being protected and cared for is transferred in our adulthood to all kinds of others: friends, coworkers, and especially our romantic intimate partners.

"Immature love" wrote Erich Fromm, "says: 'I love you because I need you.' Mature love says: 'I need you because I love you.'"[33] The closer we get to mature love, the more we experience this love as something we produce autonomously. "Paradoxically," Fromm wrote, "the ability to be alone is the condition for the ability to love." But that ability to be alone is not easy, and rarely does someone consistently remain in complete comfort with their aloneness. We often long for an immature love as a solve for existential anxiety.

The anxiety about your aloneness and accountability is the central restraining force in all change. If you feel that change will not only cause you to feel more alone, but actually make you less connected as an enduring presence in the minds of others, that anxiety is strengthened. So how can you balance your anxiety about this loneliness with your need to feel accompanied by your friends and family? One way is to not change, and to keep being recognized by others because you aren't changing.

There's a needy twentysomething and a patient careerist in each of us who struggles between the immature love that is taken and the mature practice of a love that is given, because in all of us there is always a struggle over our aloneness. It's thus very seductive to send out signals of dysfunction and problems in order to feel that warm comfort of being swaddled and held, that kind whisper of "you're not alone." Signs of trouble rivet the attention of others more than successes do, and they call out for a love that doesn't require your agency. In fact, this is evoked by your seeming lack of agency.

When comforted after a fall, you can return to the innocent ease of being a child dependent on the wisdom and care of others. You're calmly rocked, warmed, and satiated with the care you want, loving eyes looking down at you, as you blissfully fall asleep. Who wouldn't want that?

"Failure to launch": Boy, has my profession mastered the art of the insult. Not only is that term insulting, it's wrong. A person who may have a hard time leaving home isn't having a malfunction in launching per se—like some faulty rocket. It's often a problem of troubled love—but love just the same—and a fear of losing connection with the people you've been closest to most of your life. Individuals who don't leave home right after high school or return home after college are often grasping at ways to keep love going. They are afraid they'll lose it if they change. It's not a great situation, but it's very understandable. It's definitely not a failure.

Here's another amazing zinger from my profession: "enabling." Parents are often told by substance-abuse professionals that their child's inability to get sober is the result of the parents' willingness to help the kid no matter what. The narrative goes, they are enabling the son's or daughter's use because they are "enmeshed" with them, another put-down. Enabling—this perceived overprotectiveness—is part of the addictive disease, experts tell parents, a pattern indicative of a "pathological family system" (the put-downs keep coming!) in which they are complicit. Often, the professionals diagnosing the parents as enablers are young people who have not parented and have never known the unyielding worry and madness-generating anxiety that comes with parenting, especially when your child is acting in a dangerous way. When I meet with veterans of the enabling label and they tell me, typically with significant insecurity, that they are enablers— having bought the label some likely young professional applied to them—I explain that I've developed another, more accurate technical term for this behavior: *love*.

It's hard and heartbreaking to lose your connection with the people you're close to, whether that's your parents, your life coach, your tennis coach, your therapist, your AA sponsor, or your mates at the bar. But sometimes you have to change those relationships in order to move on and change yourself. And sometimes, as a child experiences with parents, the potential for the loss of cathexis is great, since losing the power of their worry means losing an intensity and exclusivity of attention and care. This leads us back to the fact that in every relationship there is always that pull of the heavy bad over the light good.

This pull to keep negative aspects of yourself intact isn't only related to your need to be connected in an unchanging way to others. It also has to do with your wish to stay connected to yourself.

Reason Not to Change #10:
Staying the same protects you from changing your relationship with yourself.

Changing yourself means changing how you relate to you.

It's fitting that this is the final Reason Not to Change. In a sense, all the previous nine reasons were about a change in your relationship with yourself: how moving forward means heading in the unknown directions in which hope takes you, adopting new postures, bending to the winds of the changes you make; how it requires that you relate to a new version of you that is alone and accountable, seriously playful and willing to consider what's next; how change requires a new relationship with yourself in the humility zone, a selfless fear of expectations, a willingness to destroy memorials to your pain and forge new or different relationships with others. That's what makes change hard: Change is fostered by a contemplative conversation between you and you, about you.

It's time for me to fess up about something, a little lie I've been retelling in the book. Here's the truth:

My office isn't really as big a mess as I've described it in the book.

When I started to write the book, I decided that an organized office would be much more conducive to the process. So I organized it, storing every unnecessary item away. And I keep it that way, always putting things away at the end of the day, and generally cleaning up. My office isn't exactly the picture of Scandinavian asceticism, but a year and a half of writing, and it's still well organized.

My organized office, however, doesn't translate to how I think about myself. After years of messy offices, and just nine months of clean office living, my self-perception is still that I'm a mess. Many years of feeling bad about my disorganization have left my mind imprinted with that image of me, frustrated, ashamed, surrounded by a junkyard of stuff. I'm sure this vision of myself isn't just about the office, and reflects decades of internalized stigma from being labeled learning disabled, its most notorious symptom being disorganization. I'm also sure other, deeper issues are at play. But for whatever reason, I would definitely feel misunderstood if someone commented to me that they are impressed with how neat I keep my office. It would feel like I was living a lie, a grifter who painted a perfect set for his con.

Things are thus upside down, since the actual scam—the one I've pulled on you, and my mind keeps pulling on me as I write—is that my office is messy. I've played the long game, keeping the con going chapter after chapter, describing my messy office in the present tense—messy as I write. Why? Why take an accomplishment and turn it upside down toward failure? The reason has to do partly with my need for some continuity between how you see me and my own self-perception. As I've written, we all have acquired "looking-glass selves," needing others' perceptions of us to confirm who we are. You're a mirroring audience to me, and I want to see in that mirror the person I believe I am. That wish for continuity—for a gestalt and wholeness in who I am—is very powerful. So powerful, in fact, that the lie I've told about my office is truer to me than the truth.

Social psychologist William Swann makes this clear in his "self-verification theory."[34] Swann says that you need to feel there is clear consistency between how you view yourself and how others view you. This need for consistency is so strong that you often choose verification of a familiar if compromised self over a more self-enhancing view, even if the latter is better supported. Swann believes that even when you have a negative view of yourself—like me with my once messy office—your need for self-verification (or self-consistency) often takes charge, so that you try to get others to see you according to your negative but familiar self-image.

There's that theater again, in which you are both actor and audience. You want to see the same performance as the people next to you. So if you feel bad about some part of you, you want them to see that too, because you want them to mirror back to you that your feelings about yourself are accurate.

I was at a party the other day and our friend's son was back from med school. James is a great kid. I've always really liked him. He's always been a very humble and thoughtful guy. Academics, however, were never easy for him, and he often had to work harder than the other kids to get where is today. He's a quiet person, never interested in attention, and I wouldn't say he got a lot of that in high school, mostly flying under the radar and hanging out with a tight group of other serious students. James and I have always shared a warm relationship.

"How's med school going?" I asked.

"Good," James replied. "I'm doing well in my classes, but it's definitely hard."

"I bet. I couldn't imagine doing it."

"I did get this award, though."

"Really!? What was that for?"

"Student of the Year."

"What! That's amazing, James! How does that feel?"

"Kinda good, and also kinda weird."

"Weird?"

"Yeah, I don't know, like it's not me who got it. Like someone else got it. Weird like that."

"Amazing though, too, right?"

"Definitely: it's a real big deal. My parents keep telling me that. The other students, they keep congratulating me. So, sure, it's amazing. But . . . I don't know, I feel like I should be more excited: like wow, that really happened, and I'm not."

"That's how it feels sometimes when you achieve something great. It's hard to integrate, right?"

"And to tell you the truth, I actually liked it better with my classmates before I got the award. Don't get me wrong, it's totally great and it's definitely going to help me get the best residencies, but still . . ."

James is not a guy who wants, needs, or expects awards. God bless him, he's not big on extrinsic goals. He does like the intrinsic reward of getting himself into better residencies later, but he can't integrate the formal, external Student of the Year award in a way that feels real, so that it aligns with how he sees himself.

GRIEF AND THE INEVITABLE DISCREPANCY OF CHANGE

The need for a gestalt of self is powerful, blocking some feelings, enhancing others, and guiding you in your most important relationships. I was reminded of this just a few months ago when Rebecca and I visited Max during his semester abroad in the Netherlands, halfway through that trip that so frightened him before he left.

Rebecca and I detrained in the small town where Max attended college, and there he was, riding up on his Dutch bike, confident, proud. Gone was the scared kid at the airport, telling me, "I'm not ready." As we continued our day with Max, I noticed how much he had changed, how mature he seemed, how independent he was—his own man. This was a parent's dream. I couldn't believe the transformation. He was moving steadily on the road to self-sufficiency.

I felt so proud and relieved. But I was also filled with other weightier feelings, ones that ended up overpowering that lighter experience of paternal pride.

I felt disoriented and roleless. Who was I now? Who was I to him? More important, how were he and I going to connect? That led to other feelings, pangs of grief and loss, the helpless sense of reaching longingly for one last touch and missing it.

There seems to be some sort of massive, beer-drenched, citywide party occurring in the Netherlands every week, and the week we visited was no exception. Max had quickly formed some very close relationships with a gang of kids in his dorm, and he clearly didn't want to miss out on any carousing. So, of course, when he asked to go out with his friends on the evenings of our first days of the trip, we willingly supported this decision. Again, this close circle of friends was a parent's dream, but not without the pain of loss. Trips, vacations: these were previously family journeys, in which I obsessively took hold of the plans. But now Max was making his own plans, and they didn't include his mom and me.

When I did get time with Max on our visit, he and I never really achieved the connection I yearned for. For the first time in our relationship, things felt awkward, for me at least. There were a lot of empty silences between us, no totem of a problem around which we could continue our tradition of the need-filled call and the protective response; no alluring heft of pain in Max that could anchor me in my parental role and him in his role as my weighty responsibility.

I'm home now from the visit, but these feelings remain. While I feel guilty and a little ashamed to write this, a big part of me yearns for that moment on the bench at the airport before Max left, when he still needed me. I want that because I know how to love him in that spot, and—much more selfishly—because being there, comforting him, gave me a gestalt between how I thought about myself and how he acted toward me that I can't have now. Up until the present, Max and I had an implicit, perhaps even unconscious, deal: I depended on Max to give me a sense of role and purpose, and a structure for how to love him, and Max depended on me for protection, warmth, sustenance, and a structure for him to love me. Damn it if Max didn't renege on that deal. Becoming more adult, he left me behind, uncomfortable, awkward, no map for the road ahead. I don't know who I am to him now, and so I don't know who I am to me. Everything is unclear. I'm unsure how to safely take the next step, or if there is any step I can take that's safe.

I'm not ready.

CHAPTER 11

THE ELEVENTH PORTRAIT AND THE BIG BOTH-AND

Invisible threads are the strongest ties.

—Friedrich Nietzsche

You've now perused the gallery of the Ten Reasons Not to Change, and I hope some or all of the portraits helped you contemplate your own tussles with change and sameness.

Each reason is a unique rendition of a shared subject: the tension between two forces that are always a part of personal change, one moving you forward toward the change, the other pulling you back toward sameness. Hope and its agent, faith, make up the upward force; existential anxiety and fear of hope comprise the downward one. It's necessary to work through the tension between these opposing arrows in order to get from where you are to where you want to be. Those particular forces, and the tensions between them, are the basic elements held within the frames of the ten portraits.

As with all endeavors to frame something, I had to keep certain elements out of my portraits in order to create some semblance of a comprehensible whole. That's the art of creating a framework: The writer's task resembles that of the painter, who must decide where the portrait begins and ends, and which elements to include in the frame and which to keep out. That's an especially tricky thing to do when it comes to ideas, since sometimes what you exclude represents other possible and important meanings.

I worry about that regarding this book. My worry is about all the other arrows pushing us forward and holding us back in every field when we attempt to get from where we are to where we want to be. It's not that I excluded these arrows completely throughout the work (I did write about them in some depth in chapter 8, regarding Peter, the soon-to-be marine biologist). But they were light, dry brushstrokes compared to the thick impasto of existential tensions.

The Arrows of Social State

The driving force of hope and the restraining force of existential anxiety are baked into any attempt to achieve personal change. They make themselves known when you try to change and when I try to change. However, there are other upward and downward arrows in each of our fields that make your attempt to change different from mine—making every field unique. Some of these arrows are individual aptitudes, talents, and strengths, but many of them have to do with our unique social experience: how connected we are to others; how much we feel valued by them; our sense of purpose in the world and thus how much we feel valued by our society; our social and economic status; and our political power. It's very important to be aware of these latter arrows—

the ones connected to your social state and mine in the world of others.

So I need to paint an eleventh portrait and hang it on the wall near the gallery's exit, something to seriously contemplate before you go. If I don't do this, I risk that my ideas will be placed in a frame where I really don't want them.

Beware the Extremists

"Whatever you hold in your mind on a consistent basis is exactly what you will experience in your life," writes the famous self-help guru, Tony Robbins.[1]

"If you can imagine it, you can make it happen," writes Jack Canfield,[2] another self-help leader and author of the *Chicken Soup for the Soul* series.

Robbins and Canfield are both students of Norman Vincent Peale's *The Power of Positive Thinking*,[3] a foundational text for a lot of self-help thought. Like their predecessor, they claim that we are the masters of our fate, and that we can control this fate by changing our emotions, attitudes, and thoughts, overcoming any barrier by simply imagining something different.

On the very thinnest of surfaces, the Ten Reasons Not to Change fit within the same frame as the ideas of Robbins, Canfield, and Peale, since they, too, speak to the idea that we are in charge of our lives, that what holds us back is often our tendency to run from this very fact, and that a better life is gained when we grasp the reins and see ourselves as masters of the existence we've been given. Yet despite our slight similarities on general principles, the picture painted by the positive thinkers represents just about the opposite of what I've written in this book. That's because they radicalize the idea of our existential aloneness, packaging it in a way that is both extreme (*You are so in charge that you can change anything through thought*) and palatable (*You can choose to be happy. Serenity Now!*).

The fact that we're alone and are accountable for doing something with our lives, and that we thus have choices to make about our experiences, is a profound truth. So profound is this truth that when it's taken to the extreme of some kind of telekinesis, in which your mind bends the spoon of your reality, it is also profoundly wrong.

That's because there's a big both-and to existential aloneness, and it's this: We are *both* alone *and* completely interconnected.

The profound, anxiety-generating truth of our deaths is a yin to a very important yang: that we are also alive. And everything that's living grows and changes, and everything that grows and changes needs the environment around it to do so. (Dust off your high school life science textbook; it's all in there.) As a human being, a big part of the environment that you depend on is other human beings.

The Big Both-And

When it comes to change, as with every human endeavor, you're *both* on a solo journey *and* in need of others to make it to your destination.

I really hope you don't forget that fact.

I would hate it if you closed this book believing that you just looked at ten perfectly framed portraits of your aloneness and accountability in which you depend only on the strength of some courage gene in your DNA, or some prescription by an expert to move forward, instead of seeing the tension of change as always surrounded by a Jackson Pollock–like web of human connection.

Imagine you have an editable version of this book on your computer, and you hit *copy* on every story I tell, then paste these stories into another book about human connecting—the desperate reach to feel close to another, the powerful disappointment of losing that closeness, the pain of isolation, and the invigorating effect of group experiences. If you did that, you would have a good portion of your connections book written (you'd also be getting a letter from my lawyer).

Mark and the pain of hope's spontaneous dance, crushed by his father; Mary and her love of team experience, and then all the losses that took her away from it; Jim and the shame about the accident, the loss of his family, and his sense he could no longer contribute to the world; Max feeling "not ready" as he struck out alone; Ann's wish to impress locals and friends with her proficiency in Spanish; the pants painters, the posers, and all that effort at premature self-completion; Peter's lost sense of his place in the world, and his nagging shame in comparison to his friends; John and his desperate need to see a thin self in the eyes of others; the extreme isolation described by Jack and Susan regarding their addiction; Alison's memorial, Dave's resentment, Emily's isolation; James's struggle to square praise with his humility; and my early experiences of stigma and ostracism.

In each of these stories of sameness or potential sameness, individuals either struggled to push up against the arrows of negative social experiences or lacked positive arrows of human connection in their lives.

When people did achieve change in these stories, the strengths and weaknesses of those arrows reversed: there were less negative social arrows pushing down on them, or they gained something socially that pushed them ahead.

Consider Bridget and the motivating force of her parent's faith; Mary's growing connections, from book group and Holly to that blessed return to teamwork; Jim's emerging social life, recovery, and sense of purpose; Sam and the vow of yes-and regarding commitment to another; Ann's friends' love of her brattiness; Max's quick connection with his mates in the Netherlands; Eric and the collaborative art of idiot cards; Peter and his sense of completion found in a chance meeting in a bar; Emily's return to LARP; Jack and Susan and the fellowship gained in AA; and my own uneven search for negative yet protective identities when I was young.

Whether ending in sameness or concluding with change, all these stories were about *both* individual concerns about existence *and* social forces that either restrain us or empower us to make singular existences as deep and meaningful as possible.

I didn't deliberately plant a theme of human connection in each of these stories in order to unearth it here. I didn't need to do that; the stories unfolded that way organically. That's because you can't tell a (true) story about making change without also telling a story about our attachments to others, or lack thereof.

That purple crayon of a creative, spontaneous, and improvised life is awesome. *But you really can't do anything with it if the upward social arrows in your field aren't strong enough, or if negative social forces are holding you down.*

THE STORY OF SOCIAL STATE IN PERSONAL CHANGE

Think about your average day. What decides whether you make good choices regarding personal goals? Speaking for myself, I'm more likely to grab a cheesesteak or a scotch (or both!) if something in my day made me feel unsettled socially. It might be something specific, like a difficult interaction with someone at work, or it could be something more general, like a dip in my overall sense of purpose and thus value to others. In either case, I'm closer to eating the sub, or taking that drink, the more social disconnectedness I feel.

This idea that our ability to get from where we are to where we want to be is partly influenced by situations outside ourselves can be frustrating. It disrupts our belief that we can depend entirely on our own inner qualities to keep moving forward despite disappointment. But a purely person-based view that reduces the roots of our perseverance to upbringing, genes, and early life lessons is only half right. This inner fortitude is always fortified by outer connections: support of friends, family, neighbors, coworkers, and larger communities.

To bring these ideas back to the themes of this book is to see our reliance on one another in this way: Our ability to take on our aloneness and accountability—the experience we must take on in order to change—depends on how much we feel *not alone*. It's a paradox: To act existentially apart from others and your environment and face your freedom takes the security that can only be attained by being *a part* of things around you.

BEING A PART TO BE APART

The infants in the studies I mentioned earlier regarding deprived attachment offer a perfect example of this paradox. Children who are securely attached to their parents don't cling to them. Instead, precisely because they are securely attached they are more likely to explore on their own than are kids who aren't as attached. The result of these kinds of secure connections, and the crowning achievement of good attachments in general is an autonomous, self-sufficient adult.

Paradoxically, it's that adult who can best metabolize connections with others in order to grow. They still need others, they're just not *needy*. "The ability to be alone is the condition for the ability to love," wrote Fromm.[4] No matter how able we are to handle the stark reality of our aloneness, we never stop attaching to others, our growth and exploration remaining dependent on the depth of these attachments. We need the stability of human connection in order to withstand the dizziness of our freedom.

Evidence that your tenacity in the face of change relies to some extent on your social connections can be found at your local neighborhood yoga studio. Most of these studios teach a prescribed, fairly standard set of positions without a lot of variation. That means that the directions, doled out by instructors in these studios, could easily be followed at home. So why do people go to the studios, forking over their hard-earned cash?

Group fitness training is the same thing. Watch one or two videos, pick up an excellent routine for strengthening your core, and you're all set. So why SoulCycle, CrossFit, or Zumba? Or WeightWatchers with their regular meetings? Peloton, a $4 billion business, sells stationary bikes with monitors that display live indoor cycling classes, virtually placing you beside others while riding in the comfort of your own basement, your only companion the water heater. Why fork over cash to sweat with virtual strangers? Because being with others and being supported by others keeps you motivated. When you go to these clubs or groups, you aren't really purchasing an education in how to stretch better, train better, or lose weight faster; you can get that online or in a book. Instead, you are purchasing something only a group activity can give you: the socially driven tenacity to keep moving forward in the face of doing something difficult and painful.[5]

Clearly, your ability to make personal change happen is very much a combination of what you personally bring to your field and what upward arrows you have access to in this field. You've likely heard plenty about that kernel within you that gives you fortitude and is indifferent to the elements: There's a cottage industry on psychological grit and resilience.[6,7,8] But the idea that your capacity to move forward despite restraining forces depends heavily on your social situation is typically ignored in our individualistic, pathologizing, fix-it culture. That's just plainly wrong.

Instead, your capacity to move forward relies in part on certain social-psychological "resources." That's the argument made by social psychologist Stevan E. Hobfolland in his work on resource conservation.[9,10]

MOBILIZING SOCIAL RESOURCES

For Hobfoll, some social resources, such as your general self-efficacy or your self-esteem, are qualities that exist somewhat within you as psychological traits, yet also rise and fall due to our actions and circumstances. Other resources exist entirely outside us, such as the amount of social support we have and our experience of belongingness.

Take the simple act of how you perceive the slope of a hill, a perfect real-life example social psychologists use to study how people perceive challenges. Turns out, your sense of purpose,[11] your social support,[12] and your experience of your own self-worth[13] all affect how you measure the effort to climb the hill—even how you perceive its degree of slope.

People estimating the effort of walking up a hill see the trek as less effortful and the slope of the hill as less steep if they have a sense of purpose, feel supported by a group, or have a heightened sense of their own self-worth.

The way you perceive challenges is half the issue when you head toward change. You look at the change in front of you and the first thing you do is measure its slope and the effort required—how much work it's going to take to get from where you are to the goal. The other half of your evaluation concerns threats: what might happen to you that won't feel good, or might even be dangerous, as you move from where you are to your goal.

As Kent Harber, my colleague in the FOH study, finds in his

"Resources and Perception" research, the way we perceive threats is also affected by our access to resources.

In one study,[14] Harber placed a live tarantula in a clear Plexiglas box attached to a fishing reel that the participant used to lower the box o' tarantula toward them. People with reduced self-worth inaccurately saw the tarantula as closer to them than it actually was. Most important for our discussion, the participants' sense of self-worth at that moment was induced by Harber and his lab-mates: those in the high-self-worth sample had raised their sense of worth by recalling a time when someone helped them in a meaningful manner; while those in the low-self-worth group had recalled a time when they didn't get support.

Through my lens, Harber's work and a lot of the social-psychological research on the relationship between social state, motivation, and the ability to measure threats and challenges is a story about the forces behind your ability to see yourself as a credible vessel to get you from here to there. Our research on fear of hope supports this point: the fewer of these kinds of resources in our subjects' lives, the higher their fear of hope. When you feel self-worth, believe you are supported by others who will back you up when you fall, have a sense of purpose in your life, and feel a strong sense of self-efficacy and esteem, among other resources, you have a sense that the big rig you're driving called YOU is powerful enough to carry the already-heavy load of existential accountability, and to get you to wherever you want to go.

Social-psychological research and just plain common sense make clear that social experiences can either support or diminish your ability to persevere. When social resources are plentiful in your life, that finish line looks close and reachable; when they're lacking, that line seems a vague shadow on the far horizon.

But why do resources matter? One answer is rather obvious. We are social animals, and perhaps the most social of all the animals. As the esteemed naturalist E. O. Wilson's work describes, our brains are wired specifically for social interactions, and we depend more on a mix of collaboration and cooperation than on instinct for our survival.[15] When we aren't connected to others, we are truly fish out of water, and so we focus more on making sure we get our basic needs met, and on our safety, than on taking the risk to improve ourselves. I think that answer is absolutely right. But it only tells us *why* we need social interaction and support to keep going. It doesn't explain *how* these help us.

The way I see it, the more you feel valued by and connected to others, the greater you're willing to risk facing your ultimate aloneness, because the more secure you feel that the net of support around you will catch you if you fall (is there anything more secure than that kind of security?). Good social experiences nurture you, providing you with a sense that, although alone, you are not isolated, not left without a person or group to securely pick you up and dust you off if things go wrong (again, it's no different from the well-attached infant).

Even Harold,[16] the wielder of purple crayons, isn't really alone. On the first page of his book, he stands perplexed, a chaotic scribble of purple lines surrounding him.

1.

But then he draws a moon.

2.

There wasn't any moon, and Harold needed a
moon for a walk in the moonlight.

The moon provides light for his journey. Once he's able to see in the moonlight, he then can draw "a long straight path, so he [doesn't] get lost," guiding him forward. With the moon above, he ventures forth, and the story begins, the moon following him from page to page, a constant in the sky, never to be drawn again. The moon is still there, in fact, after Harold returns home, gets into the bed he's illustrated, draws his sheets, and falls asleep, the crayon dropping from his hand, the moon remaining protectively in the window. That moon, I believe, represents his parents, or connection in general—something we adults often have to conjure up in order to move on. Harold was always traveling alone but in "the presence of other," in Winnicott's words:[17] He always had the sense that someone was there for him.

Who will catch me if I fall? That's the most insecure of insecure questions. *I'll be there no matter what.* That's the greatest statement of faith. Without the nurturance of social connections, it's difficult to move forward. That's true whether your parents raised you to be a tough-as-nails pit bull or a whimpering hamster.

That's why—like Mary's day of rock climbing with Holly, and Peter's chance meeting with Samantha—personal change often happens unpredictably. You plan for it, get all your ducks in a row, but can't seem to move forward. Then, if you're lucky, something unexpected—often something you can't even detect or control— occurs in the social world around you and all of a sudden *you're off*, changing at full speed.

Let me tell you one last story from my own life to make this point.

The Lift of Connection

I hate giving critical feedback to my employees and executives. Because of this, I'm no good at it. I tend to buffer the negative and emphasize the positive, and while this tendency results in very nice and polite supervisory meetings, in the long run it causes significant problems—most noticeably, a distrust of me, since people know well their imperfections and know I see them, yet I don't mention them when we meet.

After almost three decades of supervising and leading people, I set myself a goal of being clearer in my feedback. Predictably, when it came time to offer constructive criticism to one of our managers, my first attempt at sticking to this goal made me anxious. I didn't know if I could do it, and my well-worn and bad-faith promise to myself—*I'll do it next time*—was ringing louder and louder in my head. I'd even built a strong defense: *I didn't sleep well last night, it's so hot and muggy out, and the subway has made me grumpy. It's not fair to him for me to give feedback in such a horrible mood.* I was all set to kick the proverbial can down the road. But then something happened: I got on a crowded elevator with a bunch of strangers.

At the start of our climb from the lobby, the elevator jarred a bit, causing a woman to spill her coffee on the floor. As we all backed up from the puddle, a fellow passenger suggested, "Just spill a little sugar from your packet there and it will absorb most of it until someone can clean it up." We all nodded that this was a good idea. Then another person silently volunteered an extra paper napkin and placed it over the spill, all of us watching with great interest. Problem solved. A voice from the back said, "This is the best elevator ride ever!" and we all started laughing. Then, as we hit the next floor and the doors opened, a very serious-looking gentleman in a suit and tie pronounced as he left the elevator, "Same time, same date, next year: Everyone meet here!" We all cracked up. At each floor, we wished our exiting compatriots a fond farewell.

That's all it took. Between the first and eleventh floor, my faith in others, and even a little bit of my hope for humanity, went up. What's more, that general sense of faith and hope buoyed my confidence in myself. As I walked down the hall to our offices, I was able to more dispassionately contemplate what it would mean to kick the can of critical feedback yet again. On the one hand came the tried-and-true thought that I could avoid my accountability: *What's another week? I'm tired, it's going to be a long day, I don't need this right now.* But something had shifted. I could clearly see myself as accountable for completing this task and understood that I would be letting myself (and the employee) down if I didn't. My thoughts passed from bad faith on the one hand to a more playfully spirited approach on the other: *Come on! This is your chance to meet the goal of giving accurate feedback that you set for yourself. You don't want to go back to that old pattern of delaying until death.*

The convivial experience on the elevator in which strangers formed quick bonds gave me a heightened ability to stand and face my accountability. Feeling connected to these fellow riders, and by extension to all of humanity, gave me the courage to see the issue in front of me as a matter of choice that I could contemplate. The problem wasn't that I was tired or grouchy—these were bad-faith excuses for avoiding change in my behavior. With just a little lift in my step, I could see that the problem about this particular issue was like a lot of problems in my life: a struggle over what it means to change.

I had been concerned about how offering accurate, at times critical, feedback, could set off a world of unknowns—distance in a relationship with the manager who was otherwise close; a new pattern in this relationship in which he would now expect my feedback to be more clear and authentic; having a sense that if I could give feedback this time, to this person, "there's no reason I couldn't" do it again with others; the risk of disappointing myself if I didn't; and many other reasons not to change. But suddenly, I could contemplate all these cons somewhat dispassionately, while weighing them against a really big pro: changing something about myself I've always wanted to change.

I gave the feedback and the meeting went very well. It felt really good to transcend my resistance and do what I knew I needed to do.

And that one elevator ride did all that? you might be thinking, with some skepticism. Well, maybe I was at a sort of tipping point with respect to change, and the ride was the push I needed to get there. But, remember, in Harber's work, the very ability to perceive the distance of that tarantula is affected not by an enduring *trait* like good eyesight, but by a fleeting *state* of self-worth, caused when the subjects simply remembered a time when they were either supported by others or not (answering the anxious question, *Who will catch me if I fall?*). What they merely *recollected* about that past time—independent of the kind of support they were receiving in their lives in the present—changed their perception. That's how powerful our social connections are. We can recall them—*simply recall them*—and they can change the way we see the world. So, yes, one elevator ride can do that.

There is something so fragile, serendipitous, and yet deeply important about the fact that we are as alone as we are together. The message that we are interconnected is the same message that we are alive. Once you can see that you are interconnected and alive, you can also see that attempts to fix you as if you are isolated and a *thing* won't likely work, and may even be damaging.

To really contemplate your situation in your field, it's important to notice what's happening to you socially. To do so, however, means giving up on the very seductive offer of the quick fix. Once you see change as linked to your aliveness as a social being, the whole endeavor becomes very messy.

The Mess

Our evolution has brought us to that big both-and of the two human traits of individual choice and our need to hold on to others. These traits are as interdependent yet conflicted as any good marriage. The former trait is the one that separates us the most from other animals. It's also the source of innovation, a very human activity (crows can curve a piece of wire into a hook, and monkeys use grass as tools, but neither innovate in a civilization-building kind of way). That same capacity of being free to make decisions (or think of them as choices) and to innovate is also at the root of our ability to make personal change, a uniquely human attribute. The other trait, our capacity for collaboration, makes us similar to many social species, from ants to apes. Just like them, our species survived and survives by working together.

Take these two traits, mix them together, and you get a complex cocktail: an autonomous animal charged with the accountability to make its life as meaningful and deep as possible, that inherently needs its group to grow but *chooses* to join it. You're not a goose: You join the flock you need (the school, the friends, the internet chat group) through choice and decision, not the instinctual pull to fly in formation. That's heady stuff! It's very complex and makes human experience as messy as my fictionalized messy office.

If only it was just that messy. Things get worse.

That flock you choose to join? It's made up of other autonomous individuals who are also accountable for their fates. That makes the mess of human experience a giant dorm room of disorder. You are alone, you need others to make the most of your aloneness, and these people you depend on have their own squalor to deal with, and some of them depend on you to help them neaten things up.

Making personal change is a trek up a mountain, its peak the summit of all you can achieve before you descend into that shadowed valley on the other side. There are barriers on this trek, and so you can't always reach the summit in the short span of your lifetime. But you can get as far as you can, as long as you're willing to keep making decisions along the way. You feel pulled in two directions as you take each step: upward by the innate call of completeness, and downward by your fear that new heights mean more dangerous falls. There is no trail, and the hike is rugged and treacherous, deep crevasses of helpless disappointment on either side of you, and always the possibility that the direction you choose will cause you to get lost or to hit unknown and insurmountable obstacles. That's not a trek to do alone. So you make it with a climbing party, which supports you each step of the way.

Roped to them, you feel some security that they will catch you if you fall. There is no leader of this party, however, and each member is aiming for their own particular summits, some needing you to belay for them, crying out to you to hold on when they inevitably plummet into a chasm or ravine. Behind you, in front of you, and on either side of you, you hear it: falling! . . . falling! . . . falling! . . . falling! . . . falling! And then it's you . . . falling! Everyone in this climbing party is accountable for getting to their summit, but everyone is also responsible for helping the others reach theirs. The best you can ask for is some sort of controlled chaos.

The human brain is mainly built to deal with the problems that arise from this chaos (and *deal*, not always *solve*, by a long shot). Your neocortex, the thing that makes you most human, is there for generating new things through inventive collaboration with other autonomous humans. Your brain is an improviser, a yes-and organ whose purpose is to create connection in the service of growth and to generate change in yourself, others, and the society around you. When you collaborate with others, or when you are emotionally supported on a solo journey, you move ahead most efficiently. The opposite is also true.

As the science on resources shows, when you don't feel like you belong,[18] don't have a purpose, and feel you lack a role in contributing to humanity's project, and thus don't know whether you are worth something to others,[19] your social organ becomes parched, begins to malfunction, and you lose motivation and fortitude.

How do you know when your mind is withering from lack of contact? When your motivation slows or stops. What's the sign that it needs fuel? When you set yourself a goal of personal change and can't seem to reach it, and the voice in your head whispers, "Stay the same."

The dual facts that you are bequeathed the gift-curse of decision in regard to your growth, and that you need others—who are never fully reliable, and have their own journeys to navigate—to keep going despite the anxiety this gift-curse generates, means something very important and hard to grasp in our quick-fix, perfectionistic culture:

You can't always change.

That's another fact about change that makes the ideas in this book very different from the sunny philosophy of the eternally optimistic spoon benders. It's also something I hope you remember when you finish it.

Before I got on that elevator, I wanted to change, but I couldn't make it happen. But after the elevator ride, I could give difficult feedback because of things that occurred outside my control. The "couldn't" half of that story is as real as the "could" half. I might not have been able to change until something shifted in the world around me, and I was able to access the social nutrients that gave me the strength to change. Without those nutrients, my restraining forces against change were stronger than my driving ones.

That's how it works for all of us: Sometimes, no matter how much you will it to happen, change is impossible.

Impossible? Yes, impossible. I know that might sound really pessimistic and limiting, and that such a thought is almost blasphemy in the fervor of our current *go-for-it!* culture, in which "yes" is sung as if by a sacred choir of our better angels and "no" is a dirty word emanating from a defeatist underworld. But change sometimes can't happen.

Here's one more reason it sometimes can't happen. Your change is often affected not just by the minutiae of difficult or absent day-to-day connections, but by larger political forces. Sometimes the world around you doesn't permit the change, the downward arrows of political and social forces too strong for even the most hopeful of us.

That mess, within a mess, just got a whole lot messier.

The Ever-Presence of Power in Our Life Spaces

Extremism always tends to bend toward cruelty. When taken to extremes, "how-to" and "positive thinking" reach cruel conclusions. The view that your experiences are completely skull-bound, and thus your ability to make things happen in your life is completely up to you, ends with the conclusion that something's wrong with you if you're not happy and successful. The idea that your brain has the omnipotent power to bootstrap you out of every experience is most cruel when it comes to people who lack basic resources, are just trying to survive, and/or are pressed into their position due to political forces. Sometimes you can't change, in other words, because others have greedily sucked resources from a limited pool and kept them for themselves, or—through the sheer assertion of power—prevented you from accessing them.

In these situations, the idea that you can change your situation by thinking positively or imagining a better future is tantamount to blaming the victim: What's happening to you is because of you and your lousy, negative attitude. This perspective doesn't offer an answer for your lack of fulfillment; it supports and contributes to the source of your suffering—a means to keep you gazing downward at your navel of "personal troubles" and away from the horizon of "public issues," as the great sociologist C. Wright Mills[20] would describe it.

Don't get me wrong: Existential concerns are always baked into the restraining forces in your particular field—no one is immune from the worry of a short life and the heavy load of decision. However, these concerns are hardly the only things restraining you, and for many people they're the least important forces holding them back.

For a CEO returning to college to fulfill his long-held dream of finally getting that master's degree, the slope of actual effort to return to school is like a gentle hill in the Berkshires. His secretary enrolls him in his classes, purchases his books for him, and hires a car service to get him to campus. But for the cook in the cafeteria at one of this CEO's companies—an immigrant who wants to obtain a degree in order to raise her economic status—it's like K2. She borrows money from her cousin to buy the books, takes out a student loan, requests more hours at her job to pay for registration, and takes a two-hour bus ride to campus. She may have a more positive disposition than the CEO, a giant capacity for hope with little fear of it, tremendous faith in herself, a better ability to face her aloneness in the face of challenges, and greater social support than he has, *but she's still less likely to get that degree.* That's because the forces driving and restraining both these individuals in their particular fields are not just existential. They are material, existing outside the power of individual brains, grit, or gumption. These forces have to do with how certain people are granted more access to wealth, property, social standing, and upward mobility than other people.

Depending on who you are, you aren't always treated fairly by the society around you, and can—through the randomness of race, culture, gender, physical and mental ability, class, and identity—even be the target of hate and unadulterated force. In such situations, you can have all the hope in the world and still be curtailed in your growth. You can be Super Harold, and still not be able draw yourself to your unalienable right to reach your potential. You're on that trek up the mountain to all you can achieve, and due to the accidents of fate, the actual slope (not how you perceive it) is preordained.

Lewin[21] understood this about your life space. He didn't see your particular field as some fortified shell in which you operate free from larger forces. Just the opposite: He understood that these forces are always present as drivers and restraints in your particular pursuits.

Those kinds of restraints are also part of the stories I told.

In a country in which violence at home is perceived as less serious than between strangers, Mark had nowhere to go for help regarding the violence and abuse in his household; Jim worked contract jobs, the kind of nonunion work corporations currently prefer, because they make it easy to fire and hire employees. Dave, too, had little to stand on regarding his job, considering the erosion of employee rights in our country. Mary was rightfully concerned about revealing what happened with her professor, considering the level of victim blaming of women when they report such things. Alison dealt with the silencing of sexual abuse and family violence in our society by erecting a memorial of dysfunction. Emily isolated herself partly due to the shame of homophobia. John's struggle over weight, and all the shame he felt about himself, came partly from the incessant focus on thinness in our culture. And my problems growing up had to do with an orientation to learning in which schools are factories and all kids need to learn the same way, like identical widgets produced on an assembly line, in which the wrong shapes and sizes are pushed down a shoot to the defective bin.

Sometimes you can't change because of your circumstances. Sometimes the circumstances that keep you from changing are there because of structural issues. If I don't state that idea clearly here, I'm really not that different from the happy-go-lucky spoon benders selling their wares on the sunny side of the street. My idea that it's good to love sameness, and that change can be just around the corner as long as you contemplate, would be just about the same as telling you that all's good if you just accentuate the positive and eliminate the negative. For many people there's nothing around that corner, and little room to sit on a rock and consider what they want to do next.

The last thing I wanted to write is a cruel book. So please remember to consider that some or a lot of the forces holding you back are political or economic in nature, and that these forces are as or more powerful than the arrows of hope, existential anxiety, personal traits, and social connections (fig. 9).

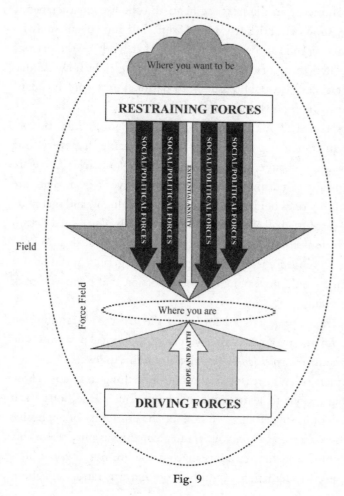

Fig. 9

The place between where you are and where you want to be is a messy kitchen sink of things that drive and restrain you. We live in a world in which particular parts of that mess are suspiciously concealed from view. From the increasing power of psychiatry in our society to make every human action definable and pathologized; all that how-to self-help garbage; all the daytime talk shows with all their experts offering simple advice like some recipe coming up in the next segment; and the pseudo-therapeutic reality shows with their twisting of suffering into voyeurism (who will get kicked off the island of rehab next week?)—the person-as-isolated-thing orientation is overpowering right now. As that orientation twists public issues into personal problems, it is dangerously disempowering.

Yes, this is a book about personal change, not politics. But no, you can't talk about change without recognizing that every time you want to change, something happens in your field. There are driving forces pushing you upward toward your goal, there are restraining ones holding you back from reaching it, and there you are—that little ball above the plastic party-gift pipe—held within the tension of these two forces. If I didn't point out that political and economic forces are often part of the gravity pushing you down, I would be leaving out a big portion that holds you back from change.

There's a perfect word for when the arrows restraining you press down on your growth from places of political power outside your control: *oppression*. That's not a restraint to love.

Sameness has its reason; restraint is something to honor. Those are big lessons to learn from this book. But please don't learn those lessons so well that you exclude the possibility of oppressive downward arrows from your frame. Sameness is only reasonable to a point, and the restraints in your life are not always things to respect. Indignation, anguish, profound frustration, agitation, and fury are necessary emotions, driving you forward when you are restrained from growth by the boot of inequality and outright prejudice. Without them, the risk of debilitating shame—the twisting of "public issues" into "personal troubles"—is very high. You look at what's going wrong in your life, don't see that it might be the result of *being wronged*, and so all you see is your own brokenness.

"It is up to you to give [life] a meaning," wrote Sartre.[22] That's mostly what he meant by existential freedom. On some level, he believed that that kind of freedom can be expressed in every situation. "Freedom," he wrote, "is what we do with what is done to us." Whether you agree with Sartre that our ability to make meaning gives you some level of freedom in the most oppressive situations (reading about the experiences of prisoners in long-term solitary confinement, I have my doubts), let's be very clear here about what he was *not* describing as freedom: happiness pulled from the magic hat of positive thoughts; the American Dream that everyone can "make it" as long as they work hard; the promises of the gurus of personal change that "you can have it all"; "total wellness," a mindful mind, a perfect existence, complete control over your destiny.

Making meaning out of your situation has absolutely nothing to do with a happy ending. It's about, well . . . meaning. And hope doesn't score more meaning points than despair.

A Quilted View

Over two decades ago, as a doctoral student at Brandeis University, I wrote my dissertation on the AIDS Memorial Quilt.[23] At that time, the quilt was made up of more than fifty-thousand standard-sheet-size panels. It has been most famously displayed as a whole on the Mall in Washington D.C., blanketing the ground from the Washington Monument to the Capital. Each panel in the quilt is a memorial for someone who died of AIDS, typically created by loved ones and friends. Part gravesite, part cemetery, part art gallery, part place of worship, part protest flag, the quilt forever changed my way of looking at the world. To this day, I simply can't see specific things as separate from universal issues, and I'm as convinced that looking at the microscopic helps us reach universal meanings as I'm sure that universal ideas make specific endeavors understandable.

Many quilt panels are comprised of small objects that belonged to the person: a teddy bear, keys, glasses, a favorite shot glass, theater tickets, photographs. These are mementos in the truest sense of the word. Likely once held in the hands of the deceased, they conjure memories of the person's uniqueness. Other panels might be made of clothing the person wore, or they might offer a quote or poem. All the panels are a testament to what Martin Luther King called "the sacredness of human personality."[24] They find something holy in the intimate. They are the antidote to dehumanization.

The panels are more specific than any tombstone. They are also valuable as individual works of art. However, they take on a different kind of value when you stand back a bit and see them as part of a gallery of panels. Now they are about a common experience, and you can see the quilt as a way of sanctifying a group of people. No longer just one memorial to one person, it is a process of commemoration: a place to worship together, a tribute to individuals who were often denied a sanctified rite of passage to the hereafter.

Back up even further, stand on the steps of the Lincoln Memorial, and look out at the entire quilt, and you now get a sense of something else: a political message. These were lives made sacred by their intricate uniqueness, but lost in massive proportions. It's like Gettysburg out there on the Mall, and it could have been prevented, if not for prejudice, neglect, and hate.

This giant political statement could not be made without the small moments of intricate stitching on each panel. At the same time, nothing is lost in the appreciation for each person memorialized, as we stand and look from the feet of the sixteenth president. On the contrary, much is gained—a voice given to the dead. The quilt summons them to speak. The uniqueness of each individual memorialized in the quilt is made more poignant, more pronounced, by their connection to a larger whole.

My hope is that by including both your social nature and the problem of the power of political restraints helps you see change in this quilted manner. Up close, you see that each of us must take on the burden of our existential aloneness and accountability if we want to change. Then you take a step back and you see that in order for each of us to take on this burden, we must be connected to others. You then take more steps back and you see that our struggle to move forward is often stymied by larger structural issues that can only be ameliorated by political change.

All these different proximities are at play in our fields. None of them negate the other. In fact, in the both-and world of change, each brings the other to life.

FEE-FI-FO-DUMB

If a man smiles all the time,
he's probably selling something that doesn't work.

—George Carlin

"Awakening the giant within" is likely Tony Robbins's[1] most famous phrase, epitomizing the view that people have concealed within them the all-powerful ability to change anything about themselves.

That kind of superpower vested only inside you means that you don't need others to help you change. In fact, it means you don't need them at all, since—with the right amount of gumption and spunk—you can change any experience on your own. And *that* means you may *want*, but don't *need* love or connection—these evolutionary gifts at the core of what makes us most human.

For giants, connection is something to attain because it's gratifying to them on their solo journey, not something that ignites their humanity. Taken to the logical conclusion, giantism is something you can create simply by thinking: simply awaken that giant and feel love—a blissful love, in fact, uncomplicated by the needs of those other, pain-in-the-ass, deciding, autonomous individuals.

The ability to have whatever you want, and an uncomplicated, self-generated experience of love: That's only an eyelash's distance from what we're currently learning about the urge of addiction, and indistinguishable from the narcissistic defense. It comes from a misguided drive for personal perfection; that fairy-tale ending so convincingly written by self-help experts, cosmetic surgeons, fitness gurus, ad executives, and life-hacking, intermittently fasting, coffee-buttering, salt-juice-drinking, DNA-splicing billionaires in Silicon Valley. There's only one problem: This state doesn't exist. It never has and it never will.

Awakening a giant within me? Personally, I'm fine with the size I am (in fact, I could lose a few pounds). I don't want to take up a lot of room, and I really don't like people who do. I am much more at ease in an elevator of human-sized coffee spillers than I am with a bunch of newly released giants.

That's because a whole lot of good happens when you give up your grandiose need to be, well, grandiose.

You and I, we're human. We're not *super*human. Very often it's really okay that you're limited in what you can make happen at any given moment. In fact, it's actually kind of nice to be in the humility zone. It's also a wonderful, wondrous thing that you're interconnected, gaining strength from others, and lending your strength when you can. It's great that you aren't a machine that only takes a few tightened bolts to fix. And it's the best thing in the world that you're never, ever, ever, fully fixed. It's even copacetic that your self-love tends to talk you into avoiding the very actions that you, a living being, are born to do: change and grow.

In fact, it's very hard to make personal change if you see your change as purely an Atlas-like act of individual fortitude, something guaranteed to you as long as you're willing to go it alone that extra mile. That's because you can't get to that loving, respecting attitude toward sameness, so necessary to change, without taking a look at your context in relation to others. When you look inward in terms of features that need fixing, without looking outward at what's happening to you because of others and because of your circumstances, your compassion for that part of you that wants to stay the same is blocked. You see the sameness, but don't see what might be occurring to keep you the same. If you can't see what's restraining you, you won't see how heroically you're driving up against this restraint. All you'll see are your supposed defects. Interpreting your inability to change as only a matter of a snoozing giant that you're just too wimpy to wake, leaves no room for self-love. Only shame.

Please remember this: It's fine—better than fine—that you are a mere mortal. There are so many amazing things you can do with your life that depend on your humble ability to accept that there are other things you can't do, and there is so much you miss out on in life if you only fly with hubris.

If I've helped you in any way, I hope it's in this humble stance toward growth, the fruits of this stance being a less judgmental attitude toward yourself about staying the same and thus a greater ability to contemplate your situation and context. If I've done my job, my gallery of portraits of sameness will help you move toward a posture of contemplation so necessary for change. I do hope the walls of this gallery are thick enough to muffle the cacophony of potential disappointment, fear of hope, and invasive clang of an individualistic, either-or, win-lose, keep-your-eye-on-your-navel culture. These noises tend to storm the barricades of your security whenever you consider change, and they are ruinous to contemplation. When they are loud, you can't hear yourself think about yourself.

To keep these sounds at bay, we have to make a deal—a little wink and a nod, a trick play to fake out our fear of hope. The deal is this: We approach staying the same as something that makes sense (which it does, most of the time), has its own value (which it has, but there are exceptions), and deserves our affection (which it should, unless is shouldn't), not in order to elevate sameness to some exalted status we should strive for, but for one purpose: to make change a whole lot easier.

Good-bye, Adieu, Later

This book is now written. But I don't have to hand it in to my editor (since I don't *have* to do anything). And there are a lot of things pulling me back from doing so. I worry, of course, about whether the book will disappoint you as well as me. But I also worry that it will be a good work and raise my expectations and the expectations of friends and colleagues about what I can do. I'm anxious about an unpredictable life without the project in front of me each day, all the spaces in my Google calendar left empty because I finished this task. I worry that I'm going to have to think about what's next soon, and know that if I can write this book "there's no reason I can't" do something else.

Mostly, however, my finger freezes, unable to hit "send," because finishing means ending my conversation with you. You, my generous audience, of which I am also a member, making the choice, page after page, to keep reading all these words. The change in my relationship with you means a big loss to me.

Of course, if you are reading these words, I did hit "send." I guess things went right enough today for me be able to say good-bye: enough distance from the last big disappointment, enough hope and faith, and a little less fear of these emotions, enough love in

my life, enough sense of purpose, enough belief that I'm valued—
things I don't always have enough of. They all gave me the strength
to look straight into the eyes of my aloneness, accept my own accountability, and take the next step. That makes me *both* grateful
for the abundance of resources that got me to this place, *and* more
than a little worried that I need them so.

Change is always both-and, and it's always both-and because
you, like me, are a both-and creature. You are *both* accountable
for your choices *and* limited by your circumstances; you are *both*
free to be your own person *and* restricted by the call of morality,
altruism, and love; you are *both* a decider on how you want to
experience what happens to you *and* very much restrained by an
unknowable future that is not fully in your control; you are *both*
free to "do with what is done to you," *and* not at all immune to
trauma; you are *both* remarkably resilient, "never surrendering"
in the face of often unspeakable hardship, *and* as brittle as ash,
your hope and faith dissolving to dust at the slightest touch of
disappointment.

All these both-ands are generated by the most singularly human
trait in the big human-defining both-and: You make decisions on
how you grow and change. While you do need the right social
resources in order to move forward in the face of the anxiety-
provoking decisions your life triggers, you're still always your own
Moses on a trek to make your life meaningful and even great in a
short span of time. Forgoing the golden calves of "Ten easy steps"
and "Imagine it and it will happen!" you're chosen to choose.

"The acorn becomes an oak by means of automatic growth;
no commitment is necessary," wrote Rollo May.[2] "But a man or
woman becomes fully human only by his or her choices and his
or her commitment to them. People attain worth and dignity by
the multitude of decisions they make from day by day. These decisions require courage."

That's so perfectly written.

Every time you grow as a person, it's the result of a decision and the courage it took to commit to this decision and to follow through on it.

Speaking your first words requires courage. Taking your first steps requires courage. Entering school requires courage. Making friends requires courage too. Leaving home requires courage. Getting a job requires courage. Finding a mate requires courage. Entering a loving partnership requires courage. Working toward a promotion requires courage, and having children requires courage. It takes courage to retire from the job you've held for years; to accept greater assistance as you age; and to design a way to die with dignity. All these things require courage (some a little, many a lot) because you don't grow automatically; you grow by deciding and choosing. And deciding and choosing are dizzying, scary things to do.

Nowhere do you so intentionally, nakedly, decide and choose your fate than at moments in which you set a goal of personal change. That's why personal change is a gutsy move. When you commit to change careers, fix your marriage, get sober, get organized, learn something new, exercise, speak up, take a stand, enter therapy, stop some ugly habit, become more considerate, listen more, stretch more, play more with your kids, schedule more "me time," and make room in your life to help others, you're taking the risk that you won't achieve your goals and will be left with difficult experiences (some mild, many strong) of helplessness and despair. Yet you do it; you do change. When you do move forward toward change, you're making the decision to endure the anxiety of your aloneness and accountability, always knowing that the option of sameness is eternally available, an easy escape any time you need it.

When you bear the unbearable tension between where you are

and where you want to be, you engage in some very beautiful, very human urges and emotions. You act on the same synapses of all human innovation, stretch and strain the Sistine tendons of all desire, longing, and love, while you fulfill the innate and even sacred itch to sculpt the blessed clay that is you.

Willingly engaged in this tension, you're pulled to go on by the evolutionary impulse to complete all unfinished things. And you courageously follow that impulse, even though nothing is ever fully completed.

Good luck on your changes.

Wish me luck on mine.

We're both going to need it.

ACKNOWLEDGMENTS

I could not have written this book without the assistance and guidance of Kent Harber and Constance Skedgell.

After decades of conversations with Kent, it's hard to decipher the exact genes of many ideas in this book. Kent also helped considerably with the writing, and the book has definitely benefited from his verbal genius, which astonishes me to this day. Most recently, our endlessly fruitful dialogue of ideas has resulted in our joint research into fear of hope. I look forward to continuing on this intellectual path. More important, however, is the path this research has forged for our continued friendship. I can't wait to see where it takes us next.

If I am anything close to a writer it's because of Connie. Long before I wrote this book, she was my day-to-day tutor, teacher, editor, and writing coach. Connie told me to write this book, argued with me when I resisted doing so, and helped me every step along the way. The fact that I've written a book and that it's now published is a particularly important victory for me; an accomplishment no one saw as possible (or advisable) when I was younger. Connie got me to this place, and I will never forget that. She's the writing instructor I wish I had had when I needed one most. With Connie standing over my shoulder, encouraging me and pointing out the mistakes I needed to firmly rub away, it's as if those painful times of stigma are also being vigorously erased.

To Hara Marano, the editor at large for *Psychology Today*. When I first started thinking about the book, this very wise individual's excitement about my ideas made me believe that I could actually do it.

To my friend Abby Ellin. She's a really gifted writer; her help with the book turned it into something far more accessible, more pleasurable, and at times more humorous, than the drafts I handed her.

To my agent, Dan Greenberg. Easygoing, kind, and direct, he made it all happen. It's been a joy to have Dan by my side throughout this process.

To Karen Rinaldi, the publisher of Harper Wave and my editor. Karen was so supportive and a real booster as she tended to me and the book. I've enjoyed talking to her about the book, but I've *loved* discussing other topics with her, because our conversations have given me a chance to hear her ideas and insights about human change, spirituality, and a host of other things. My conclusion: She's brilliant. Truly so. Karen's assistant, Rebecca Raskin, has also been just plain terrific to work with: ready to help, easy to reach, kind, smart, and precise.

To Suzi and Steve. I'm rarely at total ease in my relationships, but I am with you. Thank you for the many deep and fulfilling playdates. That's what we want from best friends: the chance for imaginative, spontaneous, and curious play—the feel of a laugh coming on. I love you two.

To the miraculous people who have sought our help at ellenhorn over the many years. It's a supremely risky act of faith to entrust your care to the hands of others. It really is the highest honor in my life that you had faith in us, and that your families did, too. Your courage to change, despite profound disappointments and a world unwelcoming of difference, is the inspiration for this book. It's my personal source of inspiration, too. My faith in my own ability to manage my life comes largely from lessons learned from you. You've made my heart break more times than I want to count, and you've also made it swell just as many times with wonder and respect.

To the amazing miracle workers at ellenhorn, here's the secret: I do what I do because I can't really do what you do. You come at your work with a kind of supreme combination of humility, curiosity, and patience that I will never muster. So thank you, Erica, Zoi, Matt, Paul, Christina, Hilary, Norana, Lisa, Ian, Diana, Michelle, Laurie, Aisha, Tim, Quinton, Maya, Annalisa, Ryan, Regina, Marie, Linda, Chad, Liam, Darren, Alexa, Jack, Carmine, Deirdre, Carolyn, Elizabeth, Himal, Kerry, Chris, Adam, Susan, Leah, Jackie, Jessica, Nick, Antonia, Shelly, Morgan, Amy, Katrina, Melissa, Pam, Justine, Serena, Heidi, Basel, Katie, Audelia, Ilda, Trevor, Lena, Andrew, Beth, Alivia, Christopher, Miranda, Kenya, Marni, Sheba, Andrins, Claudia, Joyce, Jeff, Leydy, Long-Gone Lauren and Here-Now Lauren, Sarah and Sarah, the three Amandas, both Meghans, Francesca I and Francesca II, Brian, Brian and Brian, Michael and Michael, Teresa, Theresa, Teri, and Terri, Zach, Zach and Zach, Nurse Dave, Primary Dave, and Companion Dave, Aaron and Erin, Boston Jess and New York Jess, whoever I've forgotten, and of course, Madhavi.

To Ed Levin. My business would not be where it is today without Ed's vast and mushrooming connections, the spores of his contacts creating opportunities for me I would never have imagined. The same is true of this book. It wouldn't have happened without his amazing social reach.

Dicla Circelli, my leadership partner in building my current company, and the person with whom I've had—and will ever have—the longest professional relationship, read the entire manuscript. As I predicted, her comments were thoughtful, insightful, and very helpful. Leah Kogan, my assistant at ellenhorn, was instrumental in keeping me organized, doing a lot of the work I didn't want to do—including the endnotes and the graphs—and helping in all kinds of ways.

To the young adults in my personal life who inspire me with their ability to transcend the damages of powerfully restraining events. These young Harolds wake me up every time I see them, caffeinating my existence, dilating my eyes to hope. They were my chorus of hope as I wrote the book.

To start with, there is Max "Freight Train" Ellenhorn of course; my goat-farming, spinach-drinking, soccer-playing, ocean-listening, weight-lifting, Europe-traveling, library-studying, parent-pleasing, dog's-best-friend of a son—you are a miracle of fortitude in the face of hurt, and a fine example of "the sacredness of human personality." It was very generous of you to let me use your stories in the book (even though you ignored my prompts to read them). They came to me naturally as I wrote, since the image of your locomotive bravery is always on my mind and in my heart. You, Max, take to life's highways with nothing but gusto. Please wear your seatbelt, and always keep your eyes on the road. For Dan, the gambler, and Kelsey, the Ninja, you inspire me with your efforts to venture boldly into exciting and self-created lives, and your courage to build innovative experiences of home, despite the fractured, disassembled experiences of home in your youth. For the Swann kids—Andy, Dana, and Erik. Raised right, you've all created such amazing existences despite living the tragedy every child fears most. Visit us any time you want—please—and always bring along your growing and marvelous broods. And to you, Franci: You absolutely stun me with your capacity to hope despite every indication that you should fear it. From under the weightiest of oppressive boots, there you are, beaming with that radiant smile of yours as you eat your Milk Bar ice cream. Quite honestly, I absolutely don't know how you do it. I'm so grateful to have you in our lives.

One more young person to thank: Valeria Vila, our research assistant and collaborator on the fear of hope research. Very poised, and seemingly unintimidated by Kent and me, her ideas are integral guides in our research.

To Mom. You are a profound example of the magic of curiosity; how it's portable, unimpeded by age, enduring even when your senses fail you, opening doors of excitement in the most everyday situations. It makes an introvert's life expansive. Thank you for giving me this gift. To Dad. Like the switch from my vodka to your gin martinis, I finally started reading Lewin after you passed. This book has the DNA of your particular kind of secular Jewish humanism written all over it. If it swings at all, that's because of you, too.

Rebecca, my love, you've been right all along in your funny tease: "That book's not going to write itself." It didn't; it took your husband to write it, and it now resides high up on the list of my proudest endeavors—all impossible without your faith in me, and all far from the height of my pride in our marriage. When my deep doubts about myself, my often-distorted sense of my mangled place in the world, and my actual broken, unfixable parts threaten to tear me down, you're always there, on my side. I don't know what I would do without you. I honestly don't. My comfort, my strength: you're the bridge over my troubled waters.

NOTES

INTRODUCTION: THE INFINITE POWER OF SAMENESS

1. D. Munro, "Inside the $35 Billion Addiction Treatment Industry," *Forbes*, April 27, 2015, www.forbes.com/sites/danmunro/2015/04/27/inside-the-35 -billion-addiction-treatment-industry/#d1b635117dc9.

2. "Our Twelve Traditions: A.A.'s Future in the Modern World," 25th World Service Meeting, Alcoholics Anonymous World Services, Inc., Durban, South Africa, October 2018.

3. Lance M. Dodes, *The Sober Truth: Debunking the Bad Science Behind 12-Step Programs and the Rehab Industry* (Boston: Beacon Press, 2014).

4. B. Midgley, "The Six Reasons the Fitness Industry Is Booming," *Forbes*, September 26, 2015, www.forbes.com/sites/benmidgley/2018/09/26/the-six-reasons -the-fitness-industry-is-booming/#7c24d1fe506d.

5. "New Study Finds 73% of People Who Set Fitness Goals as New Year's Resolutions Give Them Up," Bodybuilding.com press release, January 9, 2019, www.bodybuilding.com/fun/2013-100k-transformation-contest-press-release .html.

6. "The U.S. Weight Loss & Diet Control Market—Market Valued at $66 Billion in 2017—ResearchAndMarkets.com," BusinessWire, March 1, 2018, www .businesswire.com/news/home/20180301006252/en/U.S.-Weight-Loss-Diet -Control-Market.

7. "23 Exceptional Fad Diet Statistics," HRF.com, n.d., healthresearchfunding .org/23-exceptional-fad-diet-statistics/.

8. B. Goodman, "How Your Appetite Can Sabotage Weight Loss," WebMD, October 14, 2016, www.webmd.com/diet/news/20161014/how-your-appetite -can-sabotage-weight-loss#1.

9. D. Dowling, "New Year's Resolutions Are BS. Here's What You Should Do if You Actually Want to Change in 2018," Thrive Global, December 20, 2107, thriveglobal.com/stories/new-year-s-resolutions-are-bs-here-s-what-you -should-do-if-you-actually-want-to-change-in-2018/.

10. "Climate Change: How Do We Know," NASA, Global Climate Change, climate .nasa.gov/evidence/.

11. James O Prochaska, and Carlo C. DiClemente, "The Transtheoretical Approach," in *Handbook of Psychotherapy Integration*, eds. John C. Norcross and Marvin R. Goldfried, Oxford Series in Clinical Psychology, 2nd ed. (New York: Oxford University Press, 2005), 147–71.

12. M. J. Lambert, *Psychotherapy Outcome Research: Implications for Integrative and Eclectical Therapists* (New York: Basic Books, 1992), 94–129.

13. W. R. Miller and S. Rollnick, S., *Motivational Interviewing: Helping People Change* (New York: Guilford Press, 2013).

14. E. Cohen, R. Feinn, A. Arias, and H. R. Kranzler, "Alcohol Treatment Utilization: Findings from the National Epidemiologic Survey on Alcohol and Related Conditions," *Drug and Alcohol Dependence* 86 no. 2–3 (2007), 214–21.

15. Sun Tzu, *The Art of War* (CreateSpace Independent Publishing Platform, 2010).

16. N. Pagh, *Write Moves: A Creative Writing Guide and Anthology* (Peterborough, ON: Broadview Press, 2016).

17. C. R. Rogers, *On Becoming a Person: A Therapist's View of Psychotherapy*, 2nd ed. (New York: Mariner Books, 1995).

18. L. Jacobs, "Self-Realization as a Religious Value," in J. Clayton (Ed.), *Religion and the Individual*, ed. J. Clayton (New York: Cambridge University Press, 1992), 10.

19. Sun Tzu, *The Art of War.*

20. E. Fromm, *To Have or to Be?* (New York: Bloomsbury Academic, 2005).

21. E. Fromm, *The Sane Society* (New York: Holt Paperbacks, 1990).

22. R. May, *The Courage to Create* (New York: W. W. Norton, 1994).

23. M. Buber, *I and Thou* (New York: Touchstone, 1971).

24. P. Tillich, *The Courage to Be* (New Haven, CT: Yale University Press, 1952).

25. I. Illich, *Tools for Conviviality* (New York: HarperCollins Publishers, 1974).

26. R. May, *The Meaning of Anxiety,* rev. ed. (New York: W. W. Norton, 1977).

CHAPTER 1: HOW I GOT HERE

1. D. M. Foreman, "The Ethical Use of Paradoxical Interventions in Psychotherapy," *Journal of Medical Ethics* 16, no. 4 (1990): 200–205, doi:10.1136/jme .16.4.200.

2. C. R. Rogers, "The Necessary and Sufficient Conditions of Therapeutic Personality Change, *Journal of Consulting Psychology* 21, no. 2 (1957), 95–103, doi: 10.1037/h0045357.

3. J. Gleser and P. Brown, "Judo Principles and Practices: Applications to Conflict-Solving Strategies in Psychotherapy, *American Journal of Psychotherapy* 42, no.3 (1988), 437–47.

4. W. R. Miller and S. Rollnick, *Motivational Interviewing: Helping People Change* (New York: Guilford Press, 2013).

5. Valeria Vila and Christine Nazaire are a graduate student and an honors student, respectively, working with Kent Harber and Thomas Malloy, a social psychologist at Rhode Island College. The manuscript is K. D. Harber, V. Vila, T. Malloy, C. Nazaire, and R. Ellenhorn, *Fear of Hope: Measurement and Consequences*, forthcoming. The fear of hope research involved a series of seven studies. The first four were dedicated to simply confirming that the FOH measure was reliable. The remaining three all showed the results described in this book, to varying degrees, but strongly enough to give us confidence in their validity. That said, the research is yet to undergo peer review by a scientific journal, which is an important confirmatory threshold.

CHAPTER 2: THE WHERE YOU ARE/WHERE YOU WANT TO BE TENSION

1. A. Hartman, "You Can Sharpen Your Memory with the Zeigarnik Effect," Curiosity.com, July 24, 2018, curiosity.com/topics/you-can-sharpen-your-memory-with-the-zeigarnik-effect-curiosity/.

2. Bluma Zeigarnik, one of Lewin's students, went on to study and confirm this hypothesis, and the term for how people are better at remembering unfinished tasks than finished ones is now called the Zeigarnik effect. Almost ninety years later, the Zeigarnik effect would be used to set new rules for forced fouls in the NBA.

3. K. Koffka, "Perception: An Introduction to the Gestalt-Theorie," *Psychological Bulletin* 19, no. 10 (1922), 531.

4. G. Mandler, *The Language of Psychology* (Huntington, NY: R. E. Krieger, 1975).

5. K. Lewin, *A Dynamic Theory of Personality-Selected Papers* (UK: Read Books, 2013).

6. S. Holzner, "What Is a Vector?," Dummies.com, www.dummies.com/education/science/physics/what-is-a-vector/.

7. K. Lewin, *Field Theory in Social Science: Selected Theoretical Papers,* ed. D. Cartwright (New York: Harper & Brothers, 1951).

8. J. Kunst, "What Is Psychoanalysis?," *Psychology Today* online, January 15, 2014, www.psychologytoday.com/us/blog/headshrinkers-guide-the-galaxy/201401/what-is-psychoanalysis.

9. C. Hodanbosi and J. G. Fairman, "The First and Second Laws of Motion," NASA.gov, August 1966, www.grc.nasa.gov/WWW/K-12/WindTunnel/Activities/first2nd_lawsf_motion.html.

10. Ernest Becker's groundbreaking Pulitzer Prize–winning book, *The Denial of Death*, brings the point to light: Our ability to actually understand and contemplate death causes a tendency to deny it, sometimes so deeply that we don't see death as a central concern in our lives. That fight to deny death leads to all kinds of human activities, including a lot of what happens in cultural enterprises like the arts, music, and theater, and definitely in the development of

religion and concepts of an afterlife. Becker's work went on to influence the very important school of terror management theories in social psychology and evolutionary theory, exemplified in the book *The Worm at the Core: On the Role of Death in Life*. Terror management theories propose that we *manage* the terror of our death by grabbing hold of cultural beliefs, narratives, systems, and symbols, and that the more we feel the terror of death, the stronger we hold on. In President George W. Bush's 2004 reelection campaign commercial titled "Wolves," his campaign team ingeniously exploited our tendency to terror management by placing the viewers eyes at ground level, with a wolf—identified by the narrator—hunting us. Bush's campaign knew that the more people were frightened of their own death, they more they would hold on to things that kept the status quo, rather than change, and the more they would hold on to the conservative beliefs in general.

11. E. Becker, *The Denial of Death* (New York: Free Press, 1997).

12. S. Solomon, J. Greenberg, and T. Pyszczynski, *The Worm at the Core: On the Role of Death in Life* (New York: Random House, 2015).

13. Wolves advertisement, 2004 presidential campaign for George W. Bush, December 9, 2004, www.c-span.org/video/?c4496105/wolves-advertisement.

CHAPTER 3: ANXIETY, HOPE, AND FAITH: THE THREE LAWS OF PERSONAL CHANGE

1. K. Lewin, *Field Theory in Social Science: Selected Theoretical Papers,* ed. D. Cartwright (New York: Harper & Brothers, 1951).

2. C. Johnson, *Harold and the Purple Crayon* (New York: HarperCollins, 1995).

3. S. Kierkegaard, *The Concept of Dread* [*Begrebet Angest*], trans. W. Lowrie (Princeton, NJ: Princeton University Press, 1957).

4. I. R. Owen, "Introducing an Existential-Phenomenological Approach: Basic Phenomenological Theory and Research–Part I," *Counselling Psychology Quarterly* 7, no. 3 (1994), 261–73, doi:10.1080/09515079408254151.

5. Jean-Paul Sartre, *Being and Nothingness* [*L'Être et le néant: Essai d'ontologie phénoménologique*], trans. H. E. Barnes (New York: Washington Square Press, 1993).

6. K. Lewin, *Time Perspective and Morale* (Oxford, England: Houghton Mifflin, 1942) 48–70.

7. W. Churchill, "Dunkirk" in *The World's Great Speeches*, eds. L. Copeland, L. W. Lamm, and S. J. McKenna (Mineola, NY: Dover Publications, 1999), 433–39.

8. C. R. Snyder, "Hope Theory: Rainbows in the Mind," *Psychological Inquiry* 13, no. 4 (2002), 249–75.

9. I have changed the names and basic demographic information for the individuals in all the clinical examples in this book. Many of the examples are composite stories drawn from my interactions with or supervisory knowledge of more than one client.

10. Snyder, "Hope Theory."

11. A. Bandura, "Perceived Self-Efficacy in Cognitive Development and Functioning," *Educational Psychologist* 28, no. 2 (1993), 117–48.

12. M. L. King Jr., "I Have a Dream," in *The World's Great Speeches* (Mineola, NY: Dover Publications, 1999), 751f.

13. Bandura, "Perceived Self-Efficacy."

14. G. L. Clore, K. Gasper, and E. Garvin, "Affect as Information," in K. D. Harber, "Self-Esteem and Affect as Information," *Personality and Social Psychology Bulletin* 31, no. 2 (2001), 276–88, doi:10.1177/0146167204271323.

15. N. Schwarz and G. L. Clore, "Feelings and Phenomenal Experiences," in Harber, "Self-Esteem and Affect as Information."

16. G. L. Clore and S. Colcombe, "The Parallel Worlds of Affective Concepts and Feelings," quoted in Harber, "Self-Esteem and Affect as Information."

17. A. Bechara, and A .R. Damasio, "The Somatic Marker Hypothesis: A Neural Theory of Economic Decision," *Games and Economic Behavior* 52, no. 2 (2005), 336–72, doi:10.1016/j.geb.2004.06.010.

18. Clore and Colcombe, "The Parallel Worlds."

19. Harber, "Self-Esteem and Affect as Information."

20. Harber personally agrees with me on this point, and sees his research supporting this hypothesis.

21. R. D. Laing, *The Divided Self: An Existential Study in Sanity and Madness* (New York: Penguin Books, 1969).

22. R. A. Spitz and K. M. Wolf, "Anaclitic Depression: An Inquiry into the Genesis of Psychiatric Conditions in Early Childhood, II, *Psychoanalytic Study of the Child* 2, no. 1 (1946), 313–42.

23. R. A. Spitz, "Hospitalism: An Inquiry into the Genesis 0f Psychiatric Conditions in Early Childhood," *Psychoanalytic Study of the Child* 1, no. 1 (1945), 53–74.

24. M. D. S. Ainsworth, "The Bowlby-Ainsworth Attachment Theory," *Behavioral and Brain Sciences* 1, no. 3 (1978), 436–38, doi:10.1017/S0140525X00075828.

25. J. Bowlby, "The Bowlby-Ainsworth Attachment Theory," *Behavioral and Brain Sciences* 2, no. 4 (1979), 637–38, doi:10.1017/S0140525X00064955.

26. P. Waller-Bridge, H. Williams, J. Williams, H. Bradbeer, L. Hampson, J. Lewis, and S. Hammond, producers, *Fleabag*, TV series, directed by H. Bradbeer and T. Kirkby (2016, UK: BBC).

CHAPTER 4: FEAR OF HOPE

1. N. J. Roese, "Counterfactual Thinking," *Psychological Bulletin* 12, no. 1 (1997), 133.

2. These findings on future thinking and time perspective in regard to FOH were part of Christine Nazaire's senior honors thesis at Rutgers University.

3. K. Lewin, *Time Perspective and Morale* (Oxford, England: Houghton Mifflin, 1942) 48–70.

4. Laing, *The Divided Self*.

5. Thomas Jefferson, letter to Maria Cosway, October 12, 1786, Jefferson Papers, founders.archives.gov/documents/Jefferson/01-10-02-0309.

6. Peter Salovey, Laura R. Stroud, Alison Woolery, and Elissa S. Epel, "Perceived Emotional Intelligence, Stress Reactivity, and Symptom Reports: Further Explorations Using the Trait Meta-Mood Scale," *Psychology & Health* 17:5 (2002), 611-27.

CHAPTER 5: THE INGENIOUS PRESERVATION OF THE POSSUM'S POSE

1. "Dmitri Shostakovich, "Quotable Quote," Goodreads, www.goodreads.com /quotes/15049-when-a-man-is-in-despair-it-means-that-he.

2. This, by the way, is the very purpose of narrative therapy, the method I was relying on when I asked Mary to name her experience. Narrative therapy sees individuals as suffering from "problem saturation": seeing themselves as broken and incapable of generating their own recovery, due to the force of the medical model.

3. Michael White, *Maps of Narrative Practice* (New York: W.W. Norton, 1990).

4. Bill Wilson, *The Big Book of Alcoholics Anonymous*, 4th ed. (New York: Alcoholics Anonymous Worldwide, 2001).

CHAPTER 6: NO CHANGE, NO PAIN

1. Sartre, *Being and Nothingness*.

2. R. D. Ellenhorn, *Parasuicidality and Paradox: Breaking Through the Medical Model* (New York: Springer Publishing, 2007).

3. A. Tversky and D. Kahneman, "Loss Aversion in Riskless Choice: A Reference-Dependent Model," *Quarterly Journal of Economics* 106, no. 4 (1991), 1039–61.

4. B. Schwartz, *The Paradox of Choice: Why More Is Less* (New York: Harper Collins, 2009), 22.

5. H. R. Arkes and C. Blumer, "The Psychology of Sunk Cost," *Organizational Behavior and Human Decision Processes* 35, no. 1 (1985), 124–40.

6. B. M. Staw, "Knee-Deep in the Big Muddy: A Study of Escalating Commitment to a Chosen Course of Action, *Organizational Behavior and Human Performance* 16, no. 1 (1976), 27–44.

7. Staw, "Knee-Deep in the Big Muddy."

8. J. Maslin, "On the Sax, Freedom Isn't Found in Freedom," film review, *New York Times*, June 26, 1992, C12.

9. D. W. Winnicott, *Playing and Reality* (New York: Psychology Press, 1991), 99.

10. R. May, "Methods of Dealing with Anxiety, in *The Meaning of Anxiety,* 2nd ed. (New York: W. W. Norton, 1996), 363.

11. Henry Beecher, an Army doctor, found that battle-wounded World War II soldiers reported much less pain than their wounds would suggest. Beecher reasoned that the meaning of the pain affected their intensity—for these soldiers, wounds meant exit from combat and return to the States. They were, in effect, good news.

12. H. Beecher, "Pain in Men Wounded in Battle," *Annals of Surgery* 123, no. 1 (1946), 96–105.

CHAPTER 7: "THERE'S NO REASON YOU CAN'T"

1. Bandura, "Perceived Self-Efficacy," 117–48.

2. Lewin, *Time Perspective and Morale*, 48–70.

3. E. Goffman, *The Presentation of Self in Everyday Life* (New York: Anchor, 1959).

4. C. H. Cooley, "Looking-Glass Self," in Jodi O'Brien, *The Production of Reality: Essays and Readings on Social Interaction* (Thousand Oaks, CA: Sage, 2017), 261.

5. Ellenhorn, *Parasuicidality and Paradox.*

6. Erving Gottman, *Stigma: Notes on the Management of Spoiled Identity* (Englewood Cliffs, NJ: Prentice-Hall, 1963).

7. E. H. Erikson, *Identity: Youth and Crisis*, 2nd ed. (New York: W. W. Norton, 1968).

8. John Kennedy, "Do. Don't Think, Don't Hope. Do . . . Do. Act. Don't Think, Act. Eye on the Ball," Victorian Football League Grand Final, 1975, speakola.com /sports/john-kennedy-dont-think-do-1975.

9. R. E Watts, "Reflecting 'As If,'" Counseling Today, April 1, 2013, ct.counsel ing.org/2013/04/reflecting-as-if/.

CHAPTER 8: THE MIRROR OF CHANGING

1. C. Rogers, *On Becoming a Person: A Therapist's View of Psychotherapy*, 2nd ed. (New York: Mariner Books, 1995).

2. M. M. Linehan, "Dialectical Behavioral Therapy: A Cognitive Behavioral Approach to Parasuicide," *Journal of Personality Disorders* 1(4), 328–33.

3. Lewin, *Time Perspective and Morale*, 48–70.

4. Bandura, "Perceived Self-Efficacy, 117–48.

5. P. Schmuck, T. Kasser, and R.M. Ryan, "Intrinsic and Extrinsic Goals: Their Structure and Relationship to Well-Being in German and US College Students," *Social Indicators Research* 50, no. 2 (2000), 225–41.

6. P. M. Gollwitzer, "Striving for Specific Identities: The Social Reality of Self-Symbolizing," in *Public Self and Private Self* (New York: Springer, 1986), 143–59.

7. James O. Prochaska and Carlo C. DiClemente, "Transtheoretical Therapy: Toward a More Integrative Model of Change, *Psychotherapy: Theory, Research & Practice* 19, no. 3 (1982), 276.

CHAPTER 9: ARE WE THERE YET?

1. "Should You Weigh Yourself Every Day?," Harvard Health, Harvard Medical School, July 2015, www.health.harvard.edu/should-you-weigh-yourself-every-day.

2. C. R. Pacanowski and D. A. Levitsky, "Frequent Self-Weighing and Visual Feedback for Weight Loss in Overweight Adults," *Journal of Obesity* (2015), doi:10.1155/2015/763680.

3. S. Albers, *Eating Mindfully: How to End Mindless Eating and Enjoy a Balanced Relationship with Food*, 2nd ed. (Oakland, CA: New Harbinger Publications, 2012).

4. L. Marvin, *Baby Steps: A Guide to Living Life One Step at a Time* (Berkeley CA: Ross Books, 1991).

5. L. Ziskin, producer, *What About Bob?*, motion picture, directed by F. Oz, (1991: Buena Vista Pictures).

6. http.//arbanmethod.com/wyntons-twelve-ways-to-practice.

7. K. Lewin, *Time Perspective and Morale* (Oxford, England: Houghton Mifflin, 1942) 48–70.

8. A. Bandura, "Perceived Self-Efficacy in Cognitive Development and Functioning," *Educational Psychologist* 28, no. 2 (1993), 117–48.

9. Dodes, *The Sober Truth*.

CHAPTER 10: THE WEIGHT OF DESPAIR, THE LIGHTNESS OF HOPE

1. R. F. Baumeister, E. Bratslavsky, C. Finkenauer, and K. D. Vohs, "Bad Is Stronger Than Good," *Review of General Psychology* 5, no, 4 (2001), 323–70.

2. P. Brickman, D. Coates, and R. Janoff-Bulman, "Lottery Winners and Accident Victims: Is Happiness Relative?," *Journal of Personality and Social Psychology* 36 (1978), 917–27.

3. J. D. Wells, S. E. Hobfoll, and J. Lavin, "When It Rains, It Pours: The Greater Impact of Resource Loss Compared to Gain on Psychological Distress," *Personality and Social Psychology Bulletin* 25 (1999), 1172–82.

4. K. M. Sheldon, R. Ryan, and H. T. Reis, "What Makes for a Good Day? Competence and Autonomy in the Day and in the Person," *Personality and Social Psychology Bulletin* 22 (1996), 1270–79.

5. J. F. Pittman and S. A. Lloyd, "Quality of Family Life, Social Support, and Stress," *Journal of Marriage and the Family* 50 (1988), 53–67.

6. T. A. Wills, R. L. Weiss, and G. R. Patterson, "A Behavioral Analysis of the Determinants of Marital Satisfaction," *Journal of Consulting and Clinical Psychology* 6 (1974), 802–11.

7. E. O. Laumann, J. H. Gagnon, R. T. Michael, and S. Michaels, *The Social Organization of Sexuality: Sexual Practices in the United States* (Chicago: University of Chicago Press, 1994).

8. E. O. Laumann, A. Paik, and R. C. Rosen, "Sexual Dysfunction in the United States: Prevalence and Predictors," *Journal of the American Medical Association* 281 (1999), 537–44.

9. N. Rynd, "Incidence of Psychometric Symptoms in Rape Victims," *Journal of Sex Research* 24 (1988), 155–61.

10. D. C. French, G. A. Waas, S. A. Tarver-Behring, "Nomination and Rating Scale Sociometrics: Convergent Validity and Clinical Utility," *Behavioral Assessment* 8 (1986), 331–40.

11. E. L. Worthington Jr., "The New Science of Forgiveness," Greater Good, University of California-Berkeley, September 1, 2004, greatergood.berkeley.edu /article/item/the_new_science_of_forgiveness.

12. S. Lyubomirsky, *The How of Happiness* (New York: Penguin Press, 2007).

13. J. Czapinski, Negativity Bias in Psychology: An Analysis of Polish Publications," *Polish Psychological Bulletin* 16 (1985): 27–44.

14. P. H. Diamandis, "Why We Love Bad News: Understanding Negativity Bias," BigThink.com, July 19, 2013, bigthink.com/in-their-own-words/why -we-love-bad-news-understanding-negativity-bias.

15. S. P. Wood, "Bad News: Negative Headlines Get Much More Attention," *Adweek*, February 21, 2014, www.adweek.com/digital/bad-news-negative -headlines-get-much-more-attention/.

16. A. Epstein, "Here's What Happened When a News Site Only Reported Good News for a Day," Quartz, December 5, 2014, qz.com/307214/heres-what -happened-when-a-news-site-only-reported-good-news-for-a-day/.

17. G. Maté, *In the Realm of the Hungry Ghost: Close Encounters with Addiction* (Toronto: Knopf Canada, 2008).

18. J. Chaitin, "I Need You to Listen to What Happened to Me," Personal Narratives of Social Trauma in Research and Peace-Building," *American Journal of Orthopsychiatry* 84, no. 5, 475–86, doi:10.1037/ort0000023.

19. T. Frankish and J. Bradbury, "Telling Stories for the Next Generation: Trauma and Nostalgia," *Peace and Conflict: Journal of Peace Psychology* 18, no. 3 (2012), 294–306, doi:10.1037/a0029070.

20. K. C. McLean and M. Pasupathi, "Old, New, Borrowed, Blue? The Emergence and Retention of Personal Meaning in Autobiographical Storytelling," *Journal of Personality* 79, no. 1 (2011), 135–64, doi:10.1111/j.1467-6494.2010 .00676.x.

21. C. Miller and J. Boe, "Tears into Diamonds: Transformation of Child Psychic Trauma Through Sandplay and Storytelling," The Arts in Psychotherapy 17, no. 3 (1990), 247–57, doi.org/10.1016/0197-4556(90)90008-E.

22. G. Rosenthal, "The Healing Effects of Storytelling: On the Conditions of Curative Storytelling in the Context of Research and Counseling," *Qualitative Inquiry* 9, no. 6 (2003), 915–33, doi:10.1177/1077800403254888.

23. Nathaniel Hawthorne captures this act of finding justice (whether actual or imagined) in *The Scarlet Letter*. Hester Prynne continues to wear the red A long after she is required to do so. In fact, she never quits wearing it, and does so as an indictment of the town that sentenced her to wear it. She becomes her own testimony.

24. N. Hawthorne, *The Scarlet Letter* (Boston: Ticknor, Reed & Fields, 1850).

25. J. P. Burkett and L. J. Young, "The Behavioral, Anatomical and Pharmacological Parallels Between Social Attachment, Love and Addiction," *Psychopharmacology* 224, no. 1 (2012), 1–26.

26. Emily was fortunate to have LARP nearby. Many of us don't have easy access to activities that match our interests and thus provide a quick way for us to feel connected to others, to make us feel valued or have a sense of purpose. Growing theories on addiction capture this point, that addiction is closely connected to lack of opportunity for other activities that connect us. The most prominent thinker in this area is Carl Hart, a neuropsychologist who convincingly argues that the crack epidemic in African American communities was and is caused by poverty and racism, and that the popular political arguments that the problems in these communities are caused by drugs, is itself a racist argument, ignoring inequality and criminalizing behavior that is the inevitable outcome for individuals who have no other means to feel connected.

27. C. Hart, *High Price: A Neuroscientist's Journey of Self-Discovery That Challenges Everything You Know About Drugs and Society* (New York: HarperCollins, 2013).

28. Carl Hart, *High Price* (New York: HarperCollins, 2013).

29. Ellenhorn, *Parasuicidality and Paradox*.

30. D. W. Winnicott, "The Capacity to Be Alone," *International Journal of Psycho-Analysis* 39 (1958) 416–20.

31. In his book *Prisoner Without a Name, Cell Without a Number* the Jewish/Argentinian journalist Jacobo Timmerman describes his imprisonment in Argentina during the Dirty War, where thousands were "disappeared." Alone in his cell, forbidden from communicating, he was terrified. There was a slit in his steel door through which he could see only the steel door with its eye-slit opposite his. Once, looking out, he saw the eyes of another prisoner looking at him. The eyes were there, then not there, then there, then not there. The fellow prisoner was playing the simplest game, something close to "peekaboo" with toddlers. But Timmerman got the message—you are not alone. And that message, he claims, was of profound value during the first, most terrifying, days in prison.

32. J. Timerman, *Prisoner Without a Name, Cell Without a Number* [*Preso sin nombre, celda sin número*], trans. T. Talbot (Madison, WI: University of Wisconsin Press, 2002).

33. E. Fromm, *The Art of Loving* (New York: Harper & Brothers, 1956).

34. W. B. Swann Jr., "Self-Verification Theory," in *Handbook of Theories of Social Psychology* (Thousand Oaks, CA: Sage, 2011), 23–42.

CHAPTER 11: THE ELEVENTH PORTRAIT AND THE BIG BOTH-AND

1. T. Robbins, tweet, August 28, 2015.

2. J. Canfield, "If you can imagine it, you can make it happen," Facebook status update, July 9, 2016, m.facebook.com/JackCanfieldFan/photos/a.101548 36256590669.1073741840.36454130668/10153802125135669/?type=3&__tn __=C-R.

3. N. V. Peale *The Power of Positive Thinking*, 2nd ed. (New York: Touchstone, 2003).

4. Fromm, *The Art of Loving*.

5. The social-psychology term for the perseverance boost we get from others is called "social facilitation." It works best for simple tasks, like riding a bike. The presence of others can actually disrupt more complex tasks. One clever study by Robert Zajonc showed that even cockroaches benefit from social facilitation. A "runner" cockroach skittled across a runway faster when an "observer" cockroach was positioned on a Caesar-like platform overlooking the runway.

6. A. Duckworth, *Grit: The Power of Passion and Perseverance* (New York: Scribner, 2016).

7. B. Brown, *Dare to Lead* (New York: Random House, 2018).

8. C. S. Dweck, *Mindset: The New Psychology of Success* (New York: Random House, 2006).

9. S. E. Hobfoll, "Conservation of Resources: A New Attempt at Conceptualizing Stress," *American Psychologist* 44, no. 3 (1989), 513.

10. S. E. Hobfoll, *The Ecology of Stress* (Washington, DC: Hemisphere Publishing Corp., 1988).

11. A. Burrow, P. Hill, and R. Summer, "Leveling Mountains: Purpose Attenuates Links Between Perceptions of Effort and Steepness," *Personality and Social Psychology Bulletin* 42, no. 1 (2016), 94–103.

12. S. Schnall, K. D. Harber, J. K. Stefanucci, and D. R. Proffitt, "Social Support and the Perception of Geographical Slant," *Journal of Experimental Social Psychology*, 44 (2011), 1246–55.

13. Schnall et al., "Social Support."

14. K. D. Harber, D. Yeung, and A. Iacovell, "Psychosocial Resources, Threat, and the Perception of Distance and Height: Support for the Resources and Perception Model," *Emotion* 11, no. 5, (2011).

15. E. O. Wilson, *The Social Conquest of Earth* (New York: Liveright, 2013).

16. Johnson, *Harold and the Purple Crayon*.

17. Winnicott, "The Capacity to Be Alone," 416–20.

18. N. I. Eisenberger, M. D. Lieberman, and K. D Williams, "Does Rejection Hurt?: An FMRI Study of Social Exclusion," *Science* 302, no. 5643 (October 2003), 290–92, doi:10.1126/science.1089134.

19. P. E. McKnight and T. B. Kashdan, "Purpose in Life as a System That Creates and Sustains Health and Well-Being: An Integrative, Testable Theory," *Review of General Psychology* 13, no. 3 (2009), 242–51.

20. C. W. Mills, *The Sociological Imagination*, 2nd ed. (Oxford: Oxford University Press, 2000).

21. Lewin, *Time Perspective and Morale*, 48–70.

22. Jean-Paul Sartre, *Existentialism Is a Humanism*. [*L'existentialisme est un humanisme*], trans. P. Mairet (New Haven, CT: Yale University Press, 1948), 58.

23. Ross Ellenhorn, "The AIDS Memorial Quilt and the Modernist Sacred: Resurrection in a Secular World, PhD diss., Department of Sociology, Brandeis University, 1997.

24. M. L. King Jr., *A Testament of Hope: The Essential Writings of Martin Luther King, Jr.* (San Francisco: HarperSanFrancisco, 1991).

CONCLUSION

1. T. Robbins, *Awaken the Giant Within: How to Take Immediate Control of Your Mental, Emotional, Physical and Financial Destiny!* (New York: Free Press, 1992).

2. R. May, *The Courage to Create* (New York: W. W. Norton, 1994), 14.

INDEX

Page numbers of illustrations appear in italics.

ABOUT THE AUTHOR

Ross Ellenhorn, PhD, is an eminent thought leader on innovative methods and programs aimed at helping individuals diagnosed with psychiatric and substance-use issues recover in their own communities, outside of hospital or residential settings. He is the founder, owner, and CEO of ellenhorn, the most robust community integration program in the United States, with offices in Boston, New York City, and Raleigh-Durham. Dr. Ellenhorn is also the cofounder and president of the Association for Community Integration Programs, and the founder of two lecture series that aim to shift current behavioral health paradigms. He gives talks and seminars throughout the country and is an in-demand consultant to mental health agencies, psychiatric hospitals, and addiction programs in the United States and Europe. He is the executive producer of the film *Recovering Addiction: A Public Health Rescue Mission*, a documentary on new, less-oppressive means for understanding problematic substance use and other distressing habits. Dr. Ellenhorn is the first person to receive a joint PhD from Brandeis University's Florence Heller School for Social Welfare Policy and Management and the Brandeis Department of Sociology.

Don't miss Ross Ellenhorn's joyous, inventive rereading of the beloved children's book *Harold and the Purple Crayon* that celebrates our inherent "sacred originality" and establishes a new framework for self-reliance.

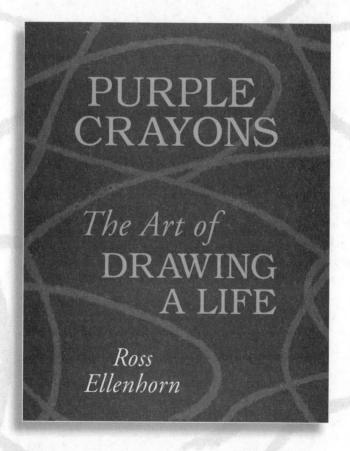

PURPLE
CRAYONS

The Art of
DRAWING
A LIFE

*Ross
Ellenhorn*